WATCH AND PRAY

WATCH

Christian Teachings on the Practice of Prayer

AND PRAY

EDITED BY LORRAINE KISLY

INTRODUCTION BY
BISHOP SERAPHIM SIGRIST

BELL TOWER · NEW YORK

Permissions to reprint from various works appear in the
acknowledgments section at the end of the book.

Copyright © 2002 by Lorraine Kisly
Introduction copyright © 2002 by Bishop Seraphim Sigrist

Published by Bell Tower, New York, New York.
Member of the Crown Publishing Group, a division of Random House, Inc.
www.randomhouse.com

Bell Tower and colophon are registered trademarks of Random House, Inc.

Printed in the United States of America

Design by Jennifer Ann Daddio

Library of Congress Cataloging-in-Publication Data

Watch and pray : Christian teachings on the practice of prayer / edited by Lorraine Kisly;
introduction by Seraphim Sigrist.
    Includes bibliographical references.
    I. Prayer—Christianity   I. Kisly, Lorraine.

BV210.3 W38 2002
248.3'2—dc21

                                                                    2001043696

ISBN 0-609-60899-1

10   9   8   7   6   5   4   3   2   I

First Edition

To my parents

CONTENTS

INTRODUCTION

Bishop Seraphim Sigrist

This is an unusual book. First, it is a remarkable anthology of writings on prayer, and this is unusual enough. I do not know any collection of comparable depth and richness, and, for that matter, sheer variety of authors. William Law and Baron von Hügel and John of the Cross and Anthony Bloom are here to be sure, but so are Jane Lead (visionary disciple of Doctor Pordage), and Martin Heidegger, and William Butler Yeats in a moment of seeing clearly into a way of devotion he perhaps did not consciously follow. Ruusbroec is here, of course, but so is André Louf, a wonderful modern Cistercian writer I met for the first time. Merton and Nouwen speak to us from the twentieth century, and Abraham of Nathpar from the sixth.

For analogy, one might go all the way to Nicodemos of Mt. Athos and his assembly of the great anthology on prayer that is the *Philokalia* in its many volumes (published in 1782). Kisly's work, if for a moment conceived as a sort of modern *philokalia*, already has a preparatory companion volume of Christian spiritual formation, *Ordinary Graces: Christian Teachings on the Interior Life.* Together they parallel the plan of the two-volume Kadloubovsky-Palmer translation of the *Philokalia*, which moves in the second to the heart of prayer.

In any case, *Watch and Pray* is divided into "cycles" marking moments of the spiritual life. I should think the cycles indicate not so much stages as permanent aspects or, precisely, cycles or circlings of a spiral around the center. These range from entry to the way, through inner healing and vision, to discussion of method and purification, to that Resurrection which is both goal and way.

If its importance as an anthology were all Lorraine Kisly's work offered, it would be much. However, I should like to suggest that as the excerpts reflect on one another, and back and forth with the editor's framing comment and structure, the whole becomes that thing still rarer than an anthology on prayer—it becomes a book about prayer.

It seems to me that the number of good books about prayer in our time is very small—I would think perhaps of *Beginning to Pray* by Anthony Bloom, C. S. Lewis's *Letters to Malcolm*, Romano Guardini's little book *Prayer in Practice* . . . perhaps you could think of others. But not many. Astoundingly few really, when you consider that prayer is that movement of heart and will toward God, which is the experience of the Christian faith.

Yet, as this collection amply attests, there is a history of deep reflection on prayer. To appreciate the full depth of this Christian reflection—that is, as far as is possible from the written record before or beside the direct and inner transmission within prayer itself—requires a gathering from many sources. And that putting together is just what *Watch and Pray* enables us to do. Here is Rudolf Bultmann showing that Jesus came to give not doctrine but a decision at every moment. And here Enzo Bianchi says that in all the days of one's life one becomes a word, a letter, to the world. Kierkegaard notes that the true man of prayer is the one who is attentive. And an anonymous old English writer tells us that truly God is neither in silence nor in speaking but between and beyond both our silence and our words.

This last, I think, goes to the heart of the matter. For if the number of good books written directly and entirely about prayer is not great, it is perhaps not because of some dryness of the theologians, or a drawing back from the intimate and living experience of prayer, as much as it is that indeed the subject of prayer so little lends itself to a manual or "how-to" book, and once opened proves to have no limit at all.

Indeed, does not the heart intuit that the whole universe is the breathing in and out of God? Prayer, that return of breath to God, then, is in its totality inclusive of the whole of our lives, imaginings, and actions. Through all of these we are ever praying—our need, then, is to know what we know, to be what we are, and not only to pray but also to know ourselves as praying.

This means that a good book on prayer will be something not at all easy to write, and once written will be no schema but an illumination of where we stand and who we are, which then opens out to include the reader, and to bring the reader into that prayer which is beyond the words and pages.

So in these selections you will find a landmark anthology of Christian reflection on prayer, past and present and immensely varied, but beyond that in the interstices between the selections and in their suggested relationships you will find (like that white fire on which the Hassids say the Torah was written in black fire, but the white being the true Law) a remarkable book on prayer, and then beyond that, if this book is read truly, the reader will surely find the beginning of prayer itself, and this is to open another book with no end at all.

FOREWORD

"Watch and pray." It is these words of Christ that have inspired the extended meditation on prayer you are about to join. "Watch," we are told, and we have at least the beginning of an idea of what is meant: awaken, remember, remain open, be mindful; attend. "And pray. . . ." Now many of us find ourselves on less sure ground. The command to pray raises resistance and uncertainty even in many who feel the need for prayer, but to watch *and* to pray together is at the center of Christian life. It is a demand for real relationship, within and without, and does not allow us to be "left alone."

The editor of this volume is among those for whom the question of prayer and watchfulness is a living one. If prayer is a lifelong practice with many stages and levels of development, where does a beginner begin? What is the difference between prayer alone and prayer with others? Is faith necessary in order to pray? If silence is true prayer, what place is there for prayers of petition and intercession, or even of praise? Is engagement with prayer an essential act? Is there true humanity without it?

Is prayer in fact ever something we *do*, or is it instead a state of being? Who prays? Is it "I" who prays? And do we ever pray alone? If prayer is like a spring flowing ceaselessly in our hearts, why are we insensible of it? What is required of us to become aware of the praying heart within? Is prayer something we reach for, or does prayer find us? When we are held in prayer, what will keep us from falling away?

The book's twelve "cycles" begin with an overture that sounds the unique themes of Christian prayer and then move from the gift of repentance to the active, informing word of God; from the meaning of intercession and petition to the place of suffering in every life; from the salvific action upon us of the Holy Spirit to the attention of the heart; from the need for struggle and the place of method and commitment to the end of egoism in the pouring out of our lives for others.

All this together is Christian prayer, a "work of the whole being."

Among the voices assembled here from the last two thousand years, an unexpected discovery was the recurring call to desire, to the finding of our own deepest need. It is only when we become dissatisfied with our small appetites that we can be led to "desire what God desires, and let God desire in us." God wishes us to have life, and to have it more abundantly, we are told. What we long for longs for us. The call to awaken this longing comes from Martin Luther, who urges us to pray the Our Father in order to "kindle the heart to stronger and greater desires," and from Teilhard de Chardin, who prays that he be granted "the desire to desire being." Many others tell us that this need, this desire, this wish to pray, is indeed already prayer itself. It is not the ability to correspond as much as the wish to do so that is prayer for us, it is the wish to say "yes," this "least sigh of desire," says Gerard Manley Hopkins, that is the life and spirit of all humanity. Awaken to this desire, says Augustine, and we shall be filled.

May we watch, and pray that this be accomplished in us.

LORRAINE KISLY

Let us desire, my brothers and sisters,
for we are to be filled.

—*Augustine of Hippo*

WATCH AND PRAY

CYCLE ONE

ANSWER
AMEN TO ME

We begin by listening. Here the great themes of Christian prayer appear: each of us is created and loved uniquely; we were created in and for relationship with God, with others, with ourselves; to open to the current of prayer within we must be willing, transparent, still; and finally, the master is within, and promises, "What you do not know I myself will teach you."

This *state of prayer* within us is something we always carry about, like a hidden treasure of which we are not consciously aware— or hardly so. Somewhere our heart is going full pelt, but we do not feel it. We are deaf to our praying heart, love's savor escapes us, we fail to see the light in which we live.

For our heart, our true heart, is asleep; and it has to be woken up, gradually—through the course of a whole lifetime. So it is not really hard to pray. It was given us long since. But very seldom are we conscious of our own prayer. Every technique of prayer is attuned to that purpose. We have to become conscious of what we have already received, must learn to feel, to distinguish it in the full and peaceful assurance of the Spirit, this prayer rooted and operative somewhere deep inside us. It must be brought to the surface of our consciousness. Little by little it will saturate and captivate our faculties, mind and soul and body. Our psyche and even our body must learn to answer to the rhythm of this prayer, be stirred to prayer from within, be incited to prayer, as dry wood is set ablaze. One of the Fathers puts it as tersely as this: "The monk's ascesis: to set wood ablaze."

Prayer then, is nothing other than that unconscious *state of prayer* which in the course of time has become completely conscious. Prayer is the *abundantia cordis,* the abundance of the heart, as the saying goes in the Gospels: "For a man's words flow out of what fills his heart" (Matt. 12:34; Luke 6:45). Prayer is a heart that overflows with joy, thanksgiving, gratitude and praise. It is the abundance of a heart that is truly awake. . . .

Each and every method of prayer has but one objective: to find the heart and alert it. It must be a form of interior alertness, watchfulness. Jesus himself set "being awake" and "praying" side by side. The phrase "be awake and pray" certainly comes from Jesus in person (Matt. 26:41; Mark 13:33). Only profound and quiet concentration can put us on the track of our heart and of the prayer within it.

All the time watchful and alert, therefore, we must first recover the way to our heart in order to free it and divest it of everything in which we have encapsulated it. With this in view we must mend our ways, come to our senses, get back to the true center of our being.

ANDRÉ LOUF (1929–)
French Cistercian abbot

Aug. 20 1880: During this retreat, which I am making at Liverpool, I have been thinking about creation. . . . I find myself with my pleasures and pains, my powers and my experiences, my deserts and guilt, my shame and sense of beauty, my dangers, hopes, fears, and all my fate, more important to myself than anything I see. And when I ask where does all this throng and stack of being, so rich, so distinctive, so important, come from/nothing I see can answer me.

And this whether I speak of human nature or of my individuality, my selfbeing. For human nature, being more highly pitched, selved, and distinctive than anything in the world, can have been developed, evolved, condensed, from the vastness of the world not anyhow or by the working of common powers, but only by one of finer or higher pitch and determination than itself and certainly than any that elsewhere we see, for this power had to force forward the starting or stubborn elements to the one pitch required.

. . . When I consider my selfbeing, my consciousness and feeling of myself, that taste of myself, of *I* and *me* above and in all things, which is more distinctive than the taste of ale or alum, more distinctive than the smell of walnutleaf or camphor, and is incommunicable by any means to another man (as when I was a child I used to ask myself: What must it be to be someone else?). Nothing else in nature comes near this unspeakable stress of pitch, distinctiveness, and selving, this selfbeing of my own. . . . Searching nature I taste *self* but at one tankard, that of my own being. The development, refinement, condensation of nothing shews any sign of being able to match this to me or give me another taste of it, a taste even resembling it. . . .

From what then do I with all my being and above all that taste of self, that selfbeing, come?

GERARD MANLEY HOPKINS (1844–1889)
English Jesuit priest and poet

For us it is *we* who experience the full measure of the intensity of reality, while other beings seem, in comparison with ourselves, to be less real; their existence seems to be more of the nature of a shadow than full reality. Our thoughts tell us that this is an illusion, that beings around us are as real as we ourselves are, and that they live just as intensely as we do. Yet fine as it is to say these things, all the same we feel ourselves at the center of reality, and we feel other beings to be removed from this center. That one qualifies this illusion as "egocentricity," or "egoism," or "*ahamkara*" (the illusion of self), or the "effect of the primordial Fall" does not matter; it does not alter the fact that we feel ourselves to be more real than others.

Now, to feel something as real in the measure of its full reality is to love. It is love which awakens us to the reality of ourselves, to the reality of others, to the reality of the world and to the reality of God. In so far as we love ourselves, we feel real. And we do not love—or we do not love as much as ourselves—other beings, who seem to us to be less real.

Now, two ways, two quite different methods exist which can free us from the illusion "me, living—you, shadow," and we have a choice. The one is to *extinguish* love of oneself and to become a "shadow amongst shadows." This is the equality of indifference. India offers us this method of liberation from *ahamkara*, the illusion of self. This illusion is destroyed by extending the indifference that one has for other beings to oneself. Here one reduces oneself to the state of a shadow equal to the other surrounding shadows. *Maya*, the great illusion, is to believe that individual beings, me and you, should be something more than shadows— appearances without reality. The formula for realizing this is therefore: "me, shadow—you, shadow."

The other way or method is that of *extending the love that one has for oneself, to other beings*, in order to arrive at the realization of the formula: "me, living—you, living." Here it is a matter of rendering other beings as real as oneself, i.e., of loving them as oneself. To be able to attain this, one has first to love one's *neighbor* as oneself. For love is not an abstract program but, rather, it is *substance* and *intensity*. It is necessary therefore that one radiates the substance and intensity of love with regard to *one* individual being in order that one can begin to ray it out in all directions. "To be able to make gold one has to have gold," say the alchemists. The spiritual counterpart of this maxim is that in order to be able to love everyone, one has to love or to have loved someone. This someone is one's "neighbor."

ANONYMOUS (20th century)
Christian hermeticist

The image of God is found essentially and personally in all mankind. Each possesses it whole, entire and undivided, and all together not more than one alone. In this way we are all one, intimately united in our eternal image, which is the image of God and the source in us of all our life.

JOHN RUUSBROEC (1293–1381)
Flemish mystic and theologian

I was crossing a little stream near Inchy Wood and actually in the middle of a stride from bank to bank, when an emotion never experienced before swept down upon me. I said, "That is what the devout Christian feels, that is how he surrenders his will to the will of God." I felt an extreme surprise, for my whole imagination was preoccupied with the pagan mythology of ancient Ireland. I was marking in red ink, upon a large map, every sacred mountain. The next morning I awoke near dawn, to hear a voice saying, "The love of God is infinite for every human soul because every human soul is unique, no other can satisfy the same need in God."

W. B. YEATS (1865–1939)
Irish poet

We ought not to understand God and creation as two things distinct from each other, but as one and the same. For both the creature, by subsisting, is in God; and God, by manifesting himself, in a marvelous and ineffable manner creates himself in the creature, the invisible making himself visible, and the incomprehensible comprehensible, and the hidden revealed, and the unknown known, and what is without form and species formed and specific, and the superessential essential, and the supernatural natural, and the simple composite, and the accident-free subject to accident, and the infinite finite, and the uncircumscribed circumscribed, and the supertemporal temporal, and the creator of all things created in all things, and the maker of all things made in all things; and eternal he begins to be, and immobile he moves into all things, and becomes all things in all things.

JOHN THE SCOT ERIUGENA (810–877)
Irish theologian and scholar

Lord, Thou has given me my being of such a nature that it can continually make itself more able to receive thy grace and goodness. And this power, which I have of Thee, wherein I have a living image of thine almighty power, is free will. By this I can either enlarge or restrict my capacity for Thy grace. . . .

When I rest in the silence of contemplation, you, Lord, speak within my heart, saying: Be you your own and I too will be yours. . . . You, Lord, can not be mine if I am not my own.

NICHOLAS OF CUSA (1401–1464)
German cardinal, theologian, and mathematician

If we want to hear something we must prepare ourselves to perceive by being still. If we ourselves are talking, or if our own thoughts, wishes and concerns are speaking within us, the noise they make will render us unable to hear. Hence directions for meditating always begin by requiring us to create inner stillness and emptiness as a means of making room for what is to be received. Mention is made of "turning off," of "concentrating" the scattered consciousness, of entering upon the "mysterious path inward" and so forth. It would, however, be reasonable to doubt that such efforts, in their mere negativity, belong to that positive readiness to listen that distinguishes Christian meditation from other kinds in which this readiness is superfluous because no Word comes from God.

The silence required of the Christian is not fundamentally and primarily of human making. Rather, believers must realize that they already possess within themselves and at the same time in God the quiet, hidden "chamber" into which they are to enter (Matt. 6:6) and in which they are with the Father. . . .

Our earthly cares and preoccupations are always on the lighter side of the scale, while the other, which sinks and is just as much ours—our being in God—possesses an "unimaginable weight" in comparison (Cor. 4:17). We need not first pave for ourselves an approach to God on our own; already and always "our life is hidden with Christ in God" (Col. 3:3). Accordingly, preparation for meditation does not first necessitate lengthy psychological adjustments but only a brief realization in faith of where our true center and emphasis permanently are. We seem to be far from God, but he is near us. We need not work our way up to him. Instead, our situation is like that described in the parable: "From a distance the father already saw him coming and was moved with pity. Running up to him, he threw his arms around his neck and kissed him" (Luke 15:20). And the son's rehearsed speech—"Father, I am not worthy to be called your son. Regard me as one of your day laborers"—is rendered useless by this gesture of the father, who calls into the house: "Quick, fetch the best garment and put it on him. Put a ring on his finger and shoes on his feet."

HANS URS VON BALTHASAR (1905–1988)

Swiss Roman Catholic theologian

There is a root or depth in you, where all these faculties come forth as lines from a center, or as branches from the body of a tree. This depth is called the center, the fund, or bottom, of the soul. This depth is the unity, the eternity, I almost said the infinity of your soul, for it is so infinite that nothing can satisfy it, or give it any rest, but the infinity of God.

Awake, then, you that sleep, and Christ, who from all eternity has been espoused to your soul, shall give you Light. Begin to search and dig in your own field for this Pearl of eternity that lies hidden in it; it cannot cost you too much, for it is all, and when you have found it you will know that all which you have sold or given away for it is as a mere nothing, as a bubble upon the water.

But if you turn from this heavenly Pearl, and trample it under your feet for the sake of being rich or great, either in Church or State, and if death finds you in this success, you cannot then say that though the Pearl is lost, yet something has been gained instead of it. For in that parting moment the things and the sounds of this world will be exactly alike; to have had an estate, or only to have heard of it, to have lived at Lambeth twenty years, or only to have twenty times passed by the palace, will be the same good or the same nothing to you.

WILLIAM LAW (1686–1761)
English contemplative and cleric

Lord, make me taste by love what I taste by knowledge; let me know by love what I know by understanding. I owe you more than my whole self, but I have no more, and by myself I cannot render the whole of it to you. Draw me to you, Lord, in the fullness of love. I am wholly yours by creation; make me all yours, too, in love.

Lord, my heart is before you. I try, but by myself I can do nothing; do what I cannot. Admit me into the inner room of your love. I ask, I seek, I knock. You who made me seek, make me receive; you who gave the seeking, give the finding; you who taught the knocking, open to my knock. . . .

By you I have desire; by you let me have fulfillment. . . . Let me be filled with your love, rich in your affection, completely held in your care. Take me and possess me wholly, who with the Father and the Holy Spirit are alone blessed to ages of ages. Amen.

ANSELM OF CANTERBURY (c. 1033–1109)
Saint and founder of medieval Scholasticism

Each of us comes forth from God in the Word and stands before him, unique in his own nature, in his own particular being, a unique expression of the divine Being; and each of us has to return to God in the Holy Spirit, in a movement of love by which we surrender ourselves to God, allow God to possess us. Our temptation is to stand upon our own dignity, to center on our selves and refuse that movement of return, of self-surrender. Sin is a failure of love, a failure to respond to the movement of grace which is ever drawing us out of ourselves into the divine life. When we refuse to respond, to acknowledge our nothingness and need, then we close in on ourselves, we become separated from God and eternal life and see ourselves as isolated selves, each shut up in our own existence and in conflict with others, alienated from our real Self, living in a world of illusion.

BEDE GRIFFITHS (1906–1993)
English Benedictine monk

Yet does not this eternal vigilance call for a continual degree of effort which is beyond our capacities? Even supposing that we have the will to try, we shall very soon be balked in spite of ourselves by weariness and exhaustion. That is why vigilance is inseparable from prayer, is impossible without prayer: neither can be realized without the other. What the New Testament commends to us is more precisely vigilance in and through prayer. Only with prayer does vigilance become spontaneous, easy, effortless, like the flow of water from the spring.

Our thoughts, words and deeds cannot in fact be motivated by the love of God unless we turn our gaze towards God in a constant attitude of love: only this loving gaze towards him can make the love of God the motive of all that we think and do and say. Now this loving gaze towards God is what constitutes the essence of prayer, and it is this which by making us alert to all the demands of the love of God produces vigilance. . . .

Thus St. Teresa of Avila could write: "There is only one way to reach God, and that is prayer; the man who tells you otherwise is a deceiver." St. Gregory of Nyssa calls prayer the "president of the chorus of virtues," and St. John Chrysostom "the source of all good, the nourishment of fruitful life, the cause of all virtue and justice, the foundation of the building, the nerve of the soul."

JEAN DAUJAT (20th century)
French Dominican monk

As soon as a man thinks with even a little attention of the divinity, he feels a certain delightful motion of the heart which testifies that God is God of the human heart. . . .

This natural inclination then which we have to love God above all things is not left for nothing in our hearts: for on God's part it is a handle by which he can hold us and draw us to himself;—and the divine goodness seems in some sort by this impression to keep our hearts tied as little birds in a string by which he can draw us when it pleases his mercy to take pity upon us—and on our part it is a mark and memorial of our first principal and creator, to whose love it moves us, giving us a secret intimation that we belong to his divine goodness; even as harts upon whom princes have had collars put with their coats of arms, though afterwards they cause them to be let loose and run at liberty in the forest, do not fail to be recognized by anyone who meets them not only as having been once taken by the prince whose arms they bear, but also as being still reserved for him.

FRANCIS DE SALES (1567–1622)
Saint, bishop of Geneva, and doctor of the church

In every encounter, God asks: "Adam, where are you? Where do you stand? How is it with you?" To answer this question, a person must be willing, lucid, transparent. Once someone has left behind the habitual prayers of childhood and has entered into the personal encounter, there is no way back. He must live in the light of God and expose and entrust himself to the light ever more unconditionally.

ADRIENNE VON SPEYR (1902–1967)
Swiss mystic, physician, and writer

An undisciplined spirit, as it first ventured forth, strayed onto the paths of error. There, eternal Wisdom in an indescribable spiritual form confronted him and drew him by means both pleasant and unpleasant until it brought him to the right path of divine truth. And, when he reflected deeply on how wondrously he had been drawn, he addressed God thus: "Dear gentle Lord, since I was a child, my spirit has been searching with unslaked thirst for something. And what this was, Lord, I have never yet fully grasped.

"For many a year, Lord, I have pursued it feverishly, yet could never attain it because I never really knew what it was; and yet it is something that draws my heart and soul to itself and without which I cannot ever really find peace. Lord, in the early days of my childhood I would search for it as I saw others do before me—in creatures. And the more I sought, the less I found; and the closer I came, the farther away I got. Concerning every form that I looked at I heard an inner voice, and before I would occupy myself with it completely or devote myself to it in peace, it would say: 'This is not what you are searching for.' Always I have had this force driving me away from all things. Lord, my heart . . . more than once sensed what it is not . . . but it is still uninstructed about what it is. . . .'"

Response of *eternal Wisdom:* "Don't you recognize it? It has, after all, lovingly embraced you and has often stood in your path until it gained you for itself alone."

The *servant:* "Lord, I never saw or heard it at all. I don't know what it is."

Response of *eternal Wisdom:* "That is not surprising. It was caused by your intimacy with creatures and your unfamiliarity with it. But now open your inner eyes and see who I am. It is I, eternal Wisdom, who chose you for myself in eternity with the embrace of my eternal providence. I have blocked your path whenever you would have been separated from me if I had let you be. You always found something repugnant in all things. This is the surest mark of my chosen ones, that I want them for myself."

The *servant:* ". . . O God, why have you waited so long to reveal yourself to me? How very long you put it off! How many a wearisome way have I plodded!"

Response of *eternal Wisdom:* "If I had acted earlier, you would not have recognized the value of my treasures as intensely as you do now."

The *servant:* "O infinite Good, how sweetly have you now poured out your goodness in me! When I did not exist, you gave me being. When I left you, you would not leave me. When I tried to escape you, you so gently took me captive. . . . Lord, you alone see and know the nature of a heart filled with love. You know that no one can love something he cannot at all know. Therefore, since I shall now love you alone, let me know you better so that I can learn to love you completely."

Response of *eternal Wisdom:* "According to the order of nature, the loftiest flowing forth of all beings from their primal origin proceeds from the highest beings to the lowest; but the return to the origin proceeds from the lowest beings to the highest. And so, if you want to see me in my uncreated Godhead, you should learn to know and love me here in my suffering humanity. This is the quickest way to eternal happiness."

HENRY SUSO (1300–1366)
German contemplative

God is to be found and seen, not through an illimitable vacancy between Himself and the spirit of man, but in and through all things that stir men to love. . . .

Christ tells us to value men and things for their own sake; we must have a passion for men if we are to have one for God. "Inasmuch as ye have done it unto one of these little ones, ye have done it unto me." It is not only of conduct that these words are true. If we are to understand Christianity, we must extend them and say—Inasmuch as ye have seen one of these little ones, ye have seen me; and—Inasmuch as ye have understood one of these little ones, ye have understood me. God is revealed to us in the known, not hidden in the unknown; and we have to find Him where we are.

ARTHUR CLUTTON-BROCK (1868–1924)
English essayist, critic, and journalist

You perceive, by the light of God, in the depth of your conscience, what grace demands of you, but you resist Him. Hence your distress. You begin to say within, it is impossible for me to undertake to do what is required of me; this is a temptation to despair. Despair as much as you please of self, but never of God; He is all good and all powerful, and will grant you according to your faith. If you will believe all things, all things shall be yours, and you shall remove mountains. If you believe nothing, you shall have nothing, but you alone will be to blame. Look at Mary, who, when the most incredible thing in the world was proposed to her, did not hesitate, but exclaimed, "Be it unto me according to thy word" (Luke 1:38).

Open, then, your heart. It is now so shut up, that you not only have not the power to do what is required of you, but you do not even desire to have it; you have no wish that your heart should be enlarged, and you fear that it will be. How can grace find room in so straitened a heart? All that I ask of you is, that you will rest in a teachable spirit of faith, and that you will not listen to self. Simply acquiesce in everything with lowliness of mind, and receive peace through recollection, and everything will be gradually accomplished for you; those things which, in your hour of temptation, seemed the greatest difficulties, will be insensibly smoothed away.

FRANÇOIS FÉNELON (1651–1715)
French Roman Catholic archbishop of Cambrai

I sought him whom my soul loves (Sg. 3:3). . . .

You would not seek him or love him unless you had first been sought and loved. Not only in one blessing have you been forestalled but in two, being loved as well as being sought. For the love is the reason for the search, and the search is the fruit of the love, and its certain proof. You are loved so that you may not suppose you are sought to be punished. You are sought so that you may not complain you are loved in vain. Both these loving and manifest favors give you courage, and drive away your diffidence, persuading you to return, and stirring your affections. From this comes the zeal and ardor to seek him whom your soul loves, because you cannot seek unless you are sought, and when you are sought you cannot but seek. . . .

One who is loved has nothing to fear. . . . Nor can I fear to look on his face, since I have sensed his tenderness. In what have I known it? In this—not only has he sought me as I am, but he has shown me tenderness, and caused me to seek him with confidence. How can I not respond to him when he seeks me, since I respond to him in tenderness? How can he be angry with me for seeking him, when he overlooked the contempt I showed for him? He will not drive away someone who seeks him, when he sought someone who spurned him. The spirit of the Word is gentle, and brings me gentle greetings, speaking to me persuasively of the zeal and desire of the Word, which cannot be hidden from him. He searches the deep things of God, and knows his thoughts—thoughts of peace and not of vengeance. How can I fail to be inspired to seek him, when I have experienced his mercy and been assured of his peace?

Brothers, to realize this is to be taught by the Word; to be convinced of it is to be found.

BERNARD OF CLAIRVAUX (1091–1153)
Cistercian abbot, saint, and theologian

"I found him," the soul says, "I found him," though previously he sought and found me like a stray sheep, like a lost coin, and in his mercy anticipated me. He forestalled me, I say, in finding me when I was lost. He anticipated me, though I deserved nothing. He found me astray; he anticipated me in my despair. He found me in my unlikeness; he anticipated me in my diffidence. He found me by pointing out my state to me; he anticipated me by recalling me to his own. He found me wandering in a labyrinth; he anticipated me with gifts when I was devoid of grace. He found me not that I might choose him but that he might choose me. He anticipated me that he might love me before I loved him.

In this way, then, chosen and loved, sought and acquired, found and anticipated, how should I not love and seek him with an effort according to my strength and with affection beyond my strength? I will seek him until gaining my desire I may utter my cry of happiness: "I have found him whom my soul loves."

GILBERT OF HOYLAND (d. 1172)
Cistercian abbot

"Let us sing a hymn to the Father, and so go to meet what lies before [us]." So he told us to form a circle, holding one another's hands, and himself stood in the middle and said, "Answer Amen to me." So he began to sing the hymn and to say,

"Glory be to thee, Father."
And we circled round him and answered him, "Amen."
"Glory be to thee, Logos:
Glory be to thee, Grace."—"Amen."
"Glory be to thee, Spirit:
Glory be to thee, Holy One:
Glory be to thy Glory."—"Amen."
"We praise thee, Father:
We thank thee, Light:
In whom darkness dwelleth not."—"Amen."
"And why we give thanks, I tell you:
I will be saved,
And I will save."—"Amen."
"I will be loosed,
And I will loose."—"Amen."

"I will be wounded,
  And I will wound."—"Amen."
"I will be born,
  And I will bear."—"Amen."
"I will eat,
  And I will be eaten."—"Amen."
"I will hear,
  And I will be heard."—"Amen." ...
"I will pipe,
  Dance, all of you."—"Amen."
"I will mourn,
  Beat you all your breasts."—"Amen." ...
"I am a lamp to you
  who see me."—"Amen."
"I am a mirror to you
  who know me."—"Amen."
"I am a door to you
  (who) knock on me."—"Amen."
"I am a way to you
  (the) traveler."—"Amen." ...
"Being moved toward wisdom
    you have me as a support;
        rest in me. ...
"What you do not know I myself will teach you. ...
    understand the whole,
and when you have understood it say,
    Glory be to thee, Father.
"Say again with me,
    Glory be to thee, Father,
        Glory be to thee, Word.
            Glory be to thee, Holy Spirit."—"Amen."

ACTS OF JOHN (150?–300?)
New Testament Apocrypha

CYCLE TWO

GATEWAY TO GRACE

Repentance is a gift of the Holy Spirit, a change of heart that leads to vigilance and recollection. It is a ray of light that at once reveals our self-satisfaction, arrogance, and heedlessness, and gathers us into the plenitude of the here and now. As repentance opens the feeling, "inward joy and gladness mingle with what we call mourning and grief, like honey in a comb."

I went away from Thee, my God, in my youth I strayed too far from Thy sustaining power, and I became to myself a barren land.

AUGUSTINE OF HIPPO (354–430)
Carthaginian saint, philosopher, and doctor of the church

Though the light and comfort of the outward world keeps even the worst of men from a constant strong awareness of that wrathful, fiery, dark and self-tormenting nature that is the essence of every fallen unregenerate soul, yet every man in the world has more or less frequent and strong intimations that it is so with him in the inmost ground of his soul. How many inventions are some people forced to have recourse to in order to keep off a certain inward uneasiness, which they are afraid of and know not whence it comes?

WILLIAM LAW (1686–1761)

English contemplative and cleric

They err in their hearts (Prov. 1:20).

This is the beginning of God's speaking. And this word which is addressed to all those who are converted in heart seems to have run on ahead; it is a word which not only calls them back but leads them back, and brings them face to face with themselves. For it is not so much a voice of power as a ray of light, telling men about their sins and at the same time revealing the things hidden in darkness. There is no difference between this inner voice and light, for they are one and the same Son of God and Word of the Father and brightness of glory. . . .

For what is the purpose of the ray of light or the Word but to bring man to know himself? Indeed, the book of conscience is opened, the wretched passage of life up to now recalled to mind; the sad story is told again; reason is enlightened and what is in the memory is unfolded as though set out before each man's eyes. But reason and memory are not so much "of" the soul, as themselves the soul, so that it is both gazer and that which is gazed upon, brought face to face with itself and overcome by the force of its realization of what it is seeing. It judges itself in its own court. Who can bear this judgment without pain? "My soul is troubled within me," says the prophet of the Lord, and do you wonder that you cannot be brought to face yourself without being aware of sin, without disturbance, without confusion?

BERNARD OF CLAIRVAUX (1091–1153)

Cistercian abbot, saint, and theologian

It is true, when I first got on shore here, and found all my ship's crew drowned, and myself spared, I was surprised with a kind of ecstasy, and some transport of soul, which, had the grace of God assisted, might have become true thankfulness; but it ended where it began, in a mere common flight of joy, or, as I may say, being glad I was alive, without the least reflection upon the distinguishing goodness of the Hand which had preserved me . . . just the same common sort of joy which seamen generally have after they are got safe ashore from a shipwreck—they drown all in the next bowl of punch, and forget almost as soon as it is over, and all the rest of my life was like it. . . . As soon as I saw but a prospect of living, and that I should not starve and perish for hunger, all the sense of my affliction wore off, and I began to be very easy. . . .

But now, when I began to be sick . . . conscience, that had slept so long, began to awake, and I began to reproach myself with my past life. . . . I now have difficulties to struggle with, too great for even Nature itself to support, and no assistance, no help, no comfort, no advice. Then I cried out, "Lord, be my help, for I am in great distress."

This was the first prayer, if I may call it so, that I had made for many years. . . . I took up the Bible, and began to read, but my head was too much disturbed with the tobacco to bear reading, at least that time; only having opened the book casually, the first words that occurred to me were these, "Call on Me in the day of trouble, and I will deliver, and thou shalt glorify Me."

The words were very apt to my case, and made some impression upon my thoughts at the time of reading them, though not so much as they did afterwards; for as being delivered, the word had no sound, as I may say, to me, the thing was so remote, so impossible in my apprehension of things. . . . But, however, the words made a great impression upon me, and I mused upon them very often.

July 3. . . . While I was thus gathering strength, my thoughts ran exceedingly upon this Scripture, "I will deliver thee"; and the impossibility of my deliverance lay much upon my mind, in bar of my ever expecting it. But as I was discouraging myself with such thoughts, it occurred to my mind. . . . Have I not been delivered, and wonderfully too, from sickness? from the most distressed condition that could be, and that was so frightful to me? and what notice had I taken of it?

Had I done my part? God had delivered me, but I had not glorified Him; that is to say, I had not owned and been thankful for that as a deliverance; and how could I expect greater deliverance? This touched my heart very much; and immediately I kneeled down, and gave God thanks aloud for my recovery from my sickness.

July 4. In the morning I took the Bible; and beginning at the New Testament, I began seriously to read it, and imposed upon myself to read awhile every morning and every night, not tying myself to the number of chapters, but as long as my thoughts should engage me. It was not long after I set seriously to this work, but I found my heart more deeply and sincerely affected with the wickedness of my past life. The impression of my dream revived, and the words, "All these things have not brought thee to repentance," ran seriously in my thought. I was earnestly begging of God to give me repentance, when it happened providentially the very day that I came to these words, "He is exalted a Prince and a Savior, to give repentance, and to give remission." I threw down the book; and, with my heart as well as my hands lifted up to heaven, in a kind of ecstasy of joy, I cried out aloud, "Jesus, Thou son of David! Jesus, Thou exalted Prince and Savior, give me repentance!"

This was the first time that I could say, in the true sense of the word, that I prayed in all my life; for now I prayed with a sense of my condition, and with a true Scripture view of hope founded on the encouragement of the Word of God; and from this time, I may say, I began to have hope that God would hear me.

Now I began to construe the words mentioned above, "Call on Me, and I will deliver you," in a different sense from what I had ever done before; for then I had no notion of anything being called deliverance but my being delivered from the captivity I was in; for though I was indeed at large in the place, yet the island was certainly a prison to me, and that in the worst sense in the world. But now I learned to take it in another sense; now I looked back upon my past life with such horror, and my sins appeared so dreadful, that my soul sought nothing of God but deliverance from the load of guilt that bore down all my comfort. As for my solitary life, it was nothing; I did not so much as pray to be delivered from it, or think of it; it was all of no consideration, in comparison to this. And I add this part here, to hint to whoever shall read it, that whenever they come to a true sense of things, they will find deliverance from a sin a much greater blessing than deliverance from affliction. . . .

My condition began now to be, though not less miserable as to my way of living, yet much easier to my mind; and my thoughts being directed, by a constant reading of the Scripture, and praying to God, to things of a higher nature, I had a great deal of comfort within, which, till now I knew nothing of.

DANIEL DEFOE (1660–1731)
English novelist, pamphleteer, and journalist

Prayer for love of God, a prayer which protests against our heart's secret and unavowed aversion from God, is our beginning of love of God and we can always make this by his grace, which is always offered to us. . . .

God hears such a prayer. For he has promised it to us in his most truthful word. For our part we should believe him rather than our own heart. If it prays for love, it loves, even if the poor heart feels little more than sorrow at still having fulfilled so little the first of all commandments.

KARL RAHNER (1904–1984)
German Jesuit theologian

The same elder was asked on another occasion, "What is repentance?" and he said, "A broken heart."

And what is humility? He replied, "Embracing a voluntary mortification in regard to everything."

And what is a merciful heart? He replied, "The heart's burning for all creation, for human beings, for birds and animals, and for demons, and everything there is. At the recollection of them and at the sight of them his eyes gush forth with tears owing to the force of the compassion which constrains his heart, so that, as a result of its abundant sense of mercy, the heart shrinks and cannot bear to hear or examine any harm or small suffering of anything in creation. For this reason he offers up prayer with tears at all times, even for irrational animals, and for the enemies of truth, and for those who harm him, and for their preservation and being forgiven. As a result of the immense compassion infused in his heart without measure—like God's—he does this even for reptiles.

"Love of God proceeds from conversing with him; this conversation of prayer comes about through stillness, and stillness comes with the stripping away of the self."

ISAAC OF NINEVEH (d.c. 700)
Monastic writer

To repent is to open our eyes to the light. In this sense, repentance is not just a single act, an initial step, but a continuing state, an attitude of heart and will that needs to be ceaselessly renewed up to the end of life. . . .

To repent is to wake up. Repentance, change of mind, leads to watchfulness. The Greek term used here, *nepsis,* means literally sobriety and wakefulness—the opposite to a state of drugged or alcoholic stupor; and so in the context of the spiritual life it signifies attentiveness, vigilance, recollection. When the prodigal son repented, it is said that "he came to himself." the "neptic" man is one who has come to himself, who does not daydream, drifting aimlessly under the influence of passing impulses, but who possesses a sense of direction and purpose. As the Gospel of Truth (mid-second century) expresses it, "He is like one who awakens from drunkenness, returning to himself. . . . He knows where he has come from and where he is going."

Watchfulness means, among other things, *to be present where we are*—at this specific point in space, at this particular moment in time. All too often we are scattered and dispersed; we are living, not with alertness in the present, but with nostalgia in the past, or with misgiving and wishful thinking in the future. While we are indeed required responsibly to plan for the future—for watchfulness is the opposite of fecklessness—we are to think about the future only so far as it depends upon the present moment. Anxiety over remote possibilities which lie altogether beyond our immediate control is sheer waste of our spiritual energies.

The "neptic" man, then, is gathered into the *here* and the *now.* He is the one who seizes the *kairos,* the decisive moment of opportunity. . . . As Meister Eckhart teaches, "He who abides always in a present *now,* in him does God beget his Son without ceasing."

The "neptic" man is the one who understands this "sacrament of the present moment," and who tries to live by it. He says to himself, in the words of Paul Evdokimov: "The hour through which you are at present passing, the man whom you meet here and

now, the task on which you are engaged at this very moment—
these are always the most important in your whole life."

KALLISTOS WARE (1934–)
Greek Orthodox archbishop

Our continual mistake is that we do not concentrate upon the
present day, the actual hour, of our life; we live in the past or in
the future; we are continually expecting the coming of some special hour when our life shall unfold itself in its full significance.
And we do not observe that life is flowing like water through our
fingers, sifting like precious grain from a loosely fastened bag.

ALEXANDER YELCHANINOV (1881–1934)
Russian priest and spiritual guide in exile in France

The greatest of sinners can and ought to pray; the one thing necessary is that he should pray as a sinner. The man of evil will,
can, and ought to pray; but he must pray according to the state
of his soul, speaking to God as he is, a man of evil will. The
lukewarm must pray as he is, the just with the prayer of the just;
each one must come to God as he is in reality.

T. R. P. DÉSURMONT (20th century)
French priest and modern exponent of the Redemptionist tradition

Almighty God, and most merciful Father, all merciful, mercy
itself; I have erred willingly and strayed willingly, nay run from
Thy ways, more like an untamed heifer than a lost or wandering
sheep. I have followed too much, even altogether, the absurd
devices and brutish desires of my own heart. I have offended
against, nay, been offended at, Thy holy, most holy, laws. I have
left undone, not done at all, those things which I ought to have

done. And I have done, done nothing else, but those things which I ought not to have done. And there is no health, no hope of health in me. But Thou, Lord, have mercy upon me, miserable, the most miserable sinner, the greatest sinner, and most unthankful for so great grace. Spare me, and all them that confess their faults. Restore me, and all them that be penitent, that desire to be penitent, that wish they were, would be glad if they were; that fear that they are not enough, and are sorry they are not more.

WILLIAM LAUD (1573–1645)
English archbishop of Canterbury

As I ponder the true nature of compunction, I find myself amazed by the way in which inward joy and gladness mingle with what we call mourning and grief, like honey in a comb. There must be a lesson here, and it surely is that compunction is properly a gift from God, so that there is a real pleasure in the soul, since God secretly brings consolation to those who in their heart of hearts are repentant.

JOHN CLIMACUS (520–603)
Father of the Eastern church

When I stopped speaking but was still trembling all over with horror, I heard behind me a soft voice saying, "Return!" I lifted my head, and I looked around to see who was calling me and where he was commanding me to return. But I saw nothing, not even my guide Searchall, for he too had already left me.

Then the voice sounded again: "Return!" Not knowing where to return or how to get out of the darkness, I began to grieve. But then the voice called out a third time: "Return whence you came, to the home of your heart, and shut the door behind you!"

I obeyed this counsel as far as I understood it, and I did well to obey God, who was counseling me; but even that was his gift. Then, collecting my thoughts as well as I could and closing my eyes, ears, mouth, nostrils, and all external passages, I entered into my heart and found that it was dark. But when with blinking eyes I looked about a little, I could see a faint light coming through the cracks, and I distinguished up above, in the vault of this little chamber, a large, round, glass window. But it was so dirty and smeared with grime that hardly any light could penetrate. . . .

The hope began to rise in me that he who had led me into this chamber by his call, whoever he might be, would make himself heard again and direct me further. For the beginnings of what I saw here began to please me. . . . I did not find rustle and clatter, the blare and clang, the commotion and whirl, the contention and violence (of which the world was full), for all was quiet.

I pondered these things within myself and awaited what was to follow. Then behold, a bright light burst forth from above. Raising my eyes toward it, I saw the upper window full of brilliance, out of which a man came down to me. In form, indeed, he was similar to us people, but in his splendor he was truly God. Although his face shone greatly, yet it could be looked upon with human eyes; nor did it inspire terror, but radiated a loveliness such as I have never seen anywhere in the world. Then he, the epitome of kindness and good will, addressed me in these most gracious words:

"Welcome, welcome, my dear son and brother." Having said this, he embraced me cheerfully and kissed me. . . . "I have watched, my son, while you wandered, but I did not want to see you stray any longer. I have led you to myself by leading you into yourself, for here I have chosen a palace for my dwelling. If you wish to dwell here with me, you will find here what you sought in vain in the world—rest, happiness, glory, and an abundance of everything. I promise you, my son, that here you will not be disappointed as you were there."

Hearing this speech and realizing that this was my Savior, Jesus Christ, of whom I had heard some mention even in the world, I clasped my hands, not with fear and doubt as in the world, but with full joy and complete trust. . . .

"Stand firm in this: be mine, call yourself mine, and remain my own. Indeed, from eternity you were and are mine, but you did not know this before. . . . I have led you to myself along strange paths, through circuitous and winding ways that you did not know. You did not perceive what I, the guide of all my chosen ones, intended by this; neither did you recognize my work within you. But I was with you everywhere, and that is why I led you through these roundabout ways, that in the end I might bring you closer to myself. Neither the world, nor your guides, nor Solomon could teach you anything. . . ."

Then I said . . . "Now I understand that I erred, wandering through the world and seeking rest in created things." . . . While I was speaking, a still greater light began to shine around me. . . . Ladders were repaired and set against the window that let in the light of heaven. Thus, I perceived that it was possible to look out. . . . "Son," he said, "I live in two places, in my glory in heaven and in the penitent heart on earth. So from this time forward, I want you also to have two dwellings: one here at home, where I have promised to dwell with you; the other with me in heaven. I give you these wings (which are the desire for eternal things and prayer) so that you might reach heaven."

JOHN AMOS COMENIUS (1592–1670)
Czech educator and bishop of Bohemian Unity of Brethren

With rare exceptions, the spiritual life comes into being in an event that is called "conversion." . . . Something we have read, an encounter, a reflection, causes a light to break forth suddenly, brilliantly. In its brightness, all is seen in its true order, as in an inspired poem that gives to everything a new and inestimable value, as in the music of Mozart. It is a religious springtime, full of joy and enthusiasm. Like the buds filled with sap, the human being feels uplifted in a surprising joy and a spontaneous sympathy for everything and everyone. This is an unforgettable time. Like a feast illumined by a thousand lights, it makes one see in God the smiling countenance of the Father coming to meet his child.

This time, however, is brief. The face of the Father takes on the face of the Son, and his cross casts its shadow within us. Our own cross stands out clearly, and there is no possible return to the simple and childlike faith of former days. Sorrowful discords tear our soul in its clear-sighted vision of evil and sin. There is an extreme tension between two states that are mutually exclusive. The brutal experience of our falls and weakness can fling us to the edge of despair. . . .

God is watching for us at this decisive moment. He expects from our faith a vigorous act, the full and conscious acceptance of our destiny. He asks us to assume it freely. No one can do it in our place, not even God himself. The cross is made of our weaknesses and our failings. It is constructed by our enthusiastic impulses and especially by the dark depths of our heart where a secret resistance and a shameful ugliness lurk, in short, by all that complexity which is at this precise moment, the authentic I.

"Love your neighbor as yourself" allows a certain love of self. It is a call to love our cross. It means perhaps the most difficult act of all—to accept ourselves as we are. We know that the proudest beings, those full of self-love, are the ones who most feel ill at ease with themselves and who secretly hate themselves. It is an infinitely serious moment when we encounter ourselves, for this requires a baring of ourselves, an immediate and total vision of ourselves even in our most secret recesses.

"He who sees himself as he is, is greater than the one who raises the dead," spiritual masters say, thus stressing the importance of this act. This vision is always frightening. We must therefore look at Christ. This is the experience of St. Paul and of every Christian. . . .

In moments of crushing solitude, only humility can help us in recognizing the radical powerlessness of human nature. It inclines us to cast our whole being at the foot of the cross, and then suddenly our heavy burden is lifted by Christ: "Learn of me . . . For my yoke is easy, and my burden light."

"Thy will be done," the *fiat*, or word of assent—"Let it be done"—springs forth. I accept it as my own. I read in this burden what God has thought of me, and I recognize in it my destiny. We are no longer self-centered, but made joyful and lighthearted. . . .

According to our spiritual teachers, the art of humility does not at all consist in becoming this or that, but of being exactly as God made us. Dostoyevski describes this vivid moment through what the pilgrim Macarius says in *The Adolescent*. With a single glance, this man envelops the universe, his life, time and eternity. He can only say finally, "All is in you, Lord; I am yours; receive me." . . . It is only after this "second birth," this personal Pentecost, that the authentic spiritual life begins.

PAUL EVDOKIMOV (1901–1970)
Russian Orthodox theologian

Prayer and helplessness are inseparable. Only those who are helpless can truly pray. . . .

Listen, my friend! Your helplessness is your best prayer. It calls from your heart to the heart of God with greater effect than all your uttered pleas. He hears it from the very moment that you are seized with helplessness, and He becomes actively engaged at once in hearing and answering the prayer of your helplessness. He hears today as He heard the helpless and wordless prayer of the man sick with the palsy. . . .

Now listen again. It is not your prayer which moves God to save you. On the contrary, your prayer is a result of the fact that Jesus has knocked at your heart's door and told you that He desires to gain access to your needs. You think that everything is closed to you because you cannot pray. My friend, your helplessness is the very essence of prayer. . . .

Be not anxious because of your helplessness. Above all, do not let it prevent you from praying. Helplessness is the real secret and the impelling power of prayer. You should therefore rather try to thank God for the feeling of helplessness which He has given you. It is one of the greatest gifts which God can impart to us. For it is only when we are helpless that we open our hearts to Jesus and let Him help us in our distress, according to His grace and mercy.

OLE HALLESBY (1879–1961)
Norwegian seminary professor and writer
imprisoned for his resistance to the Nazi regime

If it is true that penitence is the beginning of this way, "the gateway of grace," this is not to say that it is a passing moment, a stage to be left behind. It is in fact not a stage but a condition which must continue permanently, the constant attitude of those who truly aspire to union with God. The word "penitence" does not properly express the idea of this fundamental attitude of every Christian soul which turns to God. . . . The Greek *metanoia* means literally "change of mind" or "transformation of spirit." It is a "second regeneration" granted by God after baptism; a possibility of return to the Father; a continuous exodus from ourselves; a power which brings about the transformation of our nature. It is the opposite state of soul to self-sufficiency, to the spiritual complacency of the pharisee, of the "just man" who considers himself to be in a "state of grace" because he is without self-knowledge. Repentance, like the way of ascent towards God, can have no end. "Repentance," says St. Isaac the Syrian, "is fitting at all times and for all persons." . . .

The soul which is not transformed by repentance does not know grace, and thus ceases to make progress in the way of ascent. This is the "insensibility of a heart of stone," and the symptom of spiritual death. Repentance, according to St. John Climacus . . . is the fruit of baptismal grace; it is indeed that same grace when it has been acquired, appropriated by the human person, and become in it "the gift of tears"—the infallible sign that the heart has been overwhelmed by the love of God. . . . These charismatic tears, which are the consummation of repentance, are at the same time the first-fruits of infinite joy: "Blessed are ye that weep now: for ye shall laugh." Tears purify our nature, for repentance is not merely *our* effort, *our* anguish, but is also the resplendent gift of the Holy Spirit, penetrating and transforming our hearts.

VLADIMIR LOSSKY (1903–1958)
Russian Orthodox theologian

Simon the Pharisee is shocked by the attitude of Jesus to the whore. He receives the answer that the sinners have greater love than the righteous ones because more is forgiven them. It is *not* the love of the woman that brings her forgiveness, but it is the forgiveness she has received that creates her love. . . .

Jesus does not forgive the woman, but he declares that she *is* forgiven. Her state of mind, her ecstasy of love, show that something has happened to her. And nothing greater can happen to a human being than that he is forgiven. For forgiveness means reconciliation in spite of estrangement; it means reunion in spite of hostility; it means acceptance of those who are unacceptable; and it means reception of those who are rejected.

Forgiveness is unconditional, or it is not forgiveness at all. . . . There is no condition whatsoever in man which would make him worthy of forgiveness. If forgiveness were conditional, conditioned by man, no one could be accepted, and no one could accept himself. We know that this is our situation, but we are loath to face it. It is too great as a gift and too humiliating as a judgment. We want to contribute something, and if we have learned that we cannot contribute anything positive, then we try at least to contribute something negative—the pain of self-accusation and self-rejection. Then, we read our story, and the parable of the prodigal son, as if they said: These sinners were forgiven *because* they humiliated themselves and confessed that they were unacceptable; *because* they suffered about their sinful predicament, they were made worthy of forgiveness.

But this reading of the story is a misreading, and a dangerous one. If that were the way to our reconciliation with God, we would have to produce within us the feeling of unworthiness, the pain of self-rejection, the anxiety and despair of guilt. There are many Christians who try this in order to show God and themselves that they deserve acceptance. They perform an emotional work of self-punishment after they have realized that their other good works do not help them. But emotional works do not help either. God's forgiveness is independent of anything we do, even of self-accusation and self-humiliation. . . . Forgiveness creates repentance: this is declared in our story, and this is the experience of those who have been forgiven.

PAUL TILLICH (1886–1965)
German-American Protestant theologian

We can only hold ourselves in readiness to let ourselves be disturbed and emotionally moved by God. For a great deal has to happen that lies outside the reach of our good will and our natural generosity. Reversal means, not merely that we will be inwardly wounded, but that we must be shaken to our very foundations. It means that perhaps we will be broken, that something inside us will collapse—something like a concrete bunker on which we have worked perhaps for years with exemplary care but which at a given moment began to function solely as a defense system against our deepest self, against others, with the risk that in the end it would protect us even against God's grace.

That collapse is only just the beginning, even though a hopeful one. We must be on our guard not to try to build up again what grace has broken down. This is something we have to learn, for there is always a strong temptation to put scaffolding up around that crumbling facade and to tidy it up. We must learn to acquiesce in the collapse and to sit down amid the rubble without bitterness or self-reproach. . . .

Jesus' trust in and surrender to his Father through death have forever taken the sting out of God's wrath and enable us, together with Jesus, to recognize through every death and mortification the Father's love, even in our own deepest weakness. *That* is conversion, a continual switching over to sin and grace. Please note that I do not mean from sin *to* grace, but switching over to sin *and* grace. This means to let go of self-justification and of our own righteousness, to acknowledge our sin and to open ourselves to the grace of God.

This is the miracle of the sinner who continues in the conversion process, whom Jesus himself acknowledged to be the one who furnishes the greatest joy to the Father in heaven: "I tell you, in just the same way there will be more joy in heaven over one sinner who repents than over ninety-nine righteous people who have no need of repentance" (Luke 15:7).

. . . Repentance is never the fruit of good intentions or attentive effort. It is the first step of love, God's love more than ours.

Repentance is our yielding to God's urgent intervention, our surrender to the first signs of love we sense coming from him. It is surrender in the strong sense of capitulation. We capitulate; we are allowed to give up before God. All our defenses melt away before the consuming fire of his Word and glance.

ANDRÉ LOUF (1929–)
French Cistercian abbot

If we remembered that every encounter with God and every deep encounter with man is a judgment, a crisis, we would seek God both more whole-heartedly and more cautiously. We would not be bitter if this encounter did not immediately take place. We would approach God with a trembling heart. In this way we would avoid many disappointments, many useless efforts, because God would not give himself to us if we could not bear the encounter. He prepares us for it, and sometimes by a long wait. . . .

Let us be careful not to seek mystical experience when we should be seeking repentance and conversion. That is the beginning of our cry to God. "Lord, make me what I should be, change me whatever the cost." And when we have said these dangerous words, we should be prepared for God to hear them. And these words of God are dangerous because God's love is remorseless. God wants our salvation with the determination due to its importance. And God, as the Shepherd of Hermas says, "does not leave us till he has broken our heart and bones."

ANTHONY BLOOM (1914–)
Russian Orthodox monk and metropolitan of Sourozh

Wait. Listen. You must not keep quiet in this way simply in order to be able to speak about it later on. . . . Do not cast furtive glances towards some strange mystical experience. Nothing but the dispassionate clarity of truth should appear in this silence, nothing but what is pure and silent. Do not express yourself. After all, you are to accept yourself; you are not to empty yourself in self-accusation, nor to escape from yourself by too unconcerned a rejoicing, nor to enjoy your own self in a smug, small-minded way (for then you would have perceived nothing, neither of the celestial heights nor of the abysmal depths of your own existence). You must allow yourself to approach silently nearer and nearer to yourself: the past, the present and the future, in this moment of silence . . . all the waters of your life which flow away and run out and which are collected in the one basin of a heart aware of itself.

Perhaps you will then begin to feel quite horrified by what you see. Perhaps the bitter waters of disgust, of hollowness, emptiness, and boredom will rise out of the depths to the surface of your heart. Perhaps you will realize then—if you admit it honestly—how distant all those are from you with whom you are in daily contact and with whom you would ordinarily say you are united in love. Perhaps you find nothing in yourself then but weakness, wretchedness, and other things from which you would rather escape into the business of everyday life, a daily life which in such an experience appears to you as the only attainable bliss (and where it then goes under the name of work, duty, reasonableness, a sensible outlook without any illusions and similar names). Perhaps you will not be aware of anything but an uneasy feeling of emptiness and deadness. Endure yourself! You will discover how everything proclaimed in such a silence is as if encompassed by a nameless remoteness, as if suffused by something which appears like emptiness. It is not something one could chase away. It looks at us through everything, it embraces everything; frightened, one may try to force oneself to overlook it, yet one cannot remove it. . . .

"It" is the reason why we are nowhere completely at home, why we cannot be given over completely to anything we grasp, why our look and grasp find nowhere an absolute end where they would truly have arrived with no further need to look out through it and stretch out towards the undetermined. One cannot simply leave this "it" be, as a mere side-effect, and because the mysterious and the nameless are best left alone. For without "it," there would also be no space of the heart in which we can meet familiar things; without "it," nothing could be put in its right place, freedom could not say yes *and* no; without "it," there would be no true past, and no room for the future in the planning mind. . . .

One must look at the invisible and let the silent speak in stillness. Do that, but be careful. Do not call it God. Do not try to derive enjoyment from it, as if it were a part of yourself. It is a mute pointer in the direction of God, something which in its namelessness and boundlessness gives us a hint that God is more than just another thing, added to those with which we normally have to deal. It points to Him. Through it, He allows us to become aware of his presence, if we are quiet and do not take fright and run away from the mysterious being which lives and acts in this silence.

KARL RAHNER (1904–1984)
German Jesuit theologian

If we wish to pray properly, we are to think of nothing except that we stand before God's bright face, before the Holy Trinity and the choirs of His holy angels and that God tests our soul, spirit and heart in our prayers and looks on our will in a most inward manner [to see] whether it is completely directed toward Him, whether it has given itself completely to Him.

If this is so, He stirs the will with the power of His Holy Spirit and smashes it so that it is properly desirous and hungry for grace, that it begins earnestly to press out of itself and to press into God's mercy.

The will is far too weak in its own powers, but when the divine power stirs it, it is awakened so that it becomes fiery and properly desirous. In this desire God Himself works. Then a man speaks properly with God and God actually speaks with the soul of man.

JACOB BOEHME (1575–1624)

German Lutheran theosophist

Repentance itself is nothing else but a kind of circling; to return to Him by repentance, from whom by sin we have turned away . . . which circle consists of two things; which two must needs be two different motions. One is to be done with the whole heart; the other with it broken and rent: so as, one and the same it cannot be.

First, a turn, wherein we look forward to God, and with our whole heart resolve to turn to Him. Then, a turn again, wherein we look backward to our sins, wherein we have turned from God: and with beholding them, our very heart breaketh. . . . These two between them make up a complete repentance or a perfect revolution.

LANCELOT ANDREWES (1555–1626)

Anglican bishop of Winchester and Ely

Well, it says in the New Testament that man and all creation *"are subject to vanity, not willingly,"* and sigh with efforts, and desire to enter into the liberty of the children of God. The mysterious sighing of creation, the innate aspiration of every soul towards God, that is exactly what interior prayer is. There is no need to learn it, it is innate in every one of us!

ANONYMOUS RUSSIAN PILGRIM (c. 1850)

Most holy and merciful Father:
I confess to you and to the whole communion of saints in
   heaven and on earth.

I have not loved you with my whole heart, and mind, and
    strength. I have not loved my neighbors as myself. I have
    not forgiven others, as I have been forgiven.
Have mercy on me, Lord.
I have been deaf to your call to serve, as Christ served us. I
    have not been true to the mind of Christ. I have grieved
    your Holy Spirit.
Have mercy on me, Lord.
I confess to you, Lord, all my past unfaithfulness: the pride,
    hypocrisy, and impatience of my life,
I confess to you, Lord.
My self-indulgent appetites and ways, and my exploitation
    of other people,
I confess to you, Lord.
My anger at my own frustration, and my envy of those
    more fortunate than I,
I confess to you, Lord.
My intemperate love of worldly goods and comforts, and
    my dishonesty in daily life and work,
I confess to you, Lord.
My negligence in prayer and worship, and my failure to
    commend the faith that is in me,
I confess to you, Lord.
Accept my repentance, Lord, for the wrongs I have done:
    for my blindness to human need and suffering, and my
    indifference to injustice and cruelty,
Accept my repentance, Lord.
For all false judgments, for uncharitable thoughts toward
    my neighbors, and for my prejudice and contempt
    toward those who differ from me,
Accept my repentance, Lord.
For my waste and pollution of your creation, and my lack
    of concern for those who come after us,
Accept my repentance, Lord.

Restore me, good Lord, and let your anger depart from me,
  Favorably hear me for your mercy is great.
Accomplish in me and all of your church the work of your
  salvation, That I may show forth your glory in the world.
By the cross and passion of your Son our Lord, Bring me
  with all your saints to the joy of his resurrection.

LITANY OF REPENTANCE
PHYLLIS TICKLE (contemporary)
American Episcopalian writer

Notice well: Who was dearer or closer to our Lord than were the apostles? But there was no one of them who did not fall into mortal sin; they had all been mortal sinners. In the Old Law and the New he often showed this through men who afterward were by far the dearest to him. And even now one seldom finds that people attain to anything good unless first they have gone somewhat astray. Our Lord's intention in this is that we should recognize his great mercifulness; and through it he wishes to exhort us to a greater and truer humility and devotion. . . .

The weaker a man finds himself and the more have been his misdeeds, the more cause he has to bind himself to God with an undivided love in which there is no sin or weakness. . . . As godly repentance lifts itself up to God, sins vanish into God's abyss, faster than it takes me to shut my eyes, and so they become utterly nothing, as if they had never happened, if repentance is complete.

MEISTER ECKHART (1260–1327)
German Dominican mystic and theologian

THE LUMINOUS EYE

The Word of God is seen here as a "field of force," awakening and sensitizing us. It is called a mirror, a spark, a bridge, "though still, it dances about." Through meditating on the Word we witness and are witnessed, and are brought to the experience of all that "is said, and done, and doing" in ourselves. The Word of God is active, informing both the beginner's first uncertain prayer and the contemplative's silent rapture.

There are certain preparatory exercises which should occupy the attention of the contemplative apprentice: the lesson, the meditation and the petition. They may be called, for a better understanding, reading, reflecting and praying. . . . These three are so linked together that there can be no profitable reflection without previous reading, or hearing. Nor will beginners or proficients come to true prayer without previous reflection.

God's word, whether written or spoken, is like a mirror. The spiritual eye of your soul is your reason. Your spiritual face is your consciousness. And just as your bodily eyes cannot see where the dirty mark is on your bodily face without a mirror, or without someone else telling you where it is, so with your spiritual faculties. . . . Now if this mark is a particular sin, the well is the holy Church, and the water is confession, with all its elements.

And if the mark is simply the blind root with the impulse to sin, then the well is the merciful God, and the water is prayer, with all its elements.

And so you can see that beginners and proficients cannot come to proper reflection without previous reading or listening, or to prayer without previous reflection.

UNKNOWN ENGLISH MYSTIC (14th century)
The Cloud of Unknowing

You do well not to let drop from your hands the polished mirror of the holy Gospel of your Lord, for it provides the likeness of everyone who looks into it, and it shows the resemblance of all who peer into it. . . .

Though dumb, the mirror speaks: in its silence, it cries out; although you might think it was a dead object, it makes its proclamation. Though still, it dances about; though it has no body, its womb is spacious, and in those hidden chambers within it every limb is depicted. All kinds of shapes are featured in the fraction of a moment, they are created within it with a speed that is imperceptible. . . .

And just as this natural mirror is but a figure of the Gospel, so too the Gospel is but a figure of the beauty that is above which does not fade and at which all the sins of the created world are rebuked. . . .

There the kingdom of heaven is depicted, visible to those who have a luminous eye.

EPHREM THE SYRIAN (303–373)
Spiritual and theological writer

It often happens that the one who is converted has been seized by Christ and "parachuted" for a while into an experience which is decisive on the spiritual level, but which is above his usual

Christian "tools." His knowledge of doctrine is sadly lacking, or his human or moral structures are inadequate, or again perhaps he does not know how to make use of the Church's ways of expressing prayer. These gaps have to be filled by a slow and patient labor: the Lord has caught him and carried him high up and away in the air, and has then set him down again on the ground. Converted, he will have to learn how to walk on his own feet.

Meditation, the slow assimilation and rumination of the articles of faith, is most necessary in order to establish his life of prayer on a solid basis.

A CARTHUSIAN (contemporary)

Reading seeks for the sweetness of a blessed life, meditation perceives it, prayer asks for it, contemplation tastes it. Reading, as it were, puts food whole into the mouth, meditation chews it and breaks it up, prayer extracts its flavor, contemplation is the sweetness itself which gladdens and refreshes. Reading works on the outside, meditation on the pith: prayer asks for what we long for, contemplation gives us delight in the sweetness which we have found. . . .

I hear the words read: "Blessed are the pure in heart for they shall see God." This is a short text of Scripture, but it is of great sweetness, like a grape that is put into the mouth filled with many senses to feed the soul. When the soul has carefully examined it, it says to itself, There may be something good here. I shall return to my heart and try to understand and find this purity, for this is indeed a precious and desirable thing. Those who have it are called blessed. It has for its reward the vision of God which is eternal life, and it is praised in so many places in sacred Scripture. So, wishing to have a fuller understanding of this, the soul begins to bite and chew upon this grape, as though putting it in a wine press, while it stirs up its powers of reasoning to ask what this precious purity may be and how it may be had.

GUIGO DE PONTE (d. 1297)
Carthusian monk and spiritual writer

Meditation is spiritual work, sometimes difficult work. But it is a work of love and of desire. It is not something that can be practiced without effort, at least in the beginning. And the sincerity, humility and perseverance of our efforts will be proportionate to our desire. This desire in turn is a gift of grace. Anyone who imagines he can simply begin meditating without praying for the desire and the grace to do so, will soon give up. But the desire to meditate, and the grace to begin meditating, should be taken as an implicit promise of further graces. In meditation, as in anything else in the Christian life, everything depends on our correspondence with the grace of the Holy Spirit.

Meditation is almost all contained in this one idea: the idea of awakening our interior self and attuning ourselves inwardly to the Holy Spirit, so that we will be able to respond to His grace. In mental prayer, over the years, we must allow our interior perceptivity to be refined and purified. We must attune ourselves to unexpected movements of grace, which do not fit our own preconceived ideas of the spiritual life at all, and which in no way flatter our own ambitious aspirations.

We must be ready to cooperate not only with graces that console, but with graces that humiliate us. Not only with lights that exalt us, but with lights that blast our self-complacency. Much of our coldness and dryness in prayer may well be a kind of unconscious defense against grace. Without realizing it, we allow our nature to de-sensitize our souls so that we cannot perceive graces which we intuitively foresee may prove to be painful.

Meditation is then always to be associated in practice with abandonment to the will and action of God. It goes hand in hand with self-renunciation and with obedience to the Holy Spirit. Meditation that does not seek to bring our whole being into conformity with God's will must naturally remain sterile and abstract. But any sincere interior prayer that really seeks this one all-important end—our conformity to God's will in our regard—cannot fail to be rewarded by grace. It will prove, without question, to be one of the most sanctifying forces in our lives.

THOMAS MERTON (1915–1968)
American Cistercian monk

There is no standing still. Every gift we receive, every new understanding, drives us still deeper into the Word of God. We need time for God's Word. In order to understand the commandments of God correctly, we must meditate at length upon his Word. . . .

Why is it that my thoughts depart so quickly from God's Word and I find the necessary word is often not there for me in the hour of need? Do I forget to eat and drink and sleep? Why do I forget God's Word? Because I am not yet able to say with the psalmist: "My delight is in your statutes." I never forget that in which I delight. To forget or not is a matter not only of the mind but of the whole person, including the heart. That on which my life and soul depend I cannot forget. The more I begin to love the ordinances of God in creation and in his Word, the more they will be present for me at every hour. Only love guards against forgetting.

Just as you would not dissect and analyze the word spoken by someone dear to you, but would accept it just as it was said, so you should accept the Word of Scripture and ponder it in your heart as Mary did. That is all. That is meditation. Do not look for new thoughts and interconnections in the text as you would in a sermon! Do not ask how you should tell it to others, but ask what it tells you! Then ponder this word in your heart at length, until it is entirely within you and has taken possession of you.

It is not necessary every day to go through the entire text we have chosen for meditation. Often we will hold on to one word of it for the entire day. Passages that we do not understand we can simply pass over. . . .

If during meditation our thoughts move to persons who are near to us or to those we are concerned about, then let them linger there. That is a good time to pray for them. Do not pray in general, then, but in particular for the people who are on your mind. Let the Word of Scripture tell you what you ought to pray for them. As a help, we may write down the names of the people we want to remember every day. Our intercessions require their appointed time, too, if we are to be serious about them. Pay attention, though, that our intercessions do not become another means of taking flight from the most important thing: prayer for our own soul's salvation.

We begin our meditations with the prayer for the Holy Spirit, asking for proper concentration for ourselves and for all who we know are also meditating. Then we turn to the text. At the close of the meditation we want to be truly able to say a prayer of thanksgiving from a heart that is full. . . .

Whoever seriously undertakes the daily practice of meditation will soon discover great difficulties. . . . Do not become confused and upset because of your distractedness. Just sit down again every day and wait very patiently. If your thoughts keep wandering, there is no need for you to hold on to them compulsively. There is nothing wrong with letting them roam where they will; but then incorporate in your prayers the place or person to which they have gone. So you will find your way back to your text, and the minutes spent in such diversions will not be lost and will no longer be any cause for worry. . . .

Behind all our uncertainties and needs stands our great need to pray; for all too long many of us have known this need without finding any help or direction. The only help is to faithfully and patiently begin again our earliest exercises of prayer and meditation. We will be further helped by the knowledge that other brothers are also meditating, that at all times the entire holy church in heaven and on earth prays with us. That is a comfort to us in the weakness of our own prayers. And if we really do not know what we ought to pray and completely lose heart about it, we still know that the Holy Spirit prays for us with "groanings which cannot be uttered."

We dare not allow ourselves to cease from this daily engagement with the Scripture, and we must begin it right away if it is not now our practice.

DIETRICH BONHOEFFER (1906–1945)
German Lutheran pastor and theologian

There is always a danger of illuminism and false mysticism when those who are easily swayed by fancy and emotion take too seriously the vivid impulses they experience in prayer, and imagine that the voice of their own exalted feeling is really the voice of God.

The proper atmosphere of meditation is one of tranquillity and peace and balance. The mind should be able to give itself to simple and peaceful reflection. Intellectual brilliance is never required. The will should find itself directed toward the good and strengthened in its desire for union with God. It does not have to feel itself enkindled with raptures of ardent love. A good meditation may well be quite "dry" and "cold" and "dark." It may even be considerably disturbed by involuntary distractions. St. John of the Cross says somewhere that "the best fruit grows in land that is cold and dry." But this arid meditation nevertheless fills the soul with humility, peace, courage, and the determination to persevere.

THOMAS MERTON (1915–1968)
American Cistercian monk

We cannot give our attention to reading if the center of our attention is our ego. We cannot be free for God's action in us if we cling to ourselves and do not abandon ourselves totally to him.

We should therefore make an effort to reject our illusory needs, our latest idols, the false gods which we daily invent. Really, it is society that convinces us that we need so many things. Advertising and the subtle suggestions of a consumerist culture create needs in us. When people confess that they are not finding "satisfaction" in reading the Scriptures, I often ask myself if it is because they are approaching the Word in an attempt to satisfy some specific need they have. Are they expecting results from the Word that it will not give them because, like prayer, the Word is not up for sale?

ENZO BIANCHI (contemporary)
Italian Benedictine prior at Bose

The Gospel is within you, and you are its evidence; it is preached to you in your own bosom, and everything within you is a proof of the truth of it.

Ask how you shall know there is such a thing as day and night; for the fall and redemption are as manifest within you as day and night are manifest without you.

Here, in this intimate and true knowledge of yourself lies the most precious evidence of the Gospel, and is as near to you as you are to yourself; because all that is said, and declared, and recorded in the Gospel is a plain record of that which is said, and done, and doing in yourself.

And when you once feel it proved to you by its agreement with the state of your own nature, then it becomes a pearl that is dearer to you than your life; and what is best, it is then a pearl which no one can rob you of. You are then in such assurance and possession of the power and goodness of Christ as those blind men were whose eyes He had opened to see the light.

Then, all the wrangle and dispute of learned men against the truth of the Gospel will signify no more to you, nor raise any more doubt in you, than if by history and criticism they would prove that you never had any benefit from the light of the sun.

WILLIAM LAW (1686–1761)
English contemplative and cleric

Even if a thousand trumpets were to sound in the ears of the dead, they would never hear them. That is how it is with a soul . . . that has lost all memory of God, a soul that never thinks of God all day: it does not hear the sound of the Word that is calling it. The trump of the Word does not wake it. It is sunk in the sleep of death and this sleep is pleasant to it.

Being a dead soul, it is not conscious of its state and is not moved to ask for life. It is like one who has died of natural causes, or who on the level of practical obedience to the Word of God has committed suicide. It does not suffer as a result of its death and the idea of asking for a return to life does not enter its head.

The soul is dead when it never thinks of God, when it has lost all memory of God. Its powers of discernment are dead. Its desires for the things of heaven are dead. Its nature is alive, but its will is dead and its freedom has disappeared.

PHILOXENUS OF MABBUG (c. 440–c. 523)
Syrian bishop, saint, and theologian

The Holy Spirit composed the scriptures so that in them, as in a pharmacy open to all souls, we might each of us be able to find the medicine suited to our own particular illness. . . .

The Book of Psalms contains everything useful that the others have. It predicts the future, it recalls the past, it gives directions for living, it suggests the right behavior to adopt. It is, in short, a jewel case in which have been collected all the valid teachings in such a way that individuals find remedies just right for their cases.

It heals the old wounds of the soul and gives relief to recent ones. It cures the illnesses and preserves the health of the soul.

Every Psalm brings peace, soothes the internal conflicts, calms the rough waves of evil thoughts, dissolves anger, corrects and moderates profligacy.

Every Psalm preserves friendship and reconciles those who are separated. Who could actually regard as an enemy the person beside whom they have raised a song to the one God?

Every Psalm anticipates the anguish of the night and gives rest after the efforts of the day. It is safety for babes, beauty for the young, comfort for the aged, adornment for women.

Every Psalm is the voice of the Church.

BASIL THE GREAT (330–379)
Doctor of the church, saint, and bishop of Caesarea

Reading is the food of prayer. Or perhaps one can say that reading is fuel for the fire. Prayer is the flame, but you won't have a fire if you don't have fuel. If the monk is not feeding himself with the word of God, if he is not putting the logs of the word of God into the hearth of his heart, there won't be prayer. The fire will just die out in one way or another.

HUGH GILBERT, O.S.B. (contemporary)
Benedictine abbot of Pluscarden Abbey, Scotland

Lectio divina is never part of a program of self-improvement. It is a response to an invitation. The first fidelity required of a disciple is that he be open to accept guidance and concrete directives from his master. By exposing himself fully to his master's influence the disciple becomes imbued with his attitudes and values and is progressively aware of how to shape his life. In *lectio divina* we give God a chance to get at us, to guide us, to teach us, maybe to call into question some of our bright ideas and pet projects. Turning aside, for the moment, from our own beliefs and plans, we concentrate on being responsive to God's call. We go to our reading in a spirit of submission, prepared patiently to cede the initiative to Christ. . . .

Through our reading, the Holy Spirit intends to renew our lives, to reshape them according to God's plan. Because this is so, it is important that our *lectio divina* be done not in isolation from real life, from our past and present, our joys and sorrows, our pluses and minuses. The Word of God speaks to us in the here-and-now, as we are. It has now no interest in what we used to be or what we might have been. . . .

Prayer thrives in such a climate. When, during *lectio divina*, prayer comes naturally, it should not be elbowed aside but allowed to spread. When one's heart is inflamed or one's interest captivated, no pressure should be felt to keep moving. In *lectio divina* the "interruptions" are habitually more important than the reading itself. Having allowed God's Word entrance into our hearts, we should extend to it also the possibility of moving without restriction and of exercising its influence over us without stoppage or hindrance. For this to happen, any form of pressure must be eschewed. . . .

From time to time in our reading we come across something which specially appeals to us or which seems to apply very aptly to our particular situation at a given moment. We should make the most of such opportunities and spend as much time with the text in question as we can. If it helps we can write it out and keep it before us for a few days, allowing ourselves the leisure to ruminate upon it and really let it become part of us. If it is something particularly attractive to us and if fairly short, we can use it as the basis of our prayer. When occasion presents itself for brief or even momentary prayer during the day, we should take this as our starting point. In this way we are trying to give full scope to a text which the attraction of grace has signaled to us a being of special relevance. When the attraction fades we should pass on to something else without regret.

Our *lectio divina* should be conducted in such a way that we develop a sensitivity to the call of grace. In the beginning the texts which cause us to come alive will usually be of a confirmatory nature. As our sensitivity increases other texts will begin to clamor for our attention, texts which offer challenge rather than comfort. To these also we must learn to submit, knowing that it is in this way that God renews our life.

MICHAEL CASEY (contemporary)
Australian Benedictine monk of Tarrawarra Abbey

The heart of man was made to receive the Word, and the Word adapts itself to the dimensions of our human heart. The one is there for the other. . . . When the Word of God accosts our heart, then suddenly and quite unexpectedly the one may recognize the other, thanks to the one Spirit who is present in both. A bridge is made, as it were, between our heart and the Word. From heart to Word a spark is transmitted. Between the Spirit lying dormant deep within our heart and the Spirit who is active in the Word a fruitful and vitalizing dialogue begins. Engendered from an imperishable seed the heart is born again of the Word. We recognize in the Word, as in a mirror, our new countenance. By it we become witnesses to our rebirth in Christ. "The hidden man of the heart" awakens within us. . . .

The Word lays our heart quite bare. Now, and only now, can our untrammeled heart really and truly proceed to listen to God's Word. Deeper and deeper it penetrates. Word and heart mirror each other and come to resemble each other more and more. The heart is aware of itself now as a new organ, with new senses and a sensibility previously unknown.

... The Word only reaches the baptized person via the living band of brothers and sisters who have been born of this same Word before him. This may be the role of a priest; but a lay person too, can be for us the spiritual father or mother through whom the Word comes to us and by whom the new life is brought to birth in our heart. This is the normal way of attaining to an awakened heart and the practice of prayer. You do not learn this on your own. You learn it from someone else. You may learn it from the look on another's face or catch the sound of it in his heart—in a heart that lives, that radiates life and awakens others to life.

ANDRÉ LOUF (1929–)
French Cistercian abbot

What can one say about the fire when one is immersed in it? What can one say about the prayer of contemplation which comes at the end of *lectio divina* except to say that it is a glowing log which never burns out and that it inflames the believer's heart with love for the Lord? ...

Lectio divina wants to lead you there, where you can contemplate God as God's own beloved, where you can repeat the words of God's own beloved in joy, in wonder and in self-forgetfulness. This path is not always easy and straight. Don't think that you can just run along its way. Passionate love alternates with fear, gratitude with a complete absence of feeling, enthusiasm with bodily weariness, words which speak with words which are mute, God's silence with your silence: all these experiences are present and serve as the stock in trade of your *lectio divina,* day after day.

What is important is staying faithful to our daily encounter with the Lord. Sooner or later the Word will open a passageway into our hearts and clear away all the obstacles we set up, obstacles which are always present in any journey of faith and prayer. Only the person who is faithful to the Word knows God's faithfulness: that God will never fail to be available and to speak to our hearts. The faithful person knows that there are times when the Word of God seems absent, but that these times are followed by an epiphany. The Word will shine forth. The faithful person knows that these difficult, uncomfortable, dry times are a grace insofar as they remind us of the distance between our experience of God and God as God is. . . .

God needs you as an instrument in the world to help create new heavens and a new earth—a future day which awaits you when, in dying, you will see God face to face. Then you will see how you have been and still are a living letter written by Christ, a *lectio divina* for your sisters and brothers. . . .

ENZO BIANCHI (contemporary)
Italian Benedictine prior at Bose

Anyone entering the sphere of radiance of the divine word is held fast by it; he knows from experience that this word not only communicates knowledge about God, but—hidden within the garb of the letter—actually has divine qualities: in itself it is an overpowering manifestation of God's infinity and truth, his majesty and love. God's epiphany compels the hearer to kneel in humble submission. The latter had imagined that he was dealing with a word he could grasp and evaluate, like other great and profound utterances of mankind; yet once he enters its field of force, he himself is the one who is grasped and evaluated.

He had wanted to approach Jesus in order to see him ("Come and see!"), and now, under the gaze of Jesus, he finds that it is he who has long been observed, seen through, judged and accepted in grace by Jesus. All he can do now, therefore, is to fall down and worship the Word: "Master, you are the Son of God; you are the King of Israel!" This conquest, however, is only the starting point: "You shall see greater things than these. . . . You will see heaven opened, and the angels of God ascending and descending upon the Son of man" (John 1:46–51).

Contemplation's ladder, reaching up to heaven, begins with the word of scripture, and whatever rung we are on, we are never beyond this hearing of the word. In contemplation, just as we can never leave the Lord's humanity behind us, neither can we get "beyond" the word in its human form. It is in the humanity that we find God, in the world of sense that we find the Spirit.

HANS URS VON BALTHASAR (1905–1988)
Swiss Roman Catholic theologian

CYCLE FOUR

THE HEART OF
OUR DESIRE

*What is a prayer of petition? Of intercession? How do human desires relate to
the desire of God? The Gospels urge us to ask, to seek, to praise, to plead, exhort
us to be persevering and confident, but always "in his name," and "in conformity with God's nature." It is in this way we ensure in our praying that
"God is God and not an extension of my arm which is too short."*

In every request, heart and soul and mind ought to supply the
low accompaniment, "Thy will be done," but the making of any
request brings us nearer to Him. Anything large enough for a
wish to light upon, is large enough to hang a prayer upon; the
thought of Him to whom that prayer goes will purify and correct the desire.

GEORGE MACDONALD (1824–1905)
Scottish novelist and poet

Each person brings himself along when he comes to pray; and if
he is inexperienced in prayer, what he brings with him will
mostly bear the stamp of his personal problems and daily life.
Then he will learn that, in prayer, even if he asks for something

or for clarity in a matter that is important to him personally, a reorganization always takes place. What he regarded as essential may become quite unimportant from God's point of view. What seemed easy he may now find difficult. He cannot calculate how this change is going to take place, so he must be ready to fit his arrangements in with God's. . . .

So in prayer it is crucial that nature should be in a state of indifference regarding grace in order to be open and accessible to God's nature. The person who perseveres in the attitude of prayer will experience the effect of grace on nature as the real constant in his life. He will enter each succeeding prayer with an ever-growing renunciation of what he thinks of as his own and of all he has preconceived, planned, and explained, letting himself be led by grace more and more. In his own affairs he will experience the blowing of the Spirit. He will come to see that he has been handed over as a victim and that in his sacrifice and his desolation (which may be subject to very natural causes) he has been permitted to know the consolation of the experience of God. He will realize that consolation does not consist in seeing his earthly life pursuing its course according to his will and expectation, but in God adopting him into his providence and fashioning his destiny. On earth he may have to drag the same problems around with him to the very end; yet, from a Christian point of view, he may continually enjoy God's consolation, which is to experience his truth. Prayer becomes renewal, and renewal becomes truth, and truth becomes the presence of God.

ADRIENNE VON SPEYR (1902–1967)
Swiss mystic, physician, and writer

[There is a difference] between "prayed petition" and "praying prayer." The first is an expression of my desire, or rather, of my need . . . but in that search I do not really reach transcendence. "God" is brought back to our level. This is the prayer of La Hire:

"Lord, do now for La Hire what La Hire would do for you if you were La Hire and La Hire were God."

"Praying prayer," on the other hand, is, because of love, of the order of God and is not a mere petition, but prayer. Prayer is essentially communion with God and with his will. If Jesus had simply asked in the garden of Gethsemane: "Let this cup pass from me," he would only have been expressing a petition. His appeal was a prayer because he added: "Nevertheless, not as I will, but as thou wilt." In this way, God is recognized as God. True prayer ensures that God is God and not an extension of my arm which is too short.

YVES CONGAR (1904–1997)
French Dominican theologian and cardinal

In prayer, we have first to experience the dissatisfaction of our own desire, confess our own lack, and recognize in faith the absent presence of God. This should lead us to desire the desire of God himself, that is, to desire what God desires and to let God desire in us. At this point, prayer appears as the mystery of God in us and an event of the Spirit, because it is the function of the Holy Spirit to be the desire of God in God himself and also the desire of God in us. The Spirit forms, deepens, expands, and adjusts our desire to the desire of God by giving it the same object. The Spirit makes our desire live from the life of God himself, to the point where God himself comes to desire at the heart of our desire.

JEAN-CLAUDE SAGNE (contemporary)
French Roman Catholic theologian

You probably remember the two passages from St. Paul where he says "My power is manifest in weakness." Weakness is not the kind of weakness which we show by sinning and forgetting God, but the kind of weakness which means being completely supple, completely transparent, completely abandoned in the hands of God. We usually try to be strong and we prevent God from manifesting His power.

You remember how you were taught to write when you were small. Your mother put a pencil in your hand, took your hand in hers, and began to move it. Since you did not know at all what she meant to do, you left your hand completely free in hers. This is what I mean by the power of God being manifest in weakness.

ANTHONY BLOOM (1914–)
Russian Orthodox monk and metropolitan of Sourozh

It seems in fact that you have fallen between two stools: You now have neither, but are deprived of both. You are not to be too despondent about this; rather you must endure it humbly, and wait patiently on the Lord's will. For, as I see it, you are now on the spiritual ocean, being shipped across from the active state to the contemplative. . . .

As far as you can see, everything has gone—ordinary graces as well as the more special. But you must not be too disturbed, though it seems that you have every reason to be. Rather trust lovingly in our Lord, as much as you can at the time, however feebly; for he is not far off. He *will* turn his face to you, perhaps very soon, and affect you again with a touch of that same grace more ardently than you ever experienced before. . . . whenever he goes away, he will come again soon. And each time he will come more marvelously and joyfully than he did before, as long as you have that patient endurance. For his purpose in all this is to make you as close-fitting to his will spiritually as a soft leather glove is to the bodily hand.

UNKNOWN ENGLISH MYSTIC (14th century)
Letter of Private Direction

When life becomes weak it does not cease to breathe; it continues to the utmost of its capacity, restoring its strength thereby. It is similar with faith: when it weakens, we should pray to the best of our ability, restoring our faith thereby.

The same applies to those who do not yet have any faith but are searching for it. It is important that they should not merely think and read about it and discuss it; they should also dwell in prayer on it. But this should be done honestly; they cannot expect to anticipate, in prayer, certainties which they do not yet possess by faith. They must therefore establish a starting-point in their minds from which they can pray: to the Living God or the Mystery of Grace or—if it is still no more than that—to what, however remote and glimmering, they conceive to be the essential reality. If all they could say to this unknown deity were such words as: "Thou Unknown God, if Thou art, Thou shouldst know that I am ready for Thee. Make me to understand," this would be real prayer.

It is important that prayer and conduct should be closely linked and especially so in times of doubt and difficulty. When a man for the sake of his soul carries out a duty more conscientiously, overcomes temptation with greater determination or is more charitable and magnanimous towards others than he would normally be, this also affects his prayer. It opens new vistas to him, purifies his judgment, and increases his spiritual power.

Admittedly, there are times when prayer can do very little and circumstances in which man is altogether unable to pray—because he either does not know where to turn or his sense of propriety forbids him to approach God. Nevertheless, there remain for him at such times certain hidden substitutes for prayer.

He can, for example, acknowledge the sublime with special reverence wherever he encounters it and in so doing render homage to the mystery which is behind all that is noble on earth. He may make a special effort to honor all men, carefully avoiding offense in his relations with them and acknowledging the dignity that even the lowliest has; he may pay attention to the delicate, the defenseless and the tender, or be especially heedful of physical and, even more, of mental suffering. The main thing about this attitude is its intent. It aims through earthly things at things holy and divine to which, for the time being, it has no direct access. This piety can take the form of reverence towards all living things, an endeavor not to harm or destroy anything. There is nothing sentimental about this; on the contrary, it is something very calm and genuine, something born of strength— though a strength which, to be sure, has not yet found its proper channel.

ROMANO GUARDINI (1885–1968)
Italian-born German Roman Catholic monsignor
and professor of Christian philosophy

Wherever *secular* life is lived with *unreserved honesty* there *ipso facto* an essential element in religious life is already present because God loves the world in itself, endows it with grace in itself, and in no sense regards it as a rival to himself as though he were envious of it. He who responds to the world with genuine love *ipso facto* encounters in it the Cross of Christ and the inconceivability of God. He has no need whatever to conjure them up first in order for them to be present there. If he practices the virtues of the world, suffers himself to be educated by it in joyfulness, courage, devotion to duty and love, then *ipso facto* he is actively practicing a vital element in genuine religion in his life and such worldly virtues will one day open to him the innermost mystery which they contain, namely God himself.

KARL RAHNER (1904–1984)
German Jesuit theologian

Do not wish or demand any favor from God, either for your needs or for your friends. . . . Both for your interests and for theirs you must desire his will; if you pray for them, do not pray for what they choose in accordance with their own sense of values. Under cover of holy desires, the majority of souls today go astray and find their refreshment in an inferior consolation that they can grasp. This is a great pity. . . .

Nowadays this is the way everyone loves himself; people wish to live with God in consolations and repose, in wealth and power, and to share the fruition of his glory. We all indeed wish to be God with God, but God knows there are few of us who want to live as men with his Humanity, or want to carry his cross with him. . . . Indeed we can rightly discern this as regards ourselves, in that we are so little able to hold out against suffering in all respects. An unexpected sorrow, though slight, goes to our heart; or a slander, or a lie that people tell about us; or someone's robbing us of our honor, or our rest, or our own will: How quickly and deeply any of this wounds us all! And we know so well what we want or do not want, there are so many things and kinds of things for which we have an attraction or an aversion: now alike, now different; now sweetness, now bitterness; now here, now there; now off, now on; and as regards everything, we are so ready to provide for ourselves where any repose for us is in sight!

This is why we remain unenlightened in our views, inconstant in our whole manner of acting, and unreliable in our reason and our understanding. . . . we do not live with Christ as he lived; neither do we forsake all as Christ did, nor are we forsaken by all as Christ was. . . . For every advantage fills us with delight and convinces us that we are something; and precisely through this conviction we become nothing at all. And thus we ruin ourselves in all respects.

HADEWIJCH (13th century)
Flemish Beguine and contemplative writer

But we? We imitate Christ and hope he will deliver us from our own fate. Like little lambs we follow the shepherd, naturally to good pastures. No talk at all of uniting our Above and Below! On the contrary Christ and his cross deliver us from our conflict, which we simply leave alone. . . . Instead of bearing ourselves, i.e., our own cross, ourselves, we load Christ with our unresolved conflicts. We "place ourselves under his cross," but by golly not under our own. . . . The cross of Christ was borne by himself and was his. To put oneself under somebody else's cross, which has already been carried by him, is certainly easier than to carry your own cross amid the mockery and contempt of the world. That way you remain nicely ensconced in tradition and are praised as devout. This is well-organized Pharisaism and highly un-Christian. Whoever imitates Christ and has the cheek to want to take Christ's cross on himself when he can't even carry his own has in my view not yet learnt the ABC of the Christian message. . . .

In every feature, Christ's life is a prototype of individuation and hence cannot be imitated: one can only live one's own life totally in the same way with all the consequences this entails.

C. G. JUNG (1875–1961)
Swiss psychiatrist and philosopher

The gospels very frequently show us Christ at prayer: when his mission is revealed by the Father, before he calls the apostles, when he blesses God at the multiplication of the loaves, when he is transfigured on the mountain, when he heals the deaf mute, when he raises Lazarus, before he asks for Peter's confession of faith, when he teaches the disciples how to pray, when the disciples return from their mission, when he blesses the little children, when he prays for Peter.

The work of each day was closely bound up with his prayer, indeed flowed out from it. He would retire into the desert or into the hills to pray, rising very early, or spending the night as far as the fourth watch in prayer to God.

We are right in believing that he took part in public prayers, in the synagogues, which he entered on the Sabbath "as his custom was," and in the temple, which he called a house of prayer, as well as in the private prayers which devout Israelites would recite regularly every day. He used the traditional blessings of God at meals. This is expressly mentioned in connection with the multiplication of the loaves, the Last Supper, the meal at Emmaus; he also joined with the disciples in a hymn of praise.

To the very end of his life, as his Passion was approaching, at the Last Supper, in the agony in the garden, and on the cross, the divine teacher showed that prayer was the soul of his messianic ministry and paschal death. . . .

Jesus has commanded us to do as he did. On many occasions he said: "Pray," "ask," "seek," "in my name." He gave us a formula of prayer in what is known as the Lord's Prayer. He taught us that prayer is necessary, that it should be humble, vigilant, persevering, confident in the Father's goodness, singleminded, and in conformity with God's nature.

The apostles have handed on to us, scattered throughout their letters, many prayers, especially of praise and thanksgiving. They warn us that we must be urgent and persevering in prayer offered to God in the Holy Spirit through Christ. They tell us of its sure power in sanctifying and speak of the prayer of praise, of thanksgiving, of petition and of intercession on behalf of all.

From the Roman Catholic *LITURGY OF THE HOURS*

O knit my heart unto thee. (Psalm 86:11)

And here and now, as we make the most important petition we can make, "O knit my heart unto thee," the relationship of the soul to God is being reinforced by that interchange of love which is grace. The good which is like no other is continuously and unconquerably ours. Nothing that can happen to us or around us can change this central fact of faith. But it is something to be recalled into focus, over and over, or faith will die; and only God's mercy can renew its life.

MILES LOWELL YATES (1890–1956)
American Episcopalian minister

An instant of pure love is more precious in the sight of God and more profitable to the Church than all other good works put together, though it may seem as if nothing were done. . . . Let those men of zeal who think by their preaching and exterior works to convert the world, consider that they would be much more pleasing to God—to say nothing of the example they would give—if they would spend at least one-half of their time in prayer, even though they may not have attained to unitive love. Certainly they would do more, and with less trouble, by one single good work than by a thousand; because of the merit of their prayer, and the spiritual strength which it supplies.

JOHN OF THE CROSS (1542–1591)
Spanish saint and mystic

"Self-satisfaction with our good feelings, prayer for others which permits us not to do anything for them, such prayers . . . are a lie and a hypocrisy whenever we have given up our own effectiveness, our own means, in order to place all in the hands of God." . . . Surely it can seem too easy to pray at the bedside of a sick person, then to depart, leaving him alone with his sickness; to pray for a family in distress without adding to the prayer the money to resolve its problems. . . .

In the face of this position on disincarnate prayer the watchword has become: "Prayer requires that we do ourselves that which we ask God to do." . . . This new attitude carries much weight. It teaches us quite rightly that prayer does not consist of words in thin air, and that a person cannot pray unless he is fully responsible for what he is saying. He must be completely involved in the action. . . .

So we say, . . . "if I do what I can in my own sphere, then God works the miracle, which consists precisely in the fact that out of such inadequate means great things are brought to pass." That is true, and beyond dispute biblically, provided always that we do not then slip into that little variation so frequently met with today: ". . . then God performs the miracle which consists precisely in the fact that I who am bad, egotistical, sinful, that I have become capable of this love, this charity." Indeed not! The miracle is not that the disciples should be involved in the action, but that the five thousand people were fed. . . .

The deep-seated tendency now is really to place man at the center of everything. In insisting that man must himself perform that which he petitions, we no longer are saying that he should become involved in it, but that he is in fact responsible for fulfilling the prayer himself. . . .

This interpretation corresponds exactly to the society in which we find ourselves, namely, a world of means. . . . This teaching is saying to us, "Use to the full the means which this society gives you, then you will see." In other words, the proliferation of means alters the character of prayer. It is no longer a giving over of what I can do into the hands of God, upon whom I call for help from the depths of my impotence, "Out of the depths I cry to thee, O Lord!" Today there are thousands of ways to fill up the depths, or in fact to avoid them. Why call upon God?

JACQUES ELLUL (1912–1994)
French philosopher and theologian

There must always be, between us and God, a depth that we can reach—and I insist on this fact—that we should be able to reach. We should learn by the practice of the presence of God, by stopping time, by letting our being go deeper, to reach it almost at will, for it is our vocation to remain in the presence of the Lord. We should learn how to descend into ourselves when we are in the presence of our neighbor, whoever he is—not the pious one, the easy one, of whom we are ready to write in large letters: "This is an image of God!" but the difficult neighbor, the unacceptable neighbor, the one who is an insult to all that we think of God and His Incarnation—we can then meet that neighbor in the place which no means of communication would enable us to reach, because we refrain from communicating on the level of words, gestures, external relations: we are not up to that, we are too small, too weak and friable for that.

If we take on our neighbor in this way, if we accept him in silence, we are making an initial act of essential importance: it is the act of justice—not an act of social justice, which is distributive, egalitarian—but a dangerous act of justice which consists, in the first place, of accepting our neighbor just as he is and giving him the right to be as he is, even if his way means our death and our destruction. It is an act of radical justice such as we see in God, who accepted fallen man instead of rejecting and destroying him; who accepted man in his downfall, knowing that the downfall of man meant the crucifixion of the Son of God. That is the act of Christian justice; it is there that justice begins, and not when we distribute the spiritual or material wealth equally or selectively. It is the moment when we allow the other person to be himself, whatever the consequences. It is only at this price that we can look and see in the features of the other person a living and glorifying projection of the face of the Lord. . . .

Towards the end of the ninth chapter Job in his despair turns to the empty, silent, cruel heaven and says: "Where is the man who will stand between me and my Judge and put his hand on the shoulder of each of us?" Where is the one who will make an act of intercession?—for to intercede does not mean to remind the Lord of what He has forgotten. . . . What Job had sensed is that in this contestation between him and God, the only one who could place himself between the two would be someone who was the equal of each of the two, who could put his hand on the shoulder of the living God without sacrilege and on the shoulder of the man, in his agony, without destroying him. Here is a first vision of that which Christ will be, true God and true man, fully God and fully man, the One in whom and by whom the plenitude of Divinity has lived in the flesh, in our midst. And this act of Intercession by Christ which is the Incarnation—is a definitive act. Christ has not become man for a time: the Word of God is incarnated for all time.

This is what intercession is: at one and the same time an act which precedes prayer, a complete engagement which makes us simultaneously engaged and disengaged from the two sides, in solidarity with one side as well as with the other and, because of this, rejected by one as well as by the other.

ANTHONY BLOOM (1914–)
Russian Orthodox monk and metropolitan of Sourozh

The usual notion of prayer is so absurd. How can those who know nothing about it, who pray little or not at all, dare speak so frivolously of prayer? A Carthusian, a Trappist will work for years to make of himself a man of prayer, and then any fool who comes along sets himself up as judge of this lifelong effort. If it were really what they suppose, a kind of chatter, the dialogue of a madman with his shadow, or even less—a vain and superstitious sort of petition to be given the good things of this world— how could innumerable people find until their dying day, I won't even say such great "comfort"—since they put no faith in the solace of the senses—but sheer, robust, vigorous, abundant joy in prayer?

Oh, of course, "suggestion," say the scientists. Certainly they can never have known old monks, wise, shrewd, unerring in judgment, and yet aglow with passionate insight, so very tender in their humanity. What miracle enables these semi-lunatics, these prisoners of their own dreams, these sleepwalkers, apparently to enter more deeply each day into the pain of others? An odd sort of dream, an unusual opiate which, far from turning him back into himself and isolating him from his fellows, unites the individual with mankind in the spirit of universal charity.

GEORGES BERNANOS (1888–1948)
French novelist and polemicist

If we believe in a real kingdom of God—an organic fellowship of interrelated lives—prayer should be as effective a force in this interrelated social world of ours as gravitation is in the world of matter. Personal spirits experience spiritual gravitation, soul reaches after soul, hearts draw towards one another. We are no longer in the net of blind fate, in the realm of impersonal force—we are in a love system where the aspiration of one member heightens the entire group, and the need of one—even the least—draws upon the resources of the whole—even the Infinite. We are in actual Divine-human fellowship.

RUFUS JONES (1863–1948)
American Quaker

I can no longer condemn or hate a brother for whom I pray, no matter how much trouble he causes me.... The struggle we undergo with our brother in intercession may be a hard one, but that struggle has the promise that it will gain its goal.

How does this happen? Intercession means no more than to bring our brother into the presence of God, to see him under the Cross of Jesus as a poor human being and sinner in need of grace. Then everything in him that repels us falls away; we see him in all his destitution and need. His need and his sin become so heavy and oppressive that we feel them as our own, and we can do nothing else but pray: Lord, do Thou, Thou alone, deal with him according to Thy severity and Thy goodness. To make intercession means to grant our brother the same right that we have received, namely, to stand before Christ and share in his mercy.

This makes it clear that intercession is also a daily service we owe to God and our brother. He who denies his neighbor the service of praying for him denies him the service of a Christian. It is clear, furthermore, that intercession is not general and vague but very concrete: a matter of definite persons and definite difficulties and therefore of definite petitions. The more definite my intercession becomes, the more promising it is.

DIETRICH BONHOEFFER (1906–1945)
German Lutheran pastor and theologian

In 1938 a man died on Mount Athos. He was a very simple man, a peasant from Russia who came to Mount Athos when he was in his twenties and stayed for about fifty years. . . . [Starets Silouan] was a most remarkable man and for a long time he was in charge of the workshops of the monastery. The workshops of the monastery were manned by young Russian peasants who used to come for one year, for two years, in order to make some money, really farthing added to farthing, in order to go back to their villages with a few pounds, perhaps, at the utmost to be able to start a family by marrying, by building a hut and by buying enough to start their crops. One day other monks, who were in charge of other workshops, said, "Father Silouan, how is it that the people who work in your workshops work so well while you never supervise them, while we spend our time looking after them and they try continuously to cheat us in their work?" Father Silouan said, "I don't know. I can only tell you what I do about it.

"When I come in the morning, I never come without having prayed for these people and I come with my heart filled with compassion and with love for them, and when I walk into the workshop I have tears in my soul for love of them. And then I give them the task they have to perform in the day and as long as they will work I will pray for them, so I go into my cell and I begin to pray about each of them individually. I take my stand before God and I say, 'O Lord, remember Nicholas. He is young, he is just twenty, he has left in his village his wife, who is even younger than he, and their first child. Can you imagine the misery there is there that he has had to leave them because they could not survive on his work at home. Protect them in his absence. Shield them against every evil. Give him courage to struggle through this year and go back to the joy of a meeting, with enough money, but also enough courage, to face the difficulties.'" And he said, "In the beginning I prayed with tears of compassion for Nicholas, for his young wife, for the little child, but as I was praying the sense of the divine presence began to grow on me and at a certain moment it grew so powerful that I lost sight of Nicholas, his wife, his child, his needs, their village, and I could be aware only of God, and I was drawn by the sense of the divine presence deeper and deeper, until of a sudden, at the heart of this presence, I met the divine love holding Nicholas, his wife, and his child, and now it was with the love of God that I began to pray for them again, but again I was drawn into the deep and in the depths of this I again found the divine love. And so," he said, "I spend my days praying for each of them in turn, one after the other, and when the day is over I go, I say a few words to them, we pray together and they go to their rest. And I go back to fulfill my monastic office."

The Heart of Our Desire

Here you can see how contemplative prayer, compassion, active prayer was an effort and a struggle, because it was not just saying "Remember, O Lord, him, him, and him." It was hours and hours spent just praying with compassion, praying with love, both blending together.

ANTHONY BLOOM (1914–)
Russian Orthodox monk and metropolitan of Sourozh

I wonder if I can venture to tell you what is in my mind about intercessory prayer at this moment.... Well, a dear friend of mine was sick and was seemingly nigh unto death. And I was much in prayer for him that he might be spared to his family and to his friends and to his great work. And one night as I was in that intercessory prayer a Voice suddenly spake and said to me—"Are you in real earnest in what you ask? Or are you uttering, as usual, so many of your idle words in this solemn matter? Now to prove the sincerity and the integrity of your love for your friend, and to seal the truth of what you say about the value of his life, will you give Me and yourself a solid proof that you are in real earnest in what you say?" "What is the proof?" I asked, all trembling, and without looking up. And the Voice said, "Will you consent to transfer to your sick friend the half of your remaining years? Suppose you have two more years to live and work yourself, will you give over one of them to your friend? Or if you have ten years yet before you, will you let your friend have five of them?" I sprang to my feet in a torrent of sweat. It was a kind of Garden of Gethsemane to me. But, like Gethsemane, I got strength to say, "Let it be as Thou hast said. Thy will be done. Not my will but Thine be done." Till I lay down that never-to-be-forgotten night with a clean heart and a good conscience as never before both toward God and toward my much talented friend. How the matter is to end I know not. How the case is to work out I cannot tell.

Enough for me and enough for you that my story is true and is
no idle tale.

ALEXANDER WHYTE (1836–1921)
Scottish Evangelical minister

Young man, be not forgetful of prayer. Every time you pray, if
your prayer is sincere, there will be new feeling and new meaning
in it, which will give you fresh courage, and you will understand
that prayer is an education. Remember too every day, and whenever you can, repeat to yourself: "Lord, have mercy on all who
appear before Thee today." For every hour and every moment
thousands of men leave life on this earth, and their souls appear
before God. And how many of them depart in solitude,
unknown, sad, dejected; no one mourns for them or even knows
whether they have lived or not. And behold, from the other end
of the earth perhaps, your prayer for their rest will rise up to
God though you knew them not nor they you. How touching it
must be to a soul standing in dread before the Lord to feel at that
instant that, for him too, there is one to pray, that there is a fellow creature left on earth to love him. And God will look on you
both more graciously, for if you have had so much pity on him,
how much more will He have pity Who is infinitely more loving
and merciful than you. And He will forgive him for your sake.

FYODOR DOSTOEVSKY (1821–1881)
Russian novelist

We live the meaning of the mystical body of Christ in this inter-
connectedness of intercession, where our pleas for others become
pleas for ourselves and their pleas for themselves become pleas
for us. We know by direct experience that we are, as St. Paul
says, members one of another. One further confirmation of this

extraordinary fact comes to us if in our development of intercessory prayer we move into the prayer of free association. In it,
we bring together whatever names and concerns come to our
minds—or to our hearts or souls—as soon as we have selected
our first name, our first person, for whom to pray. Others follow
in remarkably fast order, in a rich, gladdening discourse with the
Spirit, each name suggesting another, and another, and another,
directly connected or loosely connected or not connected at all
except in our prayer. We do not have to hunt for people, or worry
about what may be bothering them, or work at it with any degree
of intensity. They will come to us, the people who should be filling our prayers, the needs they have or have had or are likely to
have. Some of them may have been absent from our thoughts for
years or even decades. . . . We will be surprised and occasionally
disturbed, but we will almost always feel filled up, enlarged, and
supported in ourselves by the experience.

ANN BELFORD ULANOV AND BARRY ULANOV (contemporary)
American Jungian and Christian writers

Let us suppose for a moment that the Christians of today, those
interested in their religion, in particular the more educated
among them, were not merely to talk about the Mystical Body of
Christ and discuss its theology but were to live this truth; that is
to say, suppose it were actually to be borne in upon them with
fear and trembling that we have to bear one another's burdens
and that all of us are accountable before the judgment seat of
God for the eternal destiny of one another.

Let us multiply these delightful hypotheses and these blessed
dreams (one more or less hardly matters): suppose everyone were
convinced, because he is very humble and therefore very realistic,
that such attitudes cannot be allowed to remain only a distant
ideal permitting us to enjoy a spiritual pleasure at our best

moments when we delight to feast upon our own sublime thoughts, but that they have to be put into practice, that they must be taken up anew each day, and that we have to allow ourselves to be reminded by *others* that we have need of certain gestures, certain usages, certain actions, in which these attitudes are already pre-formed and embodied; for they cannot be expected to well up out of the depths of the heart every day with power so fresh as to eliminate the need for such pre-formed and pre-established practices. Further, suppose everyone were convinced that prayer has to penetrate the whole of life, that we must pray at all times, that is to say that our will interceding with God in Christ for the welfare of all has to be a formative power in our daily life, that the prayer of the member of Christ interceding for the whole Church has to be transformed into a penitential life, into patience, love, fasting, alms-giving and into a courageous and joyful renunciation, which is able calmly to pass by many an "enjoyment" and pleasure of life. . . .

Such prayer would generate a power sufficient to transform their lives: their piety would become less egoistic and introverted. They would no longer be resentful if they themselves have to drink of that chalice of bitterness out of which all must drink the redemption of their being. They would then spontaneously begin also to *do* their part for God and his Kingdom; by witnessing to their faith, by helping their neighbor (one must first have sought him with the heart, that is in prayer, and then one's feet will also find him) and those far distant (in the missions) and so on.

They would gradually begin to feel something of that exquisite impulse of love to consume itself in service and obedience for others, until it has entirely spent and emptied itself. And perhaps they would go on from this to acquire some understanding of the heart of the Lord, of the mystery of that love which wells up out of the impenetrable depths—out of what is called the heart—of him who is the Word of God in the flesh: inexhaustible, judging and redeeming, pouring itself out in fruitless generosity and so drawing everything gloriously to itself. They would then (still more slowly, almost timidly and humbly) dare to hope that something of the love of this heart, which moves the sun and the other stars throughout the universe, might seize and transform the meditations and aspirations of their own heart, which, alas, is of itself only inclined to evil; they would perhaps at the dawn of each day with recollected heart dedicate themselves, their life and the newly-given day to this love (or at least attempt to do so).

... Everything else is left ... to the still growth of grace in the soul. It is sufficient for it that one has made a beginning which is tangible, which can be planned, which can be "resolved," which can be repeatedly renewed. But this kind of plan carried out with daily faithfulness is one of those little things which are seemingly nothing, but on which everything depends and from which the greatest consequences can flow.

KARL RAHNER (1904–1984)
German Jesuit theologian

Once again I saw him praying in me and I was as it were inside my body and I heard him praying over me, that is, over the inner man, and he was praying powerfully there, with groans. And during the whole of that time I was dumbfounded and astonished and I wondered who it was praying in me, but at the end of the prayer he spoke as if he was the Spirit, and so I woke up and recalled that the Apostle had said: "The Spirit helps us in our weakness; for we do not know how to pray as we ought, but the Spirit himself intercedes for us with sighs too deep for words."

PATRICK (d. 457)
Saint of Ireland

Inflame the light of our senses,
pour love into our hearts,
the weakness of our bodies
strengthen with lasting power. . . .

Come, Holy Spirit,
and send out a ray
of your heavenly light.

Come, father of the poor,
come, giver of gifts,
come, light of our hearts. . . .

O most blessed light,
fill the innermost hearts
of those who believe in you.

Without your divine power
there is nothing in man,
nothing that is harmless.

Wash what is unclean,
water what is arid,
heal what is wounded.

Bend what is stiff,
warm what is cold,
guide what has gone astray.

UNKNOWN (ninth century)
Veni Creator *hymn*

CYCLE FIVE

YOU ARE
RECONCILED

Blind, faithless, ignorant, self-willed, fearful—we struggle, and find ourselves further entangled in the net of self. We suffer, but "to very little purpose." The way to peace, we are told in this cycle, lies in an active acceptance of our suffering and our misery. And in patience, for "our spiritual maladies, like those of the body, while they are apt to come on horseback and express, tend to depart slowly and on foot."

The main question used to be: "What is prayer?" But now, all of a sudden, we no longer know *whether* we are still praying. We used to know that, at least. There was no doubt about praying, as such. Prayer was then one practice, one exercise, among the rest, prescribed and sometimes dished up according to rule, like other spiritual exercises. . . .

But nowadays everything has suddenly become quite different: no longer are we able to say whether we are still engaged in prayer or even whether we still believe in the possibility of prayer. In the old days prayer may have been far too easy; now it has become unspeakably difficult. . . . Prayers are no longer reeled off. There is a prevailing attitude of distrust towards set prayers "tacked on from outside" and towards the formalism they may engender. But people have come to be equally afraid of *interior* prayer, so called; and most of them no longer have any time for it. Those who do find the time are for the most part unable to achieve an interior peace and quiet.

. . . The question still arises as to what is in fact achieved by the resolve to pray. The cold walls of our own total seclusion? The storms that rage within a frustrated mind and heart? The unattainable object of wants and desires, projected into infinitude, yes, and into heaven itself? A meager consolation for having lost the courage to endure and cope with the sober realities of everyday life as an ordinary average human being? A cheap gesture of resignation because everything and everybody lay too heavy a charge upon us? Is prayer, then, a flight into unreality, into dream, illusion, romanticism? The truth is, we are at our wits' end. We have lost the scent of prayer altogether. We are caught in the blind alley of an illusion. Many of us have touched zero-point.

Thank God! For now we can make a new start. That zero-point can mean a reversal, a turn of the tide. For this is the saving grace of our time . . . that now the Lord can build everything up again, from scratch.

ANDRÉ LOUF (1929–)
French Cistercian abbot

We fear physical pain, aging, dying. We fear the force of our own distress or depression. We fear being so easily bogged down, bringing no identifiable goodness into the world.

Praying takes us right into the middle of these fears and opens their constant little trickle into a swift running stream, for in prayer every early effort to still our fears only intensifies them. We try all the familiar tricks—reciting familiar set phrases, psalms, hymns. We count numbers, we do breathing exercises. But fear persists and will not be removed by any of the consecrated relaxation procedures, by tranquilizers, by liquor, or drugs. Like the collective effort of a congress of mice in our walls, fear gnaws at us, weakening and threatening to bring down our house.

We call out to God. But nothing comes back. Bereft even of the wishes, fantasies, and images that once took us toward the divine and helped us see how close by God already was, we feel impossibly alone and helpless.

This is where prayer makes a place for fear. . . .

God does not ever altogether remove our fear. What he does is to join us in it. He is there where we are afraid. That is the way of the cross, of the tree of life. That is the way of the God who enters our life even in the face of death. That is the way of the vow of obedience in religion. It strikes to the heart of our fear. It tells us to be obedient to our love even unto death. It instructs us not to run or attempt to run from the inescapable fact of the contingency of our being. We cannot protect those we love from suffering. We cannot be sure that we will hold onto our own sanity. We cannot guarantee peace or good will on earth. There is no sure answer to these great fears. There is only one help for them—to surrender them into God's hands. We must do all we can and still give them over into God's care. Our fear brings us right to the point where we can accept the fact that we are subject to God's will and not simply to our own. . . .

Change comes at this point, a change that altogether makes over our fear. Far from being afraid that no one will answer, that nothing will be there, we are now fearfully aware that God is near and will answer. Like that prickling of antennae outdoors on a dark night when we sense an animal nearby, we feel another presence in our prayer. Fear opens us to that presence. And then we thank God, even for our fears.

ANN BELFORD ULANOV AND BARRY ULANOV (contemporary)
American Jungian and Christian writers

We can pray at moments when we become aware of our blindness—and we can include in this term whatever makes us blind to God and to all that surrounds us—and when we sense that the One who can cure us is passing near. Prayer arises at the moment when we become deeply aware of our separation and of the fact that our life is suspended over death, that nothingness is within us and lapping round us from all sides, ready to engulf us. And when we turn our gaze towards others, in place of that despair linked to an ultimate hope, which is the hope that Bartimaeus had, it is compassion which awakes in us, the capacity to suffer deeply, intensely, not the suffering of the other—for one can never suffer the suffering of another nor ever understand another—but one can suffer from the fact that he is suffering, and in a mysterious way, beyond all experience, participate within this unity of the Body of Christ, in the common suffering which is his.

ANTHONY BLOOM (1914–)
Russian Orthodox monk and metropolitan of Sourozh

People nowadays are unaware that, when they are being re-formed, they are brought into ignorance of what is true, or loneliness, or even into pain and hopelessness; and that only then do they receive comfort and help from the Lord. The reason for this ignorance is that not many people are being re-formed.

The primary purpose of this depression and loneliness is that the second-hand faith they have tried to maintain for their self-image may be broken . . . and that they may accept some perception of what is good and true. They cannot accept this until the second-hand faith derived from their self-image has been softened, so to speak. A state of anxiety and pain that reaches all the way to hopelessness accomplishes this. No one can grasp with full sensitivity what is good, what is blessed and happy, without having been in a state of not-good, not-blessed, and not-happy.

EMANUEL SWEDENBORG (1688–1772)
Swedish scientist and mystical thinker

My heart is now suffering; but it is the life of self that causes us pain; that which is dead does not suffer. If we were dead, and our life were hid with Christ in God, we should no longer perceive those pains in spirit that now afflict us. We should not only bear bodily sufferings with equanimity, but spiritual affliction also, that is to say, trouble sent upon the soul without its own immediate act. But the disturbances of a restless activity, in which the soul adds to the cross imposed by the hand of God—the burden of an agitated resistance, and an unwillingness to suffer—are only experienced in consequence of the remaining life of self.

A cross which comes purely from God, and is cordially welcomed without any self-reflective acts, is at once painful and peaceful; but one unwillingly received and repelled by the life of nature is doubly severe; the resistance within is harder to bear than the cross itself. If we recognize the hand of God, and make no opposition in the will, we have comfort in our affliction. . . . Nothing so shortens and soothes our pains as this spirit of non-resistance.

But we are generally desirous of bargaining with God; we would like at least to impose the limits and see the end of our sufferings. That same obstinate and hidden hold of life, which renders the cross necessary, causes us to reject it in part, and by a secret resistance, which impairs its virtue. We have thus to go over the same ground again and again; we suffer greatly, but to very little purpose. The Lord delivers us from falling into that state of soul in which crosses are of no benefit to us! God loves a cheerful giver, according to St. Paul; ah! what must be his love to those who, in a cheerful and absolute abandonment, resign themselves to the entire extent of his crucifying will!

FRANÇOIS FÉNELON (1651–1715)
French Roman Catholic archbishop of Cambrai

Your lively feeling of your own poverty and of your own darkness delight me, because they are a definite indication to me that the divine light is growing in you, without your knowing it, to form in you a great depth of interior humility. The time will come when the sight of this wretchedness, which horrifies you now, will fill you with joy and keep you in a delightful peace. It is only when we have reached the bottom of the abyss of our nothingness and are firmly established there that we can "walk before God in justice and truth." . . . The fruit of grace must, for the moment, remain hidden, buried as it were in the abyss of your wretchedness underneath the most lively awareness of your weakness.

JEAN-PIERRE DE CAUSSADE (1675–1751)
French Jesuit

Above all therefore it is necessary that things heard, seen, done and said, and other such things, must be received without adding things from the imagination, without mental associations and without emotional involvement, and one should not let past or future associations, implications or constructs of the imagination form and grow. For when constructs of the imagination are not allowed to enter the memory and mind, a man is not hindered, whether he be engaged in prayer, meditation, or reciting psalms, or in any other practice or spiritual exercise, nor will they recur again. So commit yourself confidently and without hesitation, all that you are, and everything else, individually and in general, to the unfailing and totally reliable providence of God, in silence and in peace, and he will fight for you. He will liberate you and comfort you more fully, more effectively and more satisfactorily than if you were to dream about it all the time, day and night, and were to cast around frantically all over the place with the futile and confused thoughts of your mind in bondage, nor will you wear out your mind and body, wasting your time, and stupidly and pointlessly exhausting your strength.

So accept everything, separately and in general, wherever it comes from and whatever its origin, in silence and peace, and with an equal mind, as coming to you from a father's hand and his divine providence. So render your imagination bare of the images of all physical things as is appropriate to your state and profession, so that you can cling to him with a bare and undivided mind, as you have so often and so completely vowed to do, without anything whatever being able to come between your soul and him, so that you can pass purely and unwaveringly from the wounds of his humanity into the light of his divinity.

ALBERT THE GREAT (c. 1200–1280)
Theologian, bishop, saint, and one of the teachers
of Meister Eckhart at the University of Paris

To die to self, or to come from under its power, is not and cannot be done by any active resistance we make to it by the powers of nature. For nature can no more overcome or suppress itself than anger can heal anger. So long as nature acts, nothing but natural works are brought forth, and therefore the more labor of this kind, the more nature is fed and strengthened with its own food.

But the one true way of dying to self is most simple and plain, it needs no arts or methods, no cells, monasteries, or pilgrimages, it is equally practicable by everybody, it is always at hand, it meets you in everything, it is free from all deceit, and is never without success.

If you ask, What is this one, true, simple, plain, immediate, and unerring way? It is the way of patience, meekness, humility, and resignation to God. This is the truth and perfection of dying to self; it is nowhere else, nor possible to be in anything else, but in this state of heart.

Could I help you to perceive or feel what a good there is in this state of heart, you would desire it with more eagerness than the thirsty hart desires the water-brooks, you would think of nothing, desire nothing, but constantly to live in it. It is a security from all evil and all delusion. Every difficulty or trial, either of body or mind, every temptation, either within you or without you, has its full remedy in this state of heart. You have no questions to ask of anybody, no new way that you need inquire after, no oracle that you need to consult; for while you shut yourself up, in patience, meekness, humility, and resignation to God, you are in the very arms of Christ, your whole heart is His dwelling-place, and He lives and works in you.

WILLIAM LAW (1686–1761)
English contemplative and cleric

The evil from which we pray to be delivered is not that which is most oppressive in life, such as poverty, worries, hardship, burdens, sacrifices, pain, injustice, tyranny and so on; it is the chain of circumstance that leads us into temptation, disturbing the balance, pushing life off-center, distorting the perspective. It will be seen at once that the so-called "good things" of life are just as liable to cause such disturbance as the painful and hard realities. These things all possess the potential power to lead or force us into temptation and by that I mean all the things that can possibly come between us and God. . . .

Man should give thought to the fact that wherever self is stressed, as in strength that glories in its own might, power that idolizes itself, life that aims at "fulfilling itself" in its own way and by its own resources, in all these, not the truth, but the negation of truth may be suspected.

ALFRED DELP (1907–1945)
German Jesuit theologian and writer

The soul which rises from out of sin to a devout life has been compared to the dawn, which does not banish darkness suddenly, but by degrees. The slow cure is always the surest, and spiritual maladies, like those of the body, while they are apt to come on horseback and express, tend to depart slowly and on foot.

So we must be brave and patient, my daughter, in this undertaking. It is sad to see souls beginning to grow disheartened because they find themselves still subject to imperfection after having made some attempt at leading a devout life . . . to give up in despair and fall back; but, on the other hand, those souls are in worse danger who, through the opposite temptation, imagine themselves purified from all imperfection at the very outset, and who count themselves as full-grown almost before they are born. Be sure, daughter, that these are in great danger of a relapse through having left their physician too soon.

FRANCIS DE SALES (1567–1622)
Saint, bishop of Geneva, and doctor of the church

These are times of great fruitfulness provided we will be patient. There is each time one crucial point . . . to form no conclusions, to take no decisions, to change nothing during such crises, and especially at such times, not to force any particularly religious mood or idea in oneself . . . for it is far, far more God who must hold us, than we who must hold Him.

FRIEDRICH BARON VON HÜGEL (1852–1925)
British Roman Catholic religious writer

It is right, I think, to feel perfectly satisfied with our prayer (after our prayer) that it *is* all right when it *feels* all wrong. . . . It is of the very essence of prayer that it does not depend on us. It depends on circumstances—our stomach, our preoccupations, much more than on our will—for the character it takes; and, naturally, on God's special grace. But possibly the *best* kind is when we seem unable to do anything, if then we throw ourselves on God, and stay contentedly before Him; worried, anxious, tired, listless, but—above all and under it all—humbled and abandoned to His will, contented with our own discontent.

If we can get ourselves accustomed to this attitude of soul, which is always possible, we have learned how to pray.

JOHN CHAPMAN (1865–1933)
English Benedictine spiritual advisor and biblical scholar

You want God as well as man to be always satisfied with you, and you want to be satisfied with yourself in all your dealings with God.

Besides, you are not accustomed to be contented with a simple good will—your self-love wants a lively emotion, a reassuring pleasure, some kind of charm or excitement. You are too much used to be guided by imagination and to suppose that your mind and will are inactive, unless you are conscious of their workings. And thus you are dependent upon a kind of excitement similar to that which the passions arouse, or theatrical representations. By trying for refinement you fall into the opposite extreme—a real coarseness of imagination. Nothing is more opposed, not only to the life of faith, but also to true wisdom. . . . It will be seen at once that the so-called "good things" of life are just as liable to cause such disturbance as the painful and hard realities. These things all possess the potential power to lead or force us into temptation, and by that I mean all the things that can possibly come between us and God. . . .

It is imagination which leads us astray; and the certainty which we seek through imagination, feeling, and taste is one of the most dangerous sources from which fanaticism springs.

This is the gulf of vanity and corruption which God would make you discover in your heart; you must look upon it with the calm and simplicity belonging to true humility. It is mere self-love to be inconsolable at seeing one's own imperfections; but to stand face to face with them, neither flattering nor tolerating them, seeking to correct oneself without becoming pettish—this is to desire what is good for its own sake, and for God's.

FRANÇOIS FÉNELON (1651–1715)
French Roman Catholic archbishop of Cambrai

Be reconciled to God; that means at the same time, be reconciled to ourselves. But we are not; we try to appease ourselves. We try to make ourselves more acceptable to our own judgment and, when we fail, we grow more hostile toward ourselves. . . . If we are often horrified by the unconscious or conscious hostility people betray toward us or about our own hostility toward people whom we believe we love, let us not forget: They feel rejected by us; we feel rejected by them. They tried hard to make themselves acceptable to us, and they failed. We tried hard to make ourselves acceptable to them, and we failed. . . . Be reconciled with God—that means, at the same time, be reconciled with the others! But it does not mean try to reconcile the others, as it does not mean try to reconcile yourselves. Try to reconcile God. You will fail. This is the message: A new reality has appeared in which you are reconciled. To enter the New Being we do not need to show anything. We must only be open to be grasped by it. . . .

Real healing is not where only a part of body or mind is reunited with the whole, but where the whole itself, our whole being, our whole personality is united with itself. The New

Creation is healing creation because it creates reunion with one-self. And it creates reunion with the others.

PAUL TILLICH (1886–1965)
German-American Protestant theologian

The peace which Christ brings is the outcome of this war faced and fought on earth: man's war with himself, in which (by God's grace) he overcomes himself, conquers himself, pacifies himself, and can at last live with himself because he no longer hates himself. But this conquest of himself can never be definitive unless it is a surrender to another: to Christ, and to our brother in Christ. For our destiny is to be one in Christ, and in order to love others as ourselves, we must first love ourselves. But in order to love ourselves we must find something in ourselves to love. This is impossible unless we find, both in ourselves and in others, the likeness of Christ.

Once again, in order to find Christ we must give up our own limited idea of Christ. He is not what we think He is. He is not, and cannot be, merely our own idealized image of ourselves.

The Christ we find in ourselves is not identified with what we vainly seek to admire and idolize in ourselves—on the contrary, He has identified Himself with what we resent in ourselves, for He has taken upon Himself our wretchedness and our misery, our poverty and our sins. We cannot find peace in ourselves if, in rejecting our misery and thrusting it away from us, we thrust away Christ Who loves in us not our human glory but our ignobility.

THOMAS MERTON (1915–1968)
American Cistercian monk

Mr. Head had never known before what mercy felt like because he had been too good to deserve any, but he felt he knew now. . . .

He stood very still and felt the action of mercy touch him again but this time he knew that there were no words in the world that could name it. He understood that it grew out of agony, which is not denied to any man and which is given in strange ways to children. He understood it was all a man could carry into death to give his Maker and he suddenly burned with shame that he had so little of it to take with him. He stood appalled, judging himself with the thoroughness of God, while the action of mercy covered his pride like a flame and consumed it. He had never thought himself a great sinner before but he saw now that his true depravity had been hidden from him lest it cause him despair. He realized that he was forgiven for sins from the beginning of time, when he had conceived in his own heart the sin of Adam, until the present, when he had denied poor Nelson. He saw that no sin was too monstrous for him to claim as his own, and since God loved in proportion as He forgave, he felt ready at that instant to enter Paradise.

FLANNERY O'CONNOR (1925–1964)
American novelist and short-story writer

Forgiving love is a possibility only for those who know they are not good, who feel themselves in need of divine mercy, who . . . know that the differences between the good man and the bad man are insignificant in [God's] sight.

REINHOLD NIEBUHR (1892–1971)
American Christian ethicist and theologian

[*Emerson's journal reminiscence of his first wife, Ellen, and his deceased brothers Charles and Edward*] Last night a remembering & remembering talk with Lidian. I went back to the first smile of Ellen on the door stone at Concord. I went back to all that delicious relation to feel as ever how many shades, how much reproach. Strange is

it that I can go back to no part of youth, no past relation without shrinking & shrinking. Not Ellen, not Edward, not Charles.
Infinite compunctions embitter each of those dear names & all
who surround them. Ah could I have felt in the presence of the
first, as now I feel my own power and hope, & so have offered her
in every word & look the heart of a man humble & wise, but
resolved to be true & perfect with God, & not as I fear it seemed,
the uneasy uncentered joy of one who received in her a good—
a lovely good—out of all proportion to his deserts, I might
haply have made her days longer & certainly sweeter & at least
have recalled her seraph smile without a pang. . . . Well O God I
will try & learn, from this sad memory to be brave & circumspect
& true henceforth & weave now a web that will not shrink.

RALPH WALDO EMERSON (1803–1882)
American poet and essayist

Come to me, all who labor and are heavy laden.

Come! For Jesus sees that those who labor and toil feel weighed
down by the weight of their burden, despondent over work, and
live in perplexity and distress; one is looking round in all directions, hoping to find relief; another keeps his eyes on the ground,
having found no consolation; a third is looking up to the sky as
though help would be coming down: but they are all searching.
That is why Jesus says, "Come!" He is not inviting those who
have stopped searching and are dismal. "Come!" For he who is
inviting knows that it is the nature of true suffering to go away
alone and plunge into silent desolation without daring to tell
anyone, far less to ask for help openly. The demoniac in the
Gospel was not the only one to be possessed by a dumb spirit;
any suffering that does not first close the sufferer's lips does not
amount to much, any more than a love which is not silent; the
malcontents who set about telling tales of their sufferings do not

labor and are not heavy laden. And that is why he who is inviting will not wait until those who are desolate under their burdens
come to him; in fullness of love, he calls them; all his eagerness
to help them might have remained ineffective had he not uttered
that word and so taken the first step; for in that cry, "Come to
me!" he comes to them.

SØREN KIERKEGAARD (1813–1855)
Danish theologian

LEAN TOWARD LOVE

This cycle tells us that we are all sought by the Holy Spirit: he comes "to save and heal," "to teach and correct," "to strengthen and console," "to give light to the mind," "to instruct and reform." As soon as he enters in, "he awakens," "he stirs and soothes and pierces the heart." Pure, subtle, and penetrating, he "brings us," he "draws us," he "calls us." And prays in us without ceasing.

No one ought to think that it is difficult to come to Him . . . for God is very zealous to be at all times with us, and teaches us that He will bring us to Himself if we will but follow. We never desire anything so earnestly as God desires to bring us to Himself, that we may know Him. God is always ready, but we are very unready; God is near to us, but we are far from Him; God is within, but we are without; God is at home, but we are strangers. The prophet saith: God guideth the redeemed through a narrow way into the broad road, so that they come into the wide and broad place; that is to say, into true freedom of the spirit, when one has become a spirit with God. May God help us to follow this course, that He may bring us to Himself. Amen.

MEISTER ECKHART (1260–1327)
German Dominican mystic and theologian

If we were on a boat and were thrown some ropes attached to a rock so as to be rescued, it is clear that we would not be drawing the rock to ourselves. Rather, we, and with us the boat, would be hauled in toward the rock. . . . And that is why . . . we must begin by prayer, not to draw toward ourselves that Power which is at one and the same time everywhere and nowhere, but to place ourselves in his hands and to be united to him.

DENIS (fifth century)
Syrian monk, mystic, and teacher

God is always infinitely near and infinitely far. We are fully aware of Him only if we experience both of these aspects. But sometimes, when our awareness of Him has become shallow, habitual—not warm and not cold—when He has become too familiar to be exciting, too near to be felt in his infinite distance, then He becomes the absent God. The Spirit has not ceased to be present. The Spiritual Presence can never end. But the Spirit of God hides God from our sight. . . .

The Spirit has shown to our time and to innumerable people in our time the absent God and the empty space that cries in us to be filled by Him. And then the absent one may return and take the space that belongs to Him, and the Spiritual Presence may break again into our consciousness, awakening us to recognize what we are, shaking and transforming us. This may happen like the coming of a storm, the storm of the Spirit, stirring up the stagnant air of our spiritual life. The storm will then recede; a new stagnancy may take place; and the awareness of the present God may be replaced by the awareness of the empty space within us. Life in the Spirit is ebb and flow—and this means, whether we experience the present or the absent God, it is the work of the Spirit.

PAUL TILLICH (1886–1965)
German-American Protestant theologian

We cry "Abba! Father!" but we say this through the Spirit, so that it is quite true to say that it is he who cries it. It is indeed difficult to say whether it is he or us. He is so deeply within us, because he has been sent "into our hearts" and, as the Holy Spirit, he is so pure, subtle and penetrating that he is able to be in all of us and in each one of us without doing violence to the person, indiscernible in his spontaneous movement. He is above all the Spirit of freedom.

YVES CONGAR (1904–1997)
French Dominican theologian and cardinal

I want to tell you of my own experience, as I promised. Not that it is of any importance. But I make this disclosure only to help you, and if you derive any profit from it I shall be consoled for my foolishness; if not, my foolishness will be revealed. I admit that the Word has also come to me—I speak as a fool—and has come many times. But although he has come to me, I have never been conscious of the moment of his coming. I perceived his presence, I remembered afterwards that he had been with me; sometimes I had a presentiment that he would come, but I was never conscious of his coming or his going. And where he comes from when he visits my soul, and where he goes, and by what means he enters and goes out, I admit that I do not know even now; as John says: "You do not know where he comes from or where he goes." There is nothing strange in this, for of him was it said, "Your footsteps will not be known." The coming of the Word was not perceptible to my eyes, for he has no color; nor to my ears, for there was no sound; nor yet to my nostrils, for he mingles with the mind, not the air; he has not acted upon the air, but created it. His coming was not tasted by the mouth, for there was no eating or drinking, nor could he be known by the sense of touch, for he is not tangible. How then did he enter? Perhaps he did not enter because he does not come from outside? He is not one of the things which exist outside us. Yet he does not come from within me, for he is good, & I know that there is no good in me. I have ascended to the highest in me, and look! the Word is towering above that. In my curiosity I have descended to explore my lowest depths, yet I found him even deeper. If I looked outside myself, I saw him stretching beyond the furthest I could see; & if I looked within, he was yet further within. Then I knew the truth of what I had read, "In him we live & move & have our being." And blessed is the man in whom he has his being, who lives for him and is moved by him.

You ask then how I knew he was present, when his ways can in no way be traced? He is life and power, and as soon as he enters in, he awakens my slumbering soul; he stirs and soothes and pierces my heart, for before it was hard as stone, and diseased. So he has begun to pluck out and destroy, to build up and to plant, to water dry places and illuminate dark ones, to open what was closed and to warm what was cold, to make the crooked straight and the rough places smooth, so that my soul may bless the Lord, and all that is within me may praise his holy name. . . . I have marveled at the depth of his wisdom when my secret faults have been revealed and made visible; at the very slightest amendment of my way of life I have experienced his goodness and mercy; in the renewal and remaking of the spirit of my mind, that is, of my inmost being, I have perceived the excellence of his glorious beauty, and when I contemplate all these things I am filled with awe and wonder at his manifold greatness.

But when the Word has left me, all these spiritual powers become weak and faint and begin to grow cold, as though you had removed the fire from under a boiling pot, and this is the sign of his going. Then my soul must needs be sorrowful until he returns, and my heart again kindles within me—the sign of his returning. . . . As long as I live the word "return," the word of recall for the recall of Word, will be on my lips.

As often as he slips away from me, so often shall I call him back. From the burning desire of my heart I will not cease to call him, begging him to return, as if after someone who is departing, and I will implore him to give back to me the joy of his salvation, and restore himself to me.

BERNARD OF CLAIRVAUX (1091–1153)
Cistercian abbot, saint, and theologian

Let us drink of living waters, welling up to eternal life. This our Savior said about the Spirit which those who believed in him were to receive. . . .

Why did he call the grace of the Holy Spirit water? Because water is of the substance of everything. Water produces green and living things. The water of the showers that come down from heaven falls as one thing, and produces many effects. Yet one source waters the whole of paradise; one and the same rain falls everywhere, and becomes white in the lily, red in the rose, purple in violets and hyacinths, and something different in all the different species. Thus in the palm tree it is one thing, another in the vine, and everything in all. In itself it is one thing, and not other than itself. For the rain does not change and fall as this or that liquid but, adapting itself to the things that receive it, it becomes what is suitable to each. Likewise the Holy Spirit is one and indivisible, giving his grace to each one as he wishes. . . . One he confirms in continence, to another he teaches the works of mercy, he instructs another in fasting and mortification, another in detachment from bodily things, another he prepares for martyrdom—acting in different ways in different people, though he himself never varies.

His coming is gentle, his presence fragrant, his yoke light. Rays of light and knowledge anticipate his appearing. He comes with the feelings of a true guardian. For he comes to save and heal, to teach and correct, to strengthen and console, to give light to the mind—first to that of the one who receives him, then, through him, to the minds of others. And just as someone, being at first in darkness and later getting a glimpse of the sun and receiving his sight, perceives what he did not see before, so the soul found worthy of the gift of the Holy Spirit is enlightened and sees, beyond human sight, what it did not know.

CYRIL OF JERUSALEM (c. 315–387)
Bishop of Jerusalem and catechetical writer

From that time onwards, more and more frequently, when I was beside the spring, you, who are without pride, did not scorn to come down (to me), but came close to me and took hold of my head, bathed it in the waters, and enabled me to see more and more clearly the light of your face. . . . You came in this way and left again and gradually you appeared more and more clearly. You flooded me with those waters and gave me the grace better to see a purer light.

You were close to me, you washed me, so it seemed to me, in the waters, you flooded me with them and plunged me into them again and again. I saw the lightning shining around me and the rays of your face mixed with the waters and I was stupefied, finding myself sprinkled with luminous water. . . . You took me and, going up to heaven again, you raised me up with you, either in my body or out of my body, I do not know. . . . Then, after a little time, when I was here below, on high the heavens opened and you deigned to show me your face, like a sun without a shape. . . .

After having shown yourself in this way again and again and concealed yourself again and again . . . I saw the lightning flashes of your face and its brilliance. . . . You showed yourself to me in this way after you had entirely purified my understanding in clarity by the light of the Holy Spirit.

SIMEON THE NEW THEOLOGIAN (949–1022)
Byzantine saint, mystic, and spiritual writer

Is there anyone who, on hearing the titles of the Holy Spirit, does not experience a certain exaltation as their mind contemplates that supreme nature? For it is called the "Spirit of God," "the Spirit of truth who proceeds from the Father," the "right Spirit," the "guiding Spirit." But the chief and distinctive title is simply "Holy Spirit." . . .

All share in the Spirit and yet the Spirit remains entire, like a sunbeam whose gentle light falls upon a person who enjoys it as though the sun shone for him alone, whereas in reality the sun is shining over land and sea and mingles with the air. In the same way, the Spirit is present to all those who are capable of receiving him as if given to each of them uniquely, and sends forth grace sufficient and great enough for all, yet without loss to itself; and we profit by sharing in this, but according to our capacity, not according to the Spirit's power.

BASIL THE GREAT (330–379)
Doctor of the church, saint, and bishop of Caesarea

God has but one design or intent towards all mankind and that is to introduce or generate His own life, light, and Spirit in them. . . . God is one, human nature is one, salvation is one, and the way to it is one; and that is, the desire of the soul turned to God. When this desire is alive and breaks forth in any creature under Heaven, then the lost sheep is found and the shepherd has it upon his shoulders. Through this desire the poor Prodigal Son leaves his husks and swine and hastens to his father: it is because of this desire that the father sees the son while yet afar off, that he runs out to meet him, falls on his neck and kisses him. See here how plainly we are taught that no sooner is this desire arisen and in motion towards God, but the operation of God's Spirit answers to it.

WILLIAM LAW (1686–1761)
English contemplative and cleric

It would never occur to a praying Christian to embrace Quietism and, on account of this indwelling, to give up his own calling on God, simply letting the Spirit pray within him. The Christian revelation never points in this direction; on the contrary it continually speaks of active "prayer in the Spirit"; the latter's own energy and personal quality is affirmed and taken up into the all-embracing activity of the Person of the Spirit. To the extent that this "activity" on man's part acknowledges the preponderance of the Spirit and surrenders to him, it can also be regarded as a mode of "passivity," just as man's inner understanding in the Holy Spirit presupposes that he is receptive to the Spirit's inspirations and illuminations. But this kind of grace-filled "passivity" can never be confused with a merely natural letting things happen; the intense heat of the Spirit, present in the believer, causes the creaturely "I" to catch fire and radiate with a heightened presence. The Spirit breaks forth out of the very core of the believer's spiritual life, showing him the way, stirring him to action, thinking, willing and praying with him; and, usually without drawing attention to himself (since the Holy Spirit's love aims primarily to glorify Father and Son), the Spirit places the contemplative in the closest intimacy with the divine truth.

HANS URS VON BALTHASAR (1905–1988)
Swiss Roman Catholic theologian

When praying fervently, either standing or sitting, or lying down or walking, and being sometimes suddenly visited by the Spirit of God and hearing His voice, we notice that He penetrates into the soul, not through the mouth, not through the nose, neither through the ears (although the Savior bestowed the Spirit through the word and breathing, and although "faith cometh by hearing"), but straight through the body into the heart, in the same manner as the Lord passed through the walls of the house when He came to the Apostles after the Resurrection, and acts suddenly, like electricity, and more rapidly than any electric current; then we feel unusually light, because we are suddenly freed from our burden of sins, the spirit of contrition for sins, the spirit of devotion, peace, and joy visits us. Remember how the angel appeared in the shut-up prison in order to deliver the Apostle Peter; the doors were shut, the keepers standing before the doors, but the angel suddenly came upon him, and at the same moment a light shined in the prison. Thus the Spirit of God suddenly visits the chamber of our soul, the body, and the light shines in it.

JOHN SERGIEFF (ST. JOHN OF KRONSTADT) (1829–1909)
Priest of the Russian Orthodox Church

Dwelling in the light, there is no occasion at all for stumbling, for all things are discovered in the light. When thou art walking abroad it is present with thee in thy bosom, thou needest not to say, Lo here, or Lo there; and as thou lyest in thy bed, it is present to teach thee and judge thy wandering mind, which wanders abroad, and thy high thoughts and imaginations, and makes them subject. For following thy thoughts, thou art quickly lost. By dwelling in this light, it will discover to thee the body of sin and thy corruptions and fallen estate, where thou art. In that light which shows thee all this, stand; go neither to the right nor to the left.

GEORGE FOX (1624–1691)
English religious leader and founder of the Society of Friends

O Holy Spirit—we pray for ourselves and for all—O Holy Spirit, Thou who dost make alive; here it is not talents we stand in need of, nor culture, nor shrewdness, rather there is here too much of all that; but what we need is that Thou take away the power of mastery and give us life. True it is that a man experiences a shudder like that of death when Thou, to become a power in him, dost take the power from him—oh, but if even animal creatures understand at a subsequent moment how well it is for them that the royal coachman took the reins, which in the first instance prompted them to shudder, and against which their mind rebelled—should not then a man be able promptly to understand what a benefaction it is towards a man that Thou takest away the power and givest life?

SØREN KIERKEGAARD (1813–1855)
Danish theologian

Have we ever kept quiet, even though we wanted to defend ourselves when we had been unfairly treated? Have we ever forgiven someone even though we got no thanks for it and our silent forgiveness was taken for granted? Have we ever obeyed, not because we had to and because otherwise things would have become unpleasant for us, but simply on account of that mysterious, silent, incomprehensible being we call God and his will? Have we ever sacrificed something without receiving any thanks or recognition for it, and even without a feeling of inner satisfaction? Have we ever been absolutely lonely? Have we ever decided on some course of action purely by the innermost judgment of our conscience, deep down where one can no longer tell or explain it to anyone, where one is quite alone and knows that one is taking a decision which no one else can take in one's place and for which one will have to answer for all eternity? Have we ever tried to love God when we are no longer being borne on the crest of the wave of enthusiastic feeling, when it is no longer possible to mistake our self, and its vital urges, for God? . . . Have we ever been good to someone who did not show the slightest sign of gratitude or comprehension and when we also were not rewarded by the feeling of having been "selfless," decent, etc.?

. . . When we let ourselves go in this experience of the spirit, when the tangible and assignable, the relishable element disappears, when everything takes on the taste of death and destruction, or when everything disappears as if in an inexpressible, as it were white, colorless and intangible beatitude—then in actual fact it is not merely the spirit but the Holy Spirit who is at work in us. Then is the hour of his grace.... This may still appear strange to us at the beginning, and we will always be tempted again to take fright and flee back into what is familiar and near to us: in fact, we will often have to and will often be allowed to do this. But we should gradually try to get ourselves used to the taste of the pure wine of the spirit, which is filled with the Holy Spirit....

Let each one of us look for the experience of grace in the contemplation of our life, but not so that we can say: there it is; I have it. One cannot "find" it so as to claim it triumphantly as one's own possession. One can only look for it by forgetting oneself; one can only find it by seeking God and by giving oneself to him in a love which forgets self, and without still returning to oneself.

KARL RAHNER (1904–1984)
German Jesuit theologian

O human heart, where are you running? Close to the shadow? Into the wind? Into the abyss? Aside from that, Who is everything? The greatest poverty? The height of wisdom? The ineffable goodness? The eternal beauty? The highest good? The infinite sea of every perfection? He hurries close to you, calling you with such strong cries and bringing new blessings, not just the old ones. Do you know whence your defects are born? It is because you do not pray, because you do not contemplate. Remaining thus, without light and without heat, it is not surprising that you fail to move yourself from works of darkness. Enter, enter now.

LAWRENCE SCUPOLI (1530–1610)
Italian Roman Catholic priest

Imagine a circle with its center and radii or rays going out from this center.... In so far as the saints move inwards within the circle towards its center, wishing to come near to God, then, in the degree of their penetration, they come closer both to God and to one another; moreover, inasmuch as they come nearer to God, they come nearer to one another, and inasmuch as they come nearer to one another, they come nearer to God. It is the same with drawing away. When they draw away from God and turn towards external things, it is clear that in the degree that they recede from the central point and draw away from God, they withdraw from one another, and as they withdraw from one another, so they draw away from God. Such is also the property of love; inasmuch as we are outside and do not love God, so each is far from his neighbor. But if we love God, inasmuch as we come near to Him by love of Him, so we become united by love with our neighbors, and inasmuch as we are united with our neighbors, so we become united with God.

ABBA DOROTHEUS (sixth century)
Saint, ascetical writer, and founder of a Palestinian monastery

I do not ask from you a love tender and emotional but only that your will should lean towards love, and notwithstanding all the corrupt desires of your heart you should prefer God before self and the whole world.

FRANÇOIS FÉNELON (1651–1715)
French Roman Catholic archbishop of Cambrai

For the desire of your heart is itself your prayer. And if the desire is constant, so is your prayer. The Apostle Paul had a purpose in saying: "Pray without ceasing." Are we then ceaselessly to bend our knees, to lie prostrate, or to lift up our hands? Is this what is meant in saying: "Pray without ceasing"? Even if we admit that we pray in this fashion, I do not believe that we can do so all the time. Yet there is another, interior kind of prayer without ceasing, namely, the desire of the heart. Whatever else you may be doing, if you but fix your desire on God's Sabbath rest, your prayer will be ceaseless. Therefore if you wish to pray without ceasing, do not cease to desire. The constancy of your desire will itself be the ceaseless voice of your prayer. And that voice of your prayer will be silent only when your love ceases. . . . If your love is without ceasing, you are crying out always; if you always cry out, you are always desiring; and if you desire, you are calling to mind your eternal rest in the Lord.

AUGUSTINE OF HIPPO (354–430)
Carthaginian saint, philosopher, and doctor of the church

It is not enough to *say* prayers, one must become, *be* prayer, prayer incarnate. It is not enough to have moments of praise. All of life, each act, every gesture, even the smile of the human face, must become a hymn of adoration, an offering, a prayer. One should offer not what one has, but what one is.

PAUL EVDOKIMOV (1901–1970)
Russian Orthodox theologian

In this passing over, if it is to be perfect,
all intellectual activities must be left behind and the height
of our affection
must be totally transferred and transformed into God.
This, however, is mystical and most secret,
which no one knows except him who receives it,
no one receives except him who desires it,
and no one desires except him
who is inflamed in his very marrow by the fire of the
Holy Spirit

whom Christ sent into the world.
And therefore the Apostle says that
this mystical wisdom is revealed by the Holy Spirit. . . .
Let us, then, die and enter into the darkness;
let us impose silence upon our cares, our desires and
our imaginings.
With Christ crucified
let us pass *out of this world to the Father*
so that when the Father is shown to us,
we may say with Philip:
It is enough for us.
Let us hear with Paul:
My grace is sufficient for you.
Let us rejoice with David saying:
My flesh and my heart have grown faint;
You are the God of my heart,
and the God that is my portion forever.
Blessed be the Lord forever
and all the people will say:
Let it be; let it be.
Amen.

BONAVENTURE (1221–1274)
Italian scholastic theologian, saint, cardinal,
and doctor of the church

CYCLE SEVEN

THE PRAYER
OF PRAYERS

The Lord's Prayer can and has been rattled off through the centuries—our word patter *comes from the practice of rushing through the words of the Pater Noster. Said attentively, however, the Our Father reveals itself as an inexhaustible meditation. Monks have been known to spend an entire day on a single repetition of this prayer. It can be said to work upon the whole person: body, mind, heart, and spirit.*

The introduction to the Lord's prayer is, "After this manner pray ye." Our Lord Jesus, in these words, gave to his disciples and to us a directory for prayer. . . . The meaning is, let this be the rule and model according to which you frame your prayers. . . . Not that we are tied to the words of the Lord's prayer. Christ says not, "After these words pray ye," but "After this manner": that is, let all your petitions agree and symbolize with the things contained in the Lord's prayer; and well may we make all our prayers consonant and agreeable to this prayer. Tertullian calls it "a breviary and compendium of the gospel"; it is like a heap of massive gold.

The exactness of this prayer appears in the dignity of the Author. A piece of work has commendation from its artificer, and this prayer has commendation from its Author; it is the Lord's prayer. As the moral law was written with the finger of God, so this prayer was dropped from the lips of the Son of God. . . .

Never was prayer so admirably and curiously composed as this. As Solomon's Song, for its excellence, is called the "Song of songs," so may this be well called the "Prayer of prayers."

The matter of it is admirable. I. For its comprehensiveness. It is short and pithy, a great deal said in a few words. . . . 2. For its clearness. It is plain and intelligible to every capacity. Clearness is the grace of speech. 3. For its completeness. It contains the chief things that we have to ask, or God has to bestow.

Use: Let us have a great esteem of the Lord's prayer; let it be the model and pattern of all our prayers. There is a double benefit arising from framing our petitions suitably to this prayer. Hereby error in prayer is prevented. It is not easy to write wrong after this copy; we cannot easily err when we have our pattern before us. Hereby mercies requested are obtained; for the apostle assures us that God will hear us when we pray "according to his will." And sure we pray according to his will when we pray according to the pattern he has set us. So much for the introduction to the Lord's prayer, "After this manner pray ye."

THOMAS WATSON (d. 1686)
English Puritan divine

Our Father, our most blessed, most holy Creator, our Savior and our Comforter; who art in heaven, in the angels, in the saints, enlightening them to know thee; because thou, O Lord, art the light that inflames them by thy divine love; because thou, O Lord, art the love which is in them and fills them to render them blessed; because thou, O Lord, art the highest good, and the eternal good, from which all good things come, and without which there is no good anywhere.

Hallowed be thy name: let the knowledge of thee become apparent to us, so that we may know how plentiful are thy blessings, how long thy promises, how lofty thy majesty, how profound thy judgments.

Thy Kingdom come; that thou shouldst reign within us with thy grace and let us come to thy Kingdom, where we will see thee face to face, and have perfect love, blessed company, and sempiternal joy.

Thy will be done on earth as it is in heaven; so that we may love thee with all our heart, thinking ever of thee; with all our soul, ever desiring thee; with all our mind, directing all our intentions to thee, and seeking thy honor in all things; and with all our strength, employing all the power of our spirit and all the senses of our body in the service of thy love, and in naught else: and that we may also love our neighbors as ourselves, drawing all men, as far as it is in our power, toward thy love, rejoicing in the good things of others and grieving at their ills as at our own, and never giving offense to anyone.

Give us this day our daily bread, that is thy beloved Son, our Lord Jesus Christ, in memory of the love he bore us, and of what he said, did, and suffered for us.

And forgive us our trespasses as we forgive those who trespass against us; and what we do not forgive entirely, make thou, O Lord, that we should forgive, so that for thy sake we should sincerely love our enemies, and intercede devoutly for them with thee, and never render evil for evil, and strive with thy help to be of assistance to all men.

And lead us not into temptation, hidden or manifest, sudden or protracted.

And deliver us from evil, past, present, and future.

So be it, with good will and without hope of reward.

FRANCIS OF ASSISI (1182–1226)
Italian monk, saint, and founder of the Franciscan order

Men will say God is their father, without wishing to obey Him like children. Hallowed be thy name, they will say, when in reality they despise and dishonor Him, preferring their own honor and will to that of God. Thy Kingdom come, they say, when all they wish is to reign in this world where they always wish to live as though God had given it to them in perpetuity. They say, Thy will be done in earth as it is in Heaven, while refusing to give way in anything to the love of God. And while praying for their daily bread they scrabble and struggle to get more for themselves than they have prayed for. They pray that He forgive them their trespasses while they love these and daily commit more. And that He will deliver them from temptation when they seek out its occasions.

PIERRE POIRET (1646–1719)
French philosopher, preacher, and mystic

At the root every conversation with God is an embarrassment, a substitute for a much deeper mutual understanding.... God does not question man until after the Fall: "Adam, where are you?" Only now begins the dialogue as between two estranged subjects, which we today call prayer: something which, at some point or another, has its basis in a bad conscience, which draws the best conclusions still possible from a baneful fact, which aims to bring those who are estranged back to God again. Thus, in the Our Father, the Son takes sin into consideration. If there were no sin we would not need to say "Hallowed be thy name," for God's name would always be hallowed; nor "Thy kingdom come," for it would be here; nor "Thy will be done on earth as it is in heaven," for God's will would be carried out equally on earth and in heaven. It would be superfluous to ask for daily bread, for all that God had created for man, even before creating him, would be available. And the remaining petitions would not apply.

In prayer God enables man to approach him once more. Most people live so estranged from God that prayer's first task must be to make them aware of their distance from God. In the light of prayer they should recognize what their life thus far has amounted to, what they owe to God the Father, Son, and Spirit for which they have not thanked him. In contrition that opens the heart they ought to try to bridge the abyss which separates them from God; they are to begin their prayer by bringing to a halt the movement that estranges them from God and so turning back toward him. Prayer is first of all *conversion*.

But perhaps they no longer know what prayer is; and they start praying as if it were the most natural thing in the world, as if it went without saying that God is ready to listen to them, to answer them and to carry out their wishes. Or they have a slight apprehension of their estrangement but try not to let it enter their consciousness too forcefully or become real in their prayer. They present themselves to God as they are and leave it to God to forget the estrangement, as they have done. But prayer cannot be built on an untruth. Every believer who tries to live by his faith will try at least once a day to consider his sin and estrangement so that he can ask God's pardon for it. He need not make this awareness the content of his prayer; indeed he must not, otherwise he will have too little time for the real approach to God, adoration and thanksgiving. But he may only dare to approach God in the recognition of his distance from him, in sorrow for his sin and in the humility of the prodigal son who accepts every grace the Father bestows on him as the most undeserved gift. Not until the pain of his estrangement burns in his soul can the divine fire of grace really burn within him.

ADRIENNE VON SPEYR (1902–1967)
Swiss mystic, physician, and writer

I and many I know began praying primarily as a reaction to feeling alone, unloved, frightened, hurt, and angry. As I became less armored against life, my prayer became "Help me," said less in desperation and more as a declaration. I was open to being helped. Increasingly surrendered, my next prayer was: "May thy will be done."

Now I hear that "May the best thing happen. May thy will be done" implies that "the best thing" is not presently happening, "thy will" is not being done now. I see that requesting any changes reveals my dissociation from the constant, seamless changing that is life.

I also feel that prayer emerges from silence, that all we have to do is listen. I see that when we listen without hope, expectation, or demand, prayer becomes a most powerful expression of our native impulse to love and be loved and so care for all beings and things, just as they are.

For me, the final prayer, just before prayer dissolves into everloving silence, is "Thank you."

ERIC LEBER (contemporary)
American layperson

It would seem, then, that this prayer, the Our Father, contains the fullness of perfection. It was the Lord Himself who gave it to us as both an example and a rule. It raises up those making use of it to that preeminent situation of which I spoke earlier. It lifts them up to that prayer of fire known to so few. It lifts them up, rather, to that ineffable prayer which rises above all human consciousness, with no voice sounding, no tongue moving, no words uttered. The soul lights up with heavenly illumination and no longer employs constricted, human speech. All sensibility is gathered together and, as though from some very abundant source, the soul breaks forth richly, bursts out unspeakably to

God, and in the tiniest instant it pours out so much more than the soul can either describe or remember when it returns again to itself.

JOHN CASSIAN (360–435)
Monk and founder of monasteries near Marseilles

Above all, let us cherish that prayer of our Lord which he himself taught us: "Thy will be done on earth as it is in heaven." Our Lord bade St. Catherine of Genoa to make a notable pause at these words whenever she said the Our Father, praying that God's holy will be fulfilled on earth with the same perfection with which the saints do it in heaven. Let this be our practice also.

FRANCIS DE SALES (1567–1622)
Saint, bishop of Geneva, and doctor of the church

The good Jesus bids us say these words which ask that this kingdom may come in us: "Hallowed be thy name: thy kingdom come in us." How great is the wisdom of our Master. It is well that we should all learn what we ask for when praying for this kingdom. His majesty says that unless he enabled us to do so by giving us his kingdom here on earth, our natural defects would render us unfit either to hallow, praise, magnify, glorify, extol the holy name of the eternal Father. Therefore the good Jesus placed the two petitions close together. I will tell you what I understand about the matter, so that you may realize for what you are praying, how important it is to ask for it, and how we should strive to please him who can bestow it.

Among the many other joys of the kingdom of heaven the principal appears to me to consist in a disregard of all earthly things and a peace and beatitude which rejoice and delight in the bliss of one's companions. The Soul dwells in perfect peace and feels supreme satisfaction at seeing that all those around it honor and praise God and bless his name, and at knowing that they never offend him. In heaven every one loves him; the soul cares for nothing but loving him: it cannot cease to do so because it knows him as he is. If only we knew him we should love him in the same way in this world, and although not so constantly and so perfectly as in heaven, yet very differently from what we do now.

TERESA OF ÁVILA (1515–1582)
Spanish Carmelite saint and mystic

Prayer—which asks, thanks, worships, and blesses—is the radiation, the breath and the warmth of the awakened heart: expressed in formulae of the articulated word, in the wordless inner sighing of the soul and, lastly, in the silence, both outward and inward, of the breathing of the soul immersed in the element of divine respiration and breathing in unison with it. . . .

One should know, dear Unknown Friend, that one never prays alone, that there are always others—above, or in the past on earth—who pray with you in the same sense, in the same spirit, and even in the same words. In praying, you always represent a visible or invisible community together with you. If you pray for healing, you represent all the sick and all healers, and the community of sick people and healers then prays with you. For this reason the Lord's prayer is not addressed to "my Father in heaven," but rather to "*our* Father in heaven," and asks the Father to "give *us* this day *our* daily bread," that he "forgive *us* our trespasses," that he "leads *us* not into temptation," and that he "delivers *us* from evil." Thus, whatever the particular intention of the one who prays the Lord's prayer may be, it is in the name of the whole of mankind that he prays.

ANONYMOUS (20th century)
Christian hermeticist

When we pray "Your will be done on earth as in heaven" we are not praying that God may accomplish what he wills, but that we may be able to do what God wills. . . .

It was the will of God, then, that Christ exemplified both in his deeds and in his teaching. It means humility in behavior, constancy in faith, modesty in conversation, justice in deeds, mercy in judgments, discipline in morals. We should be incapable of doing wrong to anyone but able to bear patiently wrongs done to us. It requires that we live at peace with our brothers and sisters, loving God with our whole heart: loving him as our Father, fearing him as our God. It means preferring nothing whatever to Christ, who preferred nothing to us . . . and that in the face of death we allow our patience to be our crown. This is what is entailed in being a co-heir with Christ. This is what it means to accomplish the commandment of God, to fulfill the will of the Father.

CYPRIAN (c. 200–258)
Father of the church and bishop of Carthage

God governs the world by authority, and not by force. If this were not so, there would be neither freedom nor law in the world; and the first three petitions of the Lord's Prayer . . . would lose all meaning. He who prays these petitions does so solely with the purpose of affirming and increasing divine *authority* and not divine power. The God who is almighty—not virtually but actually—has no need at all to be petitioned that his reign may come and that his will may be done. The meaning of this prayer is that God is powerful only in so far as his authority is freely recognized and accepted. Prayer is the act of such recognition and acceptance. One is free to be believing or unbelieving. Nothing and no one can compel us to have faith—no scientific discovery, no logical argument, no physical torture can force us to believe, i.e., to freely recognize and accept the *authority* of God. But on the other hand, once this authority is recognized and accepted, the powerless becomes powerful. Then divine power *can* manifest itself—and this is why it is said that a grain of faith is sufficient to move mountains.

ANONYMOUS (20th century)
Christian hermeticist

"Give us this day our supersubstantial bread" (Matt. 6:11). Another evangelist uses the term "daily" (Luke 11:3).

The first expression indicates that this bread has a character that is noble and substantial by virtue of which its exalted splendor and holiness surpass all substances and all creatures.

With "daily" the evangelist shows that without this bread we cannot live a spiritual life for even a day. When he says "this day" he shows that the bread must be eaten each day, that it will not be enough to have eaten yesterday unless we eat similarly today. May our daily poverty encourage us to pour forth this prayer at all times, for there is no day on which it is unnecessary for us to eat this bread so as to strengthen the heart of the person within us. . . .

And "forgive us our debts as we forgive those in debt to us." Oh, the unspeakable mercy of God! Not only has He handed to us a model of prayer, not only has He given us a discipline which will make us acceptable to Him, not only because of this necessary formula (by which He teaches us always to pray) has He pulled up the roots both of anger and of gloom, but He has also made a way and a route by which those praying to Him may call on Him to exercise a kindly and indulgent judgment over them. . . . Precisely because He did not wish us to find Him cruel and inexorable, He made clear the yardstick by which he made judgment.

JOHN CASSIAN (360–435)
Monk and founder of monasteries near Marseilles

Christ emphasizes: *"Watch and pray lest you enter into temptation."* The Apostle Peter, who walked on the waters—the waters are the temptations—began to sink, and if Christ had not reached out his hand to him, he would definitely have sunk. Peter was animated by a great desire to go towards God; Peter was moved by a great faith; he lacked prayer. At that moment he lacked that state of prayer in which we need divine help for the least thing, that help which makes our soul walk on the waters of grace. . . .

God loves us to work with Him, in Him. I will even say that He appreciates a piece of work whose aim is not always exceptional, if it is executed with prayer: help me; lead me not into temptation, I am weak. I would propose to you an image: God places His immaculate lips on the lips of our soul. That is why we must always pray, and when we discern His Will, there is nothing else to do but bend to it: we will have the strength necessary to realize it.

It is evident that in praying to God to free us from temptations, we are asking Him to free us from all that could separate us from Him. Invisibly Christ puts two weights in balance: love of God, and our own perfection. For perfection it is better for us to go through the crucible and conquer ourselves; to love God, it is better not to be perfect. How much better it is to be with Him than to compose one's perfection. I have seen souls slow their spiritual ascent because they wanted to be perfect. The construction of the marvelous temple around them prevented the Word from getting in. I will go further: to become a saint, give up the taste for holiness.

EUGRAPH KOVALEVSKY (1912–1970)
Russian founder of the French Catholic Orthodox Church

When we pray "And lead us not into temptation," we should know that the Lord is teaching us inwardly. . . . When we pray in these words we are put in touch with our vulnerability and inner weakness. We ask for help lest any should insolently exalt themselves, or become proud and conceited, or even hug to themselves the glory either of confessing their faith or of suffering [for Christ], as if it were all their own doing. The Lord himself has taught us to be humble when he said: "Watch and pray that you enter not into temptation."

CYPRIAN (c. 200–258)
Father of the church and bishop of Carthage

"Lord, do not lead us into temptation." Must we think that the Lord expects us to pray that we should never be tried at all? It is said in the Scriptures: *"He who has never been tried has not proved himself."*

And elsewhere: *"Whenever you face trial of any kind, consider it nothing but joy."*

But would not "to be tried" in our text mean "to be overwhelmed by trials"? Indeed, it may seem that this trial is a very strong current that is most difficult to cross. Those who are not overwhelmed by the trial are the only ones who can overcome it; they are, so to speak, good swimmers who are not washed away by the current. The others, as they try, drop to the bottom.

Let us take Judas, for instance; he was tempted by greed. He could not, in a way, swim across this temptation; he was lost, body and soul. Peter, on the other hand, was tempted to give up; but in the end he avoided disaster, managed to reach the other shore and was rescued. In another text the choir of saints who had remained pure sings its gratitude:

For you, O God, have tested us;
you have tried us as silver is tried
You have brought us to the net;
You laid burdens over our backs;
You let people ride over our heads;

we went through fire and water;
yet You have brought us out to a spacious place (Ps. 67:10–12).

Take good notice of the joy they experienced because they made the crossing without perishing. *"And you have brought us out,"* it is said, *"to a spacious place."* Spacious place here means: to come out of the test.

"But deliver us from evil!" If *"do not lead us into temptation"* meant to remove all trials, Jesus would not have added, "But deliver us from evil." . . . And at the end of this prayer you say: "Amen." This means that you confirm everything that is contained in this prayer.

CYRIL OF JERUSALEM (c. 315–387)
Bishop of Jerusalem, saint, and catechetical writer

God anticipates us, and Himself arranges the words and form of prayer for us, and places them upon our lips as to how and what we should pray, that we may see how heartily He pities us in our distress. . . . [the Lord's Prayer] is a great advantage indeed over all other prayers that we might compose ourselves. For in those prayers the conscience would ever be in doubt and say: I have prayed, but who knows how it pleases Him, or whether I have hit upon the right proportions and form? Hence there is no nobler prayer to be found upon earth than the Lord's Prayer which we daily pray because it has this excellent testimony, that God loves to hear it, which we ought not to surrender for all the riches of the world. . . .

But where there is to be a true prayer there must be earnestness. Men must feel their distress, and when such distress presses them and compels them to call and cry out, then prayer will be made spontaneously, as it ought to be, and men will require no teaching how to prepare for it and to attain to the proper devotion. But the distress which ought to concern us most, both as regards ourselves and every one, you will find abundantly set forth in the Lord's Prayer. Therefore it is to serve also to remind us of the same, that we contemplate it and lay it to heart, lest we become remiss in prayer. For we all have enough that we lack, but the greatest is that we neither feel nor see this lack. Therefore God also requires that you lament and plead such necessities and wants, not because He does not know them, but that you may kindle your heart to stronger and greater desires, and make wide and open your cloak to receive much.

MARTIN LUTHER (1483–1546)
German leader of the Protestant Reformation

CYCLE EIGHT

ATTENTION OF THE HEART

The root meaning of obey is to "listen," to "hyper-listen." The faculty of con-science is what opens the inner ear, enabling us to hear and to respond to the demand of every moment. It brings both the light of self-knowledge and the "unremitting consciousness of God's abiding presence deep within us."

When God made human beings, he put in them a kind of divine faculty, more alive and splendid than a spark, to illuminate the spirit and show it the difference between good and evil. It is the conscience with that law which is part of its nature. . . .

So now it depends on us whether we smother it again or allow it to shine out and give us light through our obedience.

If our conscience tells us to do something and we do it, our conscience is alive. If we do not do what it tells us, we trample on it again and bit by bit yet again we smother it. In the end it will no longer be able to speak plainly to us because of the clods of earth we throw on it. . . .

Just as in muddy water you cannot recognize your face, so we will gradually discover that we cannot perceive what our con-science is telling us. In fact, we might even imagine that we have no conscience at all.

But there is no one without a conscience. It is, as we said previously, a divine faculty and it never dies.

ABBA DOROTHEUS (sixth century)

Saint, ascetical writer, and founder of a Palestinian monastery

Saint Bonaventure teaches that "conscience is like God's herald and messenger; it does not command things on its own authority, but commands them as coming from God's authority, like a herald when he proclaims the edict of the king. This is why conscience has binding force." Thus it can be said that . . . conscience is "the witness of God himself," whose voice and judgment penetrate the depths of man's soul, calling him *"fortiler et suaviter"* to obedience. "Moral conscience does not close man within an insurmountable and impenetrable solitude, but opens him to the call, to the voice of God. In this, and not in anything else, lies the entire mystery and the dignity of the moral conscience: in being the place, the sacred place where God speaks to man." . . .

Conscience . . . is the obligation to do what the individual, through the workings of his conscience, "knows" to be a good he is called to do "here and now."

JOHN PAUL II (1920–)

Polish pope, theologian, and philosopher

Now must man know what to do and leave undone, and no standard whatsoever from the past or from the universal is available. That is the meaning of decision. . . .

Whoever sees man in the crisis of decision and recognizes this as the essential of human existence, assumes that man knows what is *now* good and evil; as has already been said, he knows, not on the basis of any past experience or rational deductions, but directly from the immediate situation. . . . It is fundamentally a mistake to look to [Jesus] for concrete ethical requirements or for his attitude toward concrete ethical problems. He always refers the questioner back to his own judgment. . . .

The demands of the Sermon on the Mount have always been regarded as particularly characteristic of the preaching of Jesus. Here we find at the beginning the new set over against the old in strong antitheses. . . .

> You have heard that it was said, Eye for eye, and tooth for tooth. But I tell you, Do not defend yourselves against injury; whoever strikes you on the right cheek, offer him the other; whoever goes to law with you about your cloak, give him your coat also; whoever forces you for a mile, go two with him (Matt. 5:38–41). . . .

In all these passages the decisive requirement is the same: the good which is to be done is to be done *completely*. He who does it partially, with reservations, just enough to fulfill the outward regulation, has not done it at all. . . .

Jesus has wholly separated obedience from legalism; hence he does not set up a better law in opposition to a less good law; he opposes the view that the fulfillment of the law is the fulfilling of the will of God. For God demands the whole man, not merely specific acts from the man. . . .

It would obviously be a complete misunderstanding to take these "But I tell you" passages as formal legal precepts of an external authority, which can be fulfilled by outward behavior. Whoever, appealing to a word of Jesus, refuses to dissolve an unendurable marriage, or whoever offers the other cheek to one who strikes him, *because* Jesus said so, would not understand Jesus. For he would have missed exactly the obedience which Jesus desires. . . . these sayings are meant to make clear by extreme examples that it is not a question of satisfying an outward authority but of being *completely* obedient. It is also wholly impossible to regard Jesus' teachings as universally valid ethical precepts by which a man can once and for all order his life. Unless the decision which is demanded in these sayings arises out of a present situation, it is not truly the decision of obedience, but an achievement which the man accomplishes. . . .

Truly when a man asks after the way of life, there is nothing in particular to say to him. He is to do what is right, what everyone knows. But if then a special demand confronts the man, it becomes plain whether the whole man was involved in that right conduct, whether that doing of what is right really rests on the decision for good. Otherwise it has no worth. . . .

For Jesus the essential meaning of human life is that man stands under the necessity of decision before God, is confronted by the demand of the will of God, which must be comprehended in each concrete moment and obeyed. Man does not have to achieve for himself particular qualities, either an especial virtue or an especial saintliness; he must simply be obedient, and for that he needs no special qualities. God is not far from him, so that a technique is necessary to approach Him; on the contrary, God speaks to him in every concrete situation, for every concrete situation is a crisis of decision. . . .

[Jesus] has no doctrine of virtue, so also he has none of duty or of the good. It is sufficient for a man to know that God has placed him under the necessity of decision in every concrete situation in life, in the here and now. And this means that he himself must know what is required of him, and that no authority and no theory can take from him this responsibility.

If a man is really capable of meeting this responsibility, he is like the good tree which bears good fruit; then his "heart" is good; and "the good man brings good out of the good treasure of his heart, and the evil man out of the evil brings evil" (Luke 6:45). Whoever sees a wounded man lying on the road knows without further command that it is right to help him. Whoever encounters the sick and oppressed knows that no Sabbath ordinance can hinder the duty to help. In all good conduct it is revealed whether the man desires to do God's will, that is, whether he wills to be completely obedient, entirely renounce his own claims, surrender his natural will with its demands. This in itself implies the requirement of truth and purity, and the casting aside of all hypocrisy, vanity, greed, and impurity. Such a man needs no particular rules for his conduct toward other men; his conduct is determined by renunciation of his own claim.

RUDOLPH KARL BULTMANN (1884–1976)
German Protestant theologian and New Testament scholar

Right relation between conduct and prayer is not that conduct is supremely important and prayer may help it, but that prayer is supremely important and conduct tests it.

WILLIAM TEMPLE (1881–1944)
English archbishop of Canterbury

Every moment of our human life is a moment of crisis; for at every moment we are called upon to make an all-important decision—to choose between the way that leads to death and spiritual darkness and the way that leads towards light and life; between interests exclusively temporal and the eternal order; between our personal will, or the will of some projection of our personality, and the will of God. . . . Here the aim is primarily to bring human beings to a state in which, because there are no longer any God-eclipsing obstacles between themselves and Reality, they are able to be aware continuously of the divine Ground of their own and all other beings; secondarily, as a means to this end, to meet all, even the most trivial, circumstances of daily living without malice, greed, self-assertion, or voluntary ignorance,

but consistently with love and understanding. . . . for the lover of
God, every moment is a moment of crisis.

ALDOUS HUXLEY (1894–1963)
English novelist, essayist, and critic

Thus self-knowledge is at the root of all real religious knowledge; and it is in vain—worse than vain—it is a deceit and a mis-
chief, to think to understand the Christian doctrines as a matter
of course, merely by being taught by books, or by attending ser-
mons, or by any outward means, however excellent, taken by
themselves. For it is in proportion as we search our hearts and
understand our own nature, that we understand what is meant by
an Infinite Governor and Judge; in proportion as we comprehend
the nature of disobedience and our actual sinfulness, that we feel
what is the blessing of the removal of sin, redemption, pardon,
sanctification, which otherwise are mere words. God speaks to us
primarily in our hearts. Self-knowledge is the key to the precepts
and doctrines of Scripture. The very utmost any outward notices
of religion can do, is to startle us and make us turn inward and
search our hearts; and then, when we have experienced what it is
to read ourselves, we shall profit by the doctrines of the Church
and the Bible.

JOHN HENRY NEWMAN (1801–1890)
English Roman Catholic cardinal

Conscience implies the faculty a man has of knowing himself. . . . this it is not possible for him to do, without the assistance of the Spirit of God. Otherwise, self-love, and, indeed,
every other irregular passion, would disguise and wholly conceal
him from himself. . . . Accordingly, the Apostle John declares to
the believers of all ages, "Ye have an unction from the Holy One,
and ye know all things." . . . So he adds, "Ye have no need that

any one should teach you, otherwise than as that anointing teach-
eth you." . . .

This St. Paul expresses various ways. . . . "Our rejoicing is
this, the testimony of our conscience, that in simplicity," with a
single eye, "and godly sincerity, we have had our conversation in the
world." Meantime he observes that this was done, "not by fleshly
wisdom"—commonly called prudence (this never did, nor ever
can produce such an effect)—"but by the grace of God," which
alone is sufficient to work this in any child of man. . . .

Therefore, if you desire to have your conscience always quick
to discern . . . if you would preserve it always sensible and tender, be sure to obey it at all events; continually listen to its admo-
nitions, and steadily follow them. Whatever it directs you to do,
according to the word of God, do.

JOHN WESLEY (1703–1791)
English founder of the Methodist Movement

Shall we be able to pray in that hour of decision, to commend
our souls into the hands of God? May God mercifully grant us
the grace to depart from this world in prayer, so that the last
thought in our minds may fit us for life everlasting. Blessed is he
who can utter a prayer of decision when the hour comes which
is for him the most decisive of all.

We do not know whether we shall be given the grace to meet
death with full consciousness, greeting it with prayer and resignation as the messenger of God. . . . Therefore we must begin in
time to tend the lamp of our faith and our love, that it may
always be filled with the oil of good works. Let us watch and
pray, so that the Lord at His coming may not find us asleep. That
prayer of decision which we wish to say in the hour of our death
must be said by us again and again during our life. We must pray
now for the decision of that future hour, and we must pray for
the grace of fortitude. . . . To think of one's death is prayer

indeed, a prayer of decision. The uncertainty of the hour of death compels us to anticipate in our everyday prayer, the prayer for the hour of death. Our everyday prayer thus becomes an intimate preparation for the ultimate prayer of decision. Let us pray unceasingly.

KARL RAHNER (1904–1984)
German Jesuit theologian

Keep your heart with all vigilance; for from it flow the springs of life (Proverbs 4:23).

The greatest difficulty is to win the heart to God; and afterwards, the greatest difficulty is to keep the heart with God.

Just this is what makes the way to life a narrow way, and the gate of heaven a strait gate; just here lies the very force and intensity of the Christian Way. Help in this great work is offered in the text above, for it first exhorts us: *Keep your heart with all vigilance;* and secondly informs: *for from it flow the springs of life.*

By keeping the heart, you should understand the diligent and constant use of all holy means to preserve the soul from error and to maintain its sweet and free communion with God. I say constant, for this obligation extends to all the states and conditions of a Christian's life, and is binding always. If the heart must be kept because *from it flow the springs of life,* then as long as these springs of life flow out of it, we are obliged to keep it.

Keep your heart. It seems that we are being told to do this work, yet at the same time we are as able to stop the sun in its course, or to make the rivers run backward, as by our own will and power to rule and order our hearts. We may as well be our own saviors as our own keepers; and yet Solomon speaks properly enough when he says, *Keep your heart,* because the duty is indeed ours, though the power is of God. What power we have depends upon the refreshing and assisting strength of Christ. Grace within us is beholden to grace without us. "Without me ye can do nothing."

Yet we are told: *Keep your heart.* The Hebrew is very emphatic; keep with all keeping; or, keep, keep; set double guards. This vehemence of expression plainly implies how difficult it is to keep our hearts, how dangerous to neglect them! *For from it flow the springs of life.* The heart is the treasury, the hand and tongue but the shops; what is in these comes from the heart; the hand and tongue always begin where the heart ends. The heart contrives, and the members execute: "a good man, out of the good treasure of his heart, bringeth forth that which is good; and an evil man, out of the evil treasure of his heart, bringeth forth that which is evil: for of the abundance of the heart his mouth speaketh."

Heart errors are like the errors made at the first step, which cannot be rectified afterward; or like the inverting of the letters in the press, which cause so many errata in all the copies that are printed. O then how important a duty is the keeping of the heart! The right managing of the heart in every condition is the one great and constant business of a Christian's life. What the philosopher says of waters applies equally to hearts: it is hard to keep them within any bounds. God has set limits to them, yet how frequently they transgress not only the bounds of grace and conscience, but even of reason and common honesty.

It is this which gives the Christian labor and watchfulness to his dying day. *Keep your heart.* To keep the heart presupposes a work of regeneration that sets the heart right by giving it a new spiritual inclination. The self is the hallmark of the unrenewed heart, which biases and moves it in all its schemes and actions; and as long as this is so, it is impossible to keep the heart with God.

This great change is the renovation of the soul after the image of God, in which self-dependence is removed by faith; self-love, by the love of God; self-will, by subjection and obedience to the will of God; and self-seeking by self-denial. The darkened understanding is illuminated, the intractable will sweetly subdued, the rebellious appetite gradually conquered. Thus the soul which sin had universally depraved is by grace restored.

To keep the heart, then, is nothing but the constant care and diligence of such a renewed person to preserve his soul in that holy state to which grace has raised it. For though grace has, in a great measure, rectified the soul, and given it an habitual heavenly temper; yet sin often discomposes it again; so that even a gracious heart is like a musical instrument, which though it be exactly tuned, a small matter brings it out of tune again; yea, hang it aside but a little, and it will need setting again before another lesson can be played upon it. If gracious hearts are in a desirable frame in one duty, yet how dull, dead, and disordered when they come to another! Therefore every act requires a particular preparation of the heart.

JOHN FLAVEL (1630–1691)
English writer and preacher

We should watch over our heart with all vigilance not only to avoid ever losing the thought of God or sullying the memory of his wonders by vain imaginations, but also in order to carry about the holy thoughts of God stamped upon our souls as an ineffaceable seal by continuous and pure recollection . . . so the Christian directs every action, small and great, according to the will of God, performing the action at the same time with care and exactitude, and keeping his thoughts fixed upon the One who gave him the work to do. In this way he fulfills the saying, "I set the Lord always in my sight; for he is at my right hand, that I be not moved," and he also observes the precept, "Whether you eat or drink or whatsoever else you do, do all to the glory of God." . . . We should perform every action as if under the eyes of the Lord and think every thought as if observed by him . . .

fulfilling the words of the Lord: "I seek not my own will but the will of him that sent me, the Father."

BASIL THE GREAT (330–379)
Doctor of the church, saint, and bishop of Geneva

The evangelical precept to watch, not to allow oneself to be weighed down by sleep, is a constant theme of Eastern asceticism, which demands full consciousness of the human person in all the degrees of its ascent towards perfect union. . . . According to St. Maximus, contemplation without action, theory which is not applied in practice, differs in no way from imagination, from fantasy without any real substance—similarly action, if it is not inspired by contemplation, is as sterile and rigid as a statue. "The very life of the spirit being the work of the heart," says St. Isaac the Syrian, "it is purity of heart which gives integrity to the contemplation of the spirit." Thus the active life consists in the purifying of the heart, and this activity is conscious, being directed by the spirit, the contemplative faculty which enters into and unites itself with the heart, coordinating and uniting the human being in grace. . . .

The human spirit, in its normal condition, is neither active nor passive: it is vigilant. This is "sobriety," the "attention of the heart," the faculty of discernment and of the judgment in spiritual matters, which are characteristic of human nature in its state of wholeness.

VLADIMIR LOSSKY (1903–1958)
Russian Orthodox theologian

St. Ignatius of Antioch grasped the relationship between the silence of God and the necessity of Christians to listen in silence to God as he speaks his Word within them: "Anyone who is really possessed of the word of Jesus can listen to his silence and so be perfect; so that he may act through his words and be known by his silence."

Inner attentiveness to the Word of God that is constantly speaking from within our hearts about the Father's infinite love for us is an obligation for all Christians. . . . Nicholas Cabasilas of the 14th century, who worked as a layman in the court of Constantinople and yet strove to live the ideal of other hesychasts who lived in monasteries or in the desert, writes to us in the modern world: "And everyone should keep his art or profession. The general should continue to command; the farmer to till the land; the artisan to practice his craft. And I will tell you why. It is not necessary to retire into the desert, to take unpalatable food, to alter one's dress, to compromise one's health, or to do anything unwise, because it is quite possible to remain in one's own home without giving up all one's possessions, and yet to practice continual meditation." . . .

For a person who has begun the inner journey into the heart, true prayer should no longer be a thing to do, an activity before God. It should become more and more a state of standing before God's loving presence, totally emptied of self, total gift to God. In complete nudity of spirit, in complete formlessness, without words, but with the "passionless passion" of the total true self, we grow daily in oneness with the triune God. . . . Prayer of the heart becomes the unremitting consciousness of God's abiding presence deep within us. It brings about the state of restfulness, tranquillity, the quelling of all inordinate movements and desires, passions and thoughts within us.

GEORGE A. MALONEY (1924–)
American Jesuit

Obedience is in general poorly understood. Philologically the term obedience in Greek, Latin, and Slavonic signifies: *listening*. Its roots go into "listening." Obedience opens the *inner ear*. It is a state which is particularly attentive, not passive. Often, the fraud of the authorities appears here. They mingle obedience to the Spirit with administrative obedience: "You must obey!" . . . All authority which crushes, whatever it may be, the authority of science, of the state, or of the Church, kills the possibility of hearing. . . . Obedience frees us, giving us the possibility of being that recipient in whom the Will of God can flow, while external discipline closes the opening. . . .

Christian obedience is not disinterestedness; we free ourselves from all we can possibly be freed from so *that we* can *"listen"* better and better to the Word.

EUGRAPH KOVALEVSKY (1912–1970)
Russian founder of the French Catholic Orthodox Church

How, then, to understand obedience? Poverty is detachment from the world, chastity is detachment from the flesh, obedience is detachment from the self. This is the most radical detachment of all. But what is the self? The self is the principle of reason and responsibility in us, it is the root of freedom, it is what makes us men. But this self is not autonomous; it is subject to a law—to what in India is called dharma, which St. Thomas Aquinas called the universal Reason, the Law of the universe. The great illusion is to consider that the self has an absolute freedom, that it is a law to itself. This is the original sin. In fact, the self can never act independently. It must either act in dependence on dharma, that is, the law of reason, or it will become subject to another law, the law of nature, of passion and desire, that is, the powers of the unconscious.

This is the drama of paradise. Man was placed in the garden of this world and given to eat of all the trees, of the senses, the feelings, the appetites, the desires—all were open to him. But the tree of knowledge of good and evil—the conscience by which we know what is right and wrong—was not left within his power. For that he is dependent on a higher power, and the moment he eats of it and seeks to make himself the master of his destiny, he loses his autonomy and becomes the slave of the powers of nature—the other gods, who take the place of the one God. The self must either be dependent on God, the universal Law, and acquire true freedom, or else it loses its freedom in subjection to nature, to the unconscious. This is the essential nature of the self; it is not a static entity, complete in itself. It is a power of self-transcendence. It is the power to give one's self totally to another, to transcend one's self by surrendering to the higher Self, the Atman, the Spirit within. . . . This is wisdom and joy and immortality. This is what man was created for—this is true obedience.

BEDE GRIFFITHS (1906–1993)
English Benedictine monk

For silence is not God, nor is speaking God; fasting is not God, nor is eating God; being alone is not God, nor is company God, nor yet any one of every such pair of contraries. He is hid between them; and he cannot be found by any work of your soul, but only by the love of your heart. He cannot be known by reason. He cannot be thought, grasped, or searched out by the understanding. But he can be loved and chosen by the true and loving desire of your heart. Choose him then, and you are silent in speaking and speaking in silence; fasting in eating and eating in fasting; and so with all the rest.

This loving choice of God, which is attentively to gather him up and seek him out with the true will of a clean heart from between such contraries—so that when they come and offer themselves as the target, the bull's-eye of our spiritual gaze, we leave them aside; this is the best searching and seeking for God that one may have or learn in this life—I speak of those who would be contemplatives. And this is true even if the person who makes this search sees nothing that can be conceived with the spiritual eye of reason. For if God is your love and your intent, the choice and the ground of your heart, this is enough for you in this life; even though you never see more of him with the eye of reason all your life long. Such a blind shot with the sharp arrow of a love that longs can never miss the bull's-eye, which is God. . . . For by love we can find him, experience him, and reach him, as he is in himself. . . .

And thus it finds and experiences, hits and pierces the target and the bull's-eye at which it aims, much sooner than it would if its sight were distracted by looking at many things as it is when reason ransacks and seeks among all these various things such as silence and speaking, extraordinary fasting and normal diet, living alone and in company, in order to find out which is better.

UNKNOWN ENGLISH MYSTIC (14th century)
Assessment of Inner Stirrings

In brief, do everything as though in the presence of God and so, in whatever you do, you need never allow your conscience to wound and denounce you, for not having done your work well.

Proceeding in this way you will smooth for yourself a true and straight path to the third method of attention and prayer which is the following: the mind should be in the heart—a distinctive feature of the third method of prayer. It should guard the heart while it prays, revolve, remaining always within, and thence, from the depths of the heart, offer up prayers to God. (Everything is in this: work in this way until you are given to taste the Lord.) When the mind, there, within the heart, at last tastes and sees that the Lord is good, and delights therein (the labor is ours, but this tasting is the action of grace in a humble heart), then it will no longer wish to leave this place in the heart . . . and will always look inwardly into the depths of the heart and will remain revolving there, repulsing all thoughts sown by the devil. (This is the third method of attention and prayer, practiced as it should be.) ...

Therefore our holy fathers, harkening to the Lord ... have renounced all other spiritual work and concentrated wholly on this one doing, that is on guarding the heart, convinced that, through this practice, they would easily attain every other virtue, whereas without it not a single virtue can be firmly established. Some of the fathers called this doing, silence of the heart; others called it attention; yet others—sobriety and opposition (to thoughts), while others called it examining thoughts and guarding the mind.

Keep your mind there (in the heart), trying by every possible means to find the place where the heart is, in order that, having found it, your mind should constantly abide there. Wrestling thus, the mind will find the place of the heart.

SIMEON THE NEW THEOLOGIAN (949–1022)
Byzantine saint, mystic, and spiritual writer

Inner unrest drives us away from the place where we should be ... the place where things really matter, where one must hold one's ground; the place where the Living God calls to the self— the place of obedience. In this exacting stillness man begins to feel uncomfortable and tries to run away. Always he flees from the holy *here* where the call reaches him, and where everything is "in its right place." It would appear that man, the more firmly he is rooted in the world, the more adrift he becomes from the place which really matters.

If he wants to pray, he must recall himself from everything and everywhere and become and remain present. . . . This becomes evident in our attempts to pray. Spiritual teachers speak of "distraction" as that state in which man lacks poise and unity, that state in which thoughts flit from object to object, in which feelings are vague and unfocused and the will ineffective. Man in this state is not really a person who speaks or who can be spoken to, but merely an uncoordinated bundle of thoughts, feelings and sensations. Collectedness means that he who prays gathers himself together, directs his attention on to what he is doing, draws in all thought—a painstaking task—so as to dedicate himself to prayer as a unified whole. This is the state in which he may, when the call comes to him, answer in the words of Moses, "Here am I." . . .

Therefore anyone able to collect himself, to be still and present, overcomes the inner brooding and heaviness. He lifts himself up and makes himself light, free and clear. He awakens the inner attention so that it may focus itself on its object. He clears the inner eye so that it may see true. He calls upon the inner preparedness so that contact becomes possible.

ROMANO GUARDINI (1885–1968)
Italian-born German Roman Catholic monsignor
and professor of Christian philosophy

In everything one must be very attentive to oneself, in all details, and not allow even the slightest lie or insincerity or flattery or man-pleasing.

ELDER MICHAEL OF VALAAM (1877–1962)
Russian Orthodox monk

Prayer, which is the fruit of true conversion, is an activity, an adventure, and sometimes a dangerous one, since there are occasions when it brings neither peace nor comfort, but challenge, conflict and new responsibility. This is why so many old ways of praying, and books about prayer, seem to have let us down. Too often when we used them we were hoping to get something for ourselves from prayer, perhaps security or a growing sensible realization and knowledge of God. To seek such things in prayer is a mistake. The essential heart of prayer is the throwing away of ourselves in self-oblation to God, so that he can do with us what he wills. Any form of prayer which does not incite a costing giving in love soon becomes sterile, dry, and a formal duty.

MOTHER MARY CLARE (1907–1988)
English Anglican nun

Even though we may really want to be sincere, we have an almost infinite resourcefulness in lying to ourselves.

The effort to be sincere keeps us face to face with our own inner contradictions. It makes it impossible for us to escape the conflict, the division within us. And this division keeps us in a state of constant anguish. The paradox that one must face, if he really takes the truth seriously, is the pragmatic fact that sincerity means insecurity. If we recognize how basic is the conflict within our hearts, we cannot settle down and take roots and become "installed" on this earth. We will know the meaning of deep, bitter, and even anguished insecurity. But we will also come to know the value of this insecurity: it is, in fact, the guarantee of our sincerity. It is, paradoxically, the sign that we are on the right road. It tells us that we are moving forward in the only direction possible for a Christian, and that we are in contact with reality.

THOMAS MERTON (1915–1968)
American Cistercian monk

Watchfulness is of as great importance to prayer as prayer is to all our other duties. No duty can be dispatched well without prayer, nor prayer without watching; for only prayer performed in a holy spiritual manner is effectual. Now, this cannot be done when the guard is off his watch. Take the Christian a napping, with his grace in a slumber, and he is no fitter to pray than a man is to work that is asleep. Whatever a man is doing, sleep, when it comes, puts an end to it. Sleep is the great leveler of the world, it makes all men alike. The strong man is as unable to defend himself from an enemy in his sleep as the child. The rich man asleep and the poor man are alike; he enjoys his estate no more than if he had none. Thus the Christian, while his graces are asleep, is even like another that hath no grace.

O how sad is this! and yet how prone are we to give way unto this drowsiness of spirit in prayer! Watch what strength and force thy soul puts to the work. In a word, thou must keep thy heart with all diligence from one end of the duty to the other, or else it will give thee the slip before thou art aware. At one moment, our hearts are warm at the work, and we pursue hard after God with full cry of our affections; but instantly we are at a loss and hunt cold again. Holy David was sensible of this, and therefore we have him in the midst of this duty begging help from God to call in his gadding heart.

WILLIAM GURNALL (1617–1679)
English pastor

Staying within means strictly speaking a conscious centering in the heart, an intensive gathering thereto of all the forces of soul and body, using the essential means, the exercises of the spiritual life. He who abides within the heart is recollected, and he who is recollected is in the heart. Around the consciousness in the heart all forces—mind, will, and feelings—must be gathered.

The gathering of the mind in the heart is attention; the gathering of will, readiness; and the gathering of the feelings, watchfulness. Attention, readiness and watchfulness are three interior works which affect the gathering of self and signify the staying within (recollection). He who has all things, without exception, within himself is within, while he who lacks even one of them is outside. Therefore, all the work of staying within, through self-gathering, consists in the following [according to Theophan the Recluse]:

"In the first moment after awakening, as soon as you come to yourself, descend into the heart, and then call, appeal, force thereto all the forces of the body and soul, by the attention of the mind, by turning the eyes thereto, by readiness of will with a certain tensing of the muscles, and by watchfulness over the feelings. Repress feelings of pleasure, especially of the flesh, and do this until consciousness has firmly established itself in the heart as on a throne. Remain there all the time while you still have consciousness. Repeat often this exercise because self-gathering needs continuous renewal and strengthening." Every spiritual work requires great concentration. The Kingdom of God is within us and in order to find it we must, according to the Savior, enter into the room of our heart. He who enters the heart and gathers there all his forces is a flaming spirit.

SERGIUS BOLSHAKOFF (20th century)
Russian Orthodox monk and writer

It sometimes happens that you go to your prayer after having spent the whole day dissipated and without recollection; it is no wonder you are distracted, for you well deserve it. You follow your own inclinations, you are cross-grained and resentful in your obedience, lacking in sweetness and condescension towards your neighbor, and then you go boldly to prayer in order to unite yourself to God and to have consolation and sweetness.

If you find the door shut, why should you be surprised?

JANE DE CHANTAL (1572–1641)
French saint and founder of the Order of the Visitation

We must seek to be before prayer what we want to be and to do in prayer. The attitudes and thoughts of our heart during prayer depend on the state we were in as we begin to pray. As we kneel to pray, the same actions, words and feelings we have known are reborn from our imagination. . . .

First of all, we must totally suppress all anxiety concerning the flesh. Then concerns—and more, the memory even—of every matter that occupies or absorbs our interest must be absolutely dismissed. After this, we ought also to renounce slander, idle conversation, gossip, and foolish speech. Above all, strike at the root of anger or sadness. . . .

Once these vices and their companions—even those which escape the human eye—have been entirely removed and destroyed; after the purification we have described has been begun and we are on the way to purity, simplicity, and innocence, we can lay the unshakable foundations of a deep humility. . . . Finally, withhold your soul from seeking escape in wayward or flighty thoughts, so that you may thus begin to ascend, gradually, to the contemplation of God and of spiritual realities.

All the strange ideas we would be free of during the time of prayer must thus be banished with a care drawn from the temple of our heart before we begin to pray. Then we shall be able to heed the admonition of the Apostle: "Pray without ceasing!"

AUGUSTINE OF HIPPO (354–430)
Carthaginian saint, philosopher, and doctor of the church

When we come to prayer we bring with us, although perhaps unknowingly, all the disquiet that we have imposed on ourselves during the preceding hours or days. If we have not beforehand tried to keep our heart or our body in a state of order, truth and beauty, we cannot expect them to be suddenly transformed, just because we shut our eyes and want to be in the presence of God.

The quality of our prayer is a function of the way we live throughout the day. If there is wisdom and order in our approach towards the whole rhythm of our daily activities—our sleep, the way we take our meals, the times of rest—then these will be the remote preparation for our recollection during the times specially set apart for prayer. . . .

We have to admit that we often become slaves to work because we renounce all custody of our heart. We engage passionately in whatever it is we are doing. We allow this to become our real center of interest.

A CARTHUSIAN (contemporary)

Because of the workings of memory whatever has preoccupied our mind before the time for prayer must of necessity intrude on our actual prayers. Therefore in advance of prayer we must strive to dispose ourselves as we would wish to be during prayer. The praying spirit is shaped by its own earlier condition. As we prostrate ourselves for prayer our deeds, words, and fastings rise up in our imagination. They are as they were before our prayer, and they move us to anger or gloom. We turn back toward desire or worldly affairs. Stupidly—and I am ashamed to say it—we laugh as we recall some clownish word or act, and the mind flits back to the earlier concerns of our talk. . . .

The soul may quite sensibly be compared to the finest down and the lightest feather which, if spared the onset and penetration of dampness from without, have a nature so mobile that at the slightest breeze they rise up of themselves to the highest points of the sky. But if they are weighed down by any splash, any dampening of moisture, not only will there be no natural impulse to fly up into the air but the pressure of the absorbed liquid will drag them downward to earth.

So too with our soul. If sin and worldly preoccupation have not weighed it down, if dangerous passion has not sullied it, then, lifted up by the natural goodness of its purity, it will rise to the heights on the lightest breath of meditation and, leaving the lowly things, the things of earth, it will travel upward to the heavenly and the invisible.

And so we are quite rightly admonished by the Lord's command: "See to it that your hearts are not weighed down in drunkenness and intoxication and in the concerns of every day." . . . We should take care to observe the reasons mentioned by the Lord for the loading down of the mind. He was not talking of adultery, of fornication, of murder, of blasphemy, of robbery. These, as everyone knows, bring death and damnation. But what He mentioned were drunkenness, intoxication, and earthly worries and concerns. . . .

But after this preliminary work of purification has received its crown of innocent simplicity and purity, the foundations must be laid: unshakable foundations of a *deep humility,* capable of bearing the tower that is to rise even to the heavens.

JOHN CASSIAN (360–435)
Monk and founder of monasteries near Marseilles

My purpose is to impress on you the importance of weighing your thoughts and desires as they arise, for you must learn to reject the least of them that might lead you to sin. . . . And so to stand firmly and avoid pitfalls, keep to the path you are on. Let your longing relentlessly beat upon the *cloud of unknowing* that lies between you and your God. Pierce that cloud with the keen shaft of your love, spurn the thought of anything less than God, and do not give up this work for anything. For the contemplative work of love by itself will eventually heal you of all the roots of sin. . . . Genuine goodness is a matter of habitually acting and responding appropriately in each situation, as it arises, moved always by the desire to please God. He alone is the pure source of all goodness and if a person is motivated by some thing else besides God, even though God is first, then his virtue is imperfect. This is evident in the case of two virtues in particular, humility and brotherly love. Whoever acquires these habits of mind and manner needs no others, for he will possess everything.

UNKNOWN ENGLISH MYSTIC (14th century)
The Cloud of Unknowing

Human perfection consists in knowing the greatness of God and our own nothingness.

The more you are tempted, the more must you persevere in prayer. . . . For through prayer you are enlightened, through prayer you are set free from temptation, through prayer you are cleansed, through prayer you are united to God. Prayer is nothing else than the awareness of God and of oneself . . . and it is then that true humility appears. For humility consists in the soul beholding God and itself as it should. Then the soul is in a state of deep humility, and the deeper the humility the greater the divine grace that springs forth and increases from this mutual gaze.

The more the divine grace humbles the soul, the more quickly does this same grace increase and spring afresh out of the depths of that humility. And the more the grace increases the more deeply does the soul abase itself in true humility through continuing in true prayer. Thus do grace and light divine grow ever within the soul, and the soul is ever prostrate in true humility.

ANGELA OF FOLIGNO (1248–1309)
Umbrian mystic

Feeling His presence before you, surrender yourself to His almighty power, all-seeing and omniscient, in worshipful submission laying all your activities before him, in such a way that in every action, word and thought you remember God and His holy will. Such, in brief, is the spirit of prayer. Whoever has a love for prayer must without fail possess this spirit, and, as far as possible, must submit his understanding to God's understanding by means of constant attention of the heart, humbly and reverently obeying the commands of God. In the same way he should submit his wishes and desires to God's will, and surrender himself completely to the designs of God's providence.

In all possible ways we should combat the spirit of arbitrary self-will and the impulse to shake off all restraint. It is a spirit that whispers to us: This is beyond my strength, for that I have no time, it is too soon yet for me to undertake this, I should wait . . . —and plenty of other excuses of like kind. He who listens to this spirit will never acquire the habit of prayer. Closely connected with this spirit is the spirit of self-justification: when we have been carried away into wrongdoing by the spirit of willful arbitrariness and are therefore worried by our conscience, this second spirit approaches and sets to work on us. In such a case the spirit of self-justification uses all kinds of wiles to deceive the conscience and to present our wrong as being right.

AGAPII (19th century)

Monk of Valamo monastery, Russia

The Apostle writes: "For our rejoicing is this, the testimony of our conscience" (2 Cor. 1:12). Simeon the New Theologian says: "If our conscience is pure, we are given the prayer of mind and heart; but without a pure conscience we cannot succeed in any spiritual endeavor."

IGUMEN VARLAAM (18th century)

Monk of Valamo monastery, Russia

When thou hast shut thy door (Matt. 6:6).

Nothing could be plainer, and more impressive, than our Lord's words to us in the text. Just as you do every day—He says to us—in your household and business life, so do, exactly, in your religious life. Fix on times; set apart times. He does not say how often, or how long. He leaves all that to each man to find out for himself. . . .

Let us shut our door tonight. We are in no hurry of business or of pleasure tonight. Let us go back upon the morning, upon the forenoon, upon the whole day, upon the week, upon the year. Let us recollect for whom, and for what, we prayed in secret this morning—or did not pray. Let us recall what we read, what we heard, and with what feelings: with whom we conversed, about what: all the things that tried us, tempted us, vexed us, or helped, comforted, and strengthened us. Let us do that tonight, and we shall not want matter for repentance and prayer tonight: nor for prayer, and purpose, and a plan of life for tomorrow. . . . Begin with the first action of the day; and proceed, step by step; and let no time, place, or action be overlooked. "An examination," an expert says, "so managed, will, in a little time, make you as different from yourself as a wise man is different from an idiot. It will give you such a newness of mind, such a spirit of wisdom, and such a desire of perfection, as you were an entire stranger to before."

ALEXANDER WHYTE (1836–1921)
Scottish Evangelical minister

Father, help me to realize that now is eternity and that there is only the dimension of the now in which to awaken to Thy unquenchable love that will not let me go. Strip me of all further evasion and postponement, that this very hour I may abandon my heart to Thee. Amen.

BERNARD OF CLAIRVAUX (1091–1153)
Cistercian abbot, saint, and theologian

CYCLE NINE

LIBERTY OF
THE SPIRIT

To be spiritually free requires that we not be enslaved by our emotional, intellectual, and bodily impulses. But how? Efforts to "rectify the exterior" can backfire when we try to "turn to God without turning from ourselves." Yet, Jung tells us, "no Christian is meant to sleep in a safe pew." What supports the undeniable need for struggle, inhibition, and detachment?

The tragedy of original sin is that the world is turned upside down. The spirit should be nourished by God and breathe Him; the soul should be nourished by the spirit and breathe it; the body should be nourished by the soul and breathe it; and the world should be nourished by the human body and breathe it.

Having turned away from God, having turned its values upside down, cut off the contact between itself and the Creator—which is the first death—the human spirit lost its true nourishment and breathing.

. . . Food-prayer and breath-prayer reveal the essentials of human anthropology to us. Man is composed of three elements: spirit (pneuma), soul (psyche) and body (soma). What is the food of the body? Whether it is vegetables, meat, or fish, it is communion with the cosmos, with animals and plants, contact with nature which penetrates us, communion with the universe.

The need to eat in order to live is also the mystery of the unity of nature, if I may say so, it is a "natural Mass."

The food of the soul is composed of relationships with beings, cultures, arts. As far as food is concerned, our epoch particularly prizes a healthy diet. . . . Yet books are a kind of food: devoured without discernment they cause a disorder, anxiety, which could be described as due to lack of hygiene. We certainly do not observe fasts of the soul! . . . If its taste is well developed, our palate does not eat just anything; but consider your soul: it swallows anything, music, film, books, meetings. Hygiene of the psyche is absent.

God is the sole food of our spirit, and He communicates Himself to us through prayer. Neither human contact, nor books, nor thoughts, nor feelings, nor what belongs to culture, to civilization, or to religion, will feed that which is divine in us. Only the Divine, God, can feed the divine. . . . Food-prayer par excellence is liturgical prayer; breath-prayer is interior prayer. . . . Without prayer, the spirit wilts and dies: the body lives; the soul is moved but the spirit is dead. Prayer is the indispensable, the vital food.

Obviously, as a person eats, he opens his mouth, takes a fork, chews, then digests. As he breathes, he inhales and exhales the air, and he can learn to breathe properly. But if the physical movements of eating and breathing demand an effort of us, they are harmful. We should receive, assimilate, and not wish to act. I say this for food-prayer and for breath-prayer. Every voluntary decision restricts the possibility of health. . . . Let the soul imitate a cup, a receptacle, a "vessel," as the Medieval texts say—religious initiations are symbolized by a cup—a cup in which God pours His wine, His grace, His power. Let the soul resemble a lotus, a tulip which catches the sun's rays or the heavenly dew of the morning. Let the soul become a rose, the heart of which is the sun.

Cup, lotus, tulip, rose, something which opens itself to receive and be fed. Your gestures, your position, should not demand of you more effort than that of being well seated at a banquet.

I have emphasized this behavior, as many people worry. They think that food-prayer depends on an interior activity in which we must become taut, must imagine, desire, fix, and concentrate, instead of protecting, thrusting aside what hinders, and hollowing out the inner cup which God penetrates.

Concentration and intellectual conception are domes which close so that grace cannot spread within them.

EUGRAPH KOVALEVSKY (1912–1970)
Founder of the French Catholic Orthodox Church

The Christian world worships the Crucifix, i.e., the image expressing the paradox of almighty God reduced to a state of extreme powerlessness. . . . The only Son of the eternal Father nailed to the cross *for our sake*—this is what is divinely impressed upon all open souls, including the robber crucified to the right. This impression is unforgettable and inexpressible. It is the immediate breath of God which has inspired and still inspires thousands of martyrs, confessors of the faith, virgins and recluses. But it is not so that every human being finding himself facing the Crucifix may be thus divinely moved. There are those who react in the opposite way. It was so at the time of Calvary; it is so today.

> And those who passed by derided him, wagging their heads and saying: . . . If you are the Son of God, come down from the cross. (Matt. 27:39–40)

The chief sacrificers, with the scribes and elders, also mocked him, saying

> He saved others; he cannot save himself! If he is the king of Israel, let him come down now from the cross, and we

will believe in him. He trusts in God; let God deliver him now, if he loves him! (Matt. 27: 42–43)

This is the other reaction. Nowadays we encounter exactly the same. . . . It is the dogma or philosophical principle which states that *truth and power are identical;* that which is powerful is true and that which is powerless is false. According to this dogma or philosophical principle (which has become that of modern technological science) power is the absolute criterium and supreme ideal of truth. Only that which is powerful is of the Divine.

Now there are open and secret worshippers of the idol of power (for it *is* an idol, the source of all idolatry)—also in Christian factions or in religious and spiritual circles in general. . . .

It is they who teach that God has created souls predestined to eternal damnation and others predestined to salvation; it is they who make God responsible for the entire history of the human race, including all its atrocities. God, they say, "chastises" his disobedient children by means of wars, revolutions, tyrannies and other similar things. How could it be otherwise? God is almighty, therefore all that happens is only able to happen through his action or with his consent.

The idol of power has such a hold on some human minds that they prefer a God who is a mixture of good and evil, provided that he is powerful, to a God of love who governs only by the intrinsic authority of the Divine—by truth, beauty, and goodness—i.e., they prefer a God who is actually almighty to the *crucified God.*

However, the father in the parable of the prodigal child had neither sent his son far from his paternal home in order to lead a life of debauchery, nor had he prevented him from leaving and forced him to lead a life which was pleasing to him (the father). All he did was to await his return and to go and meet him when the prodigal son was approaching his father's home. Everything which took place in the story of the prodigal son, save for his return to the father, was clearly *contrary* to the will of the father.

Now the history of the human race since the Fall is that of the prodigal son.... And the key formula of the history of humanity is to be found neither in the progress of civilization nor in the process of evolution or in any other "process" but rather in the parable of the prodigal son, in the words:

Father, I have sinned against heaven and before you; I am no longer worthy to be called your son; treat me as one of your hired servants. (Luke 15:18–19)

Is mankind therefore solely responsible for its history? Without a doubt—because it is not God who has willed it to be as such. God is crucified in it.

One understands this when one takes account of the significance of the fact of human freedom.... Freedom is nothing other than the real and complete existence of a being created by God. To be free and to exist are synonymous from a moral and spiritual point of view.... Freedom is the spiritual existence of beings.

ANONYMOUS (20th century)
Christian hermeticist

What constantly marked the life of Jesus was not nonviolence but in every situation the choice not to use power. This is infinitely different.

JACQUES ELLUL (1912–1994)
French philosopher and theologian

We may venture to define liberty of spirit as the subordination of spiritual means to the one spiritual end. It is a liberty from attachment to anything, even the means of perfection, except so far as they promote perfection. In the *Legatus* of St. Gertrude, our Lord Himself has deigned to give a definition of liberty of spirit. It chanced that once a certain devout person, being in prayer, asked our Lord what it was that pleased Him most in His chosen servant; and our Lord vouchsafed to answer that it was her "liberty of heart." The questioner did not understand this, and he ventured to express his astonishment. "I thought, O Lord," he continued, "that it was because she was so high in the knowledge and the love of Thee." And our Lord again replied, "So it is; but the cause or instrument of this perfection is her liberty. There is never a moment in which she is not prepared for My gifts, because she never permits her heart to cling to anything which may be an obstacle to Me." . . . the shortest way to attain contemplation is thus to remove obstacles. A Greater than ourselves is within us. Hinder Him not, do not contristate Him, and "there is no need that any man should teach us."

BEDE FROST (1877–?)
English Benedictine

For prayer is the expression of a wish to God and, since God searches the heart, the conceiving even of the wish is prayer in God's eyes. . . . looked at in itself, such a nothing is the creature before its creator; it is found to be no more than the mere wish, discernible by God's eyes, that it might do as he wishes, might correspond, might say Yes to him; correspondence on man's side is not so much corresponding as the wish to correspond, and this least sigh of desire, this one aspiration, is the life and spirit of man.

GERARD MANLEY HOPKINS (1844–1889)
English Jesuit priest and poet

And because an act of the will is quite distinct from feeling, it is by an act that the will is united with God and rests in Him; that act is love. This union is never wrought by feeling or exertion of the desire; for these remain in the soul as aims and ends. It is only as motives of love that feelings can be of service, if the will is bent on going onwards, and for nothing else. . . .

He, then, is very unwise who, when sweetness and spiritual delight fail him, thinks for that reason that God has abandoned him; and when he finds them again, rejoices and is glad, thinking that he has in that way come to possess God.

More unwise still is he who goes about seeking for sweetness in God, rejoices in it, and dwells upon it; for in so doing he is not seeking after God with the will grounded in the emptiness of faith and charity, but only in spiritual sweetness and delight, which is a created thing, following herein in his own will and fond pleasure. . . . It is impossible for the will to attain to the sweetness and bliss of the divine union otherwise than in detachment, in refusing to the desire every pleasure in the things of heaven and earth.

The soul that is attached to anything, however much good there may be in it, will not arrive at the liberty of divine union. For whether it be a strong wire rope or a slender and delicate thread that holds the bird, it matters not, if it really holds it fast; for, until the cord be broken, the bird cannot fly. So the soul, held by the bonds of human affections, however slight they may be, cannot, while they last, make its way to God.

JOHN OF THE CROSS (1542–1591)
Spanish saint and mystic

The most powerful prayer, and almost the strongest of all to obtain everything, and the most honorable of all works, is that which proceeds from an empty spirit. The emptier the spirit, the more is the prayer and the work mighty, worthy, profitable, praiseworthy and perfect. The empty spirit can do everything.

What is an empty spirit?

An empty spirit is one that is confused by nothing, attached to nothing, has not attached its best to any fixed way of acting, and has no concern whatever in anything for its own gain, for it is all sunk deep down into God's dearest will and has forsaken its own. A man can never perform any work, however humble, without it gaining strength and power from this.

We ought to pray so powerfully that we should like to put our every member and strength, our two eyes and ears, mouth, heart and all our senses to work; and we should not give up until we find that we wish to be one with him who is present to us and whom we entreat, namely God.

MEISTER ECKHART (1260–1327)
German Dominican mystic and theologian

The life of a good Christian is an experience of an ever deepening desire for God. What you desire you cannot, as yet, see; but the desire gives you the capacity, so that when you eventually see you are satisfied. Imagine that you are filling some sort of bag. You know the bulk of what you will be given so you stretch the opening of the sack or the skin or whatever it is to accommodate it. You know how big the object is but you realise that the bag is too small so you increase its capacity by stretching it. In the same way, by deferring our hope, God is stretching our desire, and by deepening our desire he is expanding our soul and increasing its capacity.

Let us desire, my brothers and sisters, for we are to be filled. In the Scriptures we witness the apostle Paul stretching wide his heart to embrace whatever was to come. He says, "Not that I have already achieved this or am already perfect; my friends, I do not reckon that I have made it my own as yet." What, then, Paul, are you doing in this life if you have not yet made it your own?

"But one thing I do: forgetting what lies behind me and reaching out for that which lies ahead, I press on towards the goal to win the prize, which is God's call to the life above in Christ Jesus." He describes himself as "reaching out" and "pressing on." He felt himself inadequate to embrace "what eye has not seen nor ear heard, what has not entered into the human heart." This is the pattern of our life, an experience of being expanded by desire.

But we are expanded by our desire for God only insofar as we have severed our various yearnings of love of this world. I have already said, "Empty out that which is to be filled." . . . Imagine that God wants to fill you with honey. If you are already full of vinegar where is the honey to go? That is why what was in the vessel must not only be poured out, but the container itself be washed, cleansed and scoured. It may be hard work, but it is necessary in order to make it fit to house something else, whatever it may be. Whether we call it honey or gold or wine is immaterial because the reality we are describing cannot be named, and whatever we want to say is summed up in one word: "God." And when we have said "God," what in fact have we said? That one syllable is the distillation of all we hope for. Whatever is in our power to say must in reality be less than God. So, let us stretch ourselves, reaching out to God so that when he comes he may indeed fill us.

AUGUSTINE OF HIPPO (354–430)
Carthaginian saint, philosopher, and doctor of the church

Of its very nature, work is a multiple factor in detachment, provided a man gives himself to it faithfully and without rebellion. In the first place it implies effort and a victory over inertia. And then, however interesting and intellectual it may be (and the more intellectual it is, the truer this becomes), work is always accompanied by the painful pangs of birth. Man can escape the terrible boredom of monotonous and commonplace duty only by facing the inner tension and the anxieties of "creation."

To create, or organize material energy, or truth, or beauty, brings with it an inner torment which prevents those who face its hazards from sinking into the quiet and closed-in life wherein grows the vice of egoism and attachment. An honest workman not only surrenders his tranquillity and peace once and for all, but must learn to abandon over and over again the form which his labor or art or thought first took, and go in search of new forms. To pause, so as to enjoy or possess results, would be a betrayal of action. Over and over again he must transcend himself, tear himself away from himself, leaving behind him his most cherished beginnings.

PIERRE TEILHARD DE CHARDIN (1881–1955)
French paleontologist and Jesuit priest

Poverty, chastity and obedience—the renunciation of the world, the flesh and the ego—are the basis not only of all religious life but of all human life. Detachment is the universal law. You cannot enjoy anything until you have learned to be detached from it. It is not the drunkard who enjoys wine, or the glutton who enjoys food, or the sensualist who enjoys love. The perfect artist—whether dancer or actor or athlete—is not one who indulges the body but one who has mastered the body. His art becomes a yoga—a means of union, union of the powers of the body in harmony, union of body and soul in harmony, union of body and soul with the inner Spirit. But this is only attained when body and soul are "sacrificed" to the Spirit. As long as they retain their independence, there can be no yoga, no harmony. This is the death which body and soul have to undergo, the sacrifice of their autonomy, their surrender to the inner Spirit.

BEDE GRIFFITHS (1906–1993)
English Benedictine monk

Would you know why it is that so many have deceived themselves and others with false fire and false light, laying claim to information, illumination and opening of the divine Life, particularly that they are to do wonders under extraordinary calls from God? It is this: they have turned to God without turning from themselves; they wish to be alive to God before they are dead to their own nature. Now, religion in the hands of self, or corrupt nature, promotes vices of a far worse kind than nature left to itself. From this come all the disorderly passions of religious men, which burn in a worse flame than passions about merely worldly matters; pride, self-exaltation, hatred, and persecution, under a cloak of religious zeal, will sanctify actions which nature, left to itself, would be ashamed to own.

WILLIAM LAW (1686–1761)
English contemplative and cleric

By what rule or manner can I bind this body of mine? By what precedent can I judge him? Before I can bind him he is let loose, before I can condemn him I am reconciled to him, before I can punish him I bow down to him and feel sorry for him. How can I hate him when my nature disposes me to love him? How can I break away from him when I am bound to him forever? How can I escape from him when he is going to rise with me? How can I make him incorrupt when he has received a corruptible nature? How can I argue with him when all the arguments of nature are on his side?

If I try to bind him through fasting, then I am passing judgment on my neighbor who does not fast—with the result that I am handed over to him again. If I defeat him by not passing judgment I turn proud—and I am in thrall to him once more. He is my helper and my enemy, my assistant and my opponent, a protector and a traitor. I am kind to him and he assaults me. If I wear him out he gets weak. If he has a rest he becomes unruly.

If I upset him he cannot stand it. If I mortify him I endanger myself. If I strike him down I have nothing left by which to acquire virtues. I embrace him. And I turn away from him.

What is this mystery in me? What is the principle of this mixture of body and soul? How can I be my own friend and my own enemy? Speak to me! Speak to me, my yoke-fellow, my nature! I cannot ask anyone else about you. How can I remain uninjured by you? How can I escape the danger of my own nature?

JOHN CLIMACUS (520–603)
Father of the Eastern Church

St. Paul writes of this: "I find then a law, that, when I would do good, evil is present with me. For I delight in the law of God after the inward man: but I see another law in my members, warring against the law of my mind, and bringing me into captivity to the law of sin which is in my members" (Rom. 7:21–23). And he gives to all the rule: "Walk in the Spirit, and ye shall not fulfill the lust of the flesh" (Gal. 5:16). And this cannot be accomplished without struggling with the flesh.

A particularly great effort and laborious toil must be experienced to start with by those who, before deciding to change their worldly and carnal life to a righteous one and to give themselves up to the practices of love and sincere service of God, had enmeshed themselves in evil habits through frequent satisfaction of the desires of their carnal and passionate will. Although the demands of their intelligent will, which they wish to follow, stand on one side of their free will and are made active by God, yet on the other side there stand the desires of the carnal and passionate will, towards which they still feel a certain sympathy. Opposing the former, these desires pull it towards their side with the same force as a beast of burden is pulled by its halter; and only the grace of God gives them strength to remain firm in the

decision they have taken. Long-drawn resistance and not yielding
them victory saps the strength of carnal desires; yet this does not
end the struggle.

So let no one dream of acquiring a true Christian disposition
and Christian virtue, and of working for God as he should, if he
does not want to compel himself to renounce and overcome all
the passionate impulses of the will of the flesh, whether great or
small, which he was formerly accustomed to satisfy willingly and
fondly. The chief reason why so few people attain to Christian
perfection is exactly their reluctance, through self-pity, to force
themselves to deny themselves absolutely everything. But if, having overcome great passionate tendencies, they do not wish,
thereafter, to compel themselves to overcome small ones, which
seem unimportant, then, since these small tendencies are the outcome and expression of the great, by indulging in them they
inevitably feed the latter, and so make them continue to live and
act in the heart, in spite of the fact that they no longer manifest
themselves on a large scale. And so the heart remains passionate
and impure, and, above all, in no whit freed from self-indulgence
and self-pity, which always make any practice to please God of
doubtful value.

UNSEEN WARFARE

No Christian is meant to sleep in a safe pew.... I have discovered in my private life that a true Christian is not bedded
upon roses and he is not meant for peace and tranquillity of
mind but for war. And again I am realizing profoundly that
not everybody's nature is as bellicose as mine, although I have
attained—*Deo concedente*—a certain state of peace within, paid
for by a rather uncomfortable state of war without. But even if
a peaceful nature has reached a certain higher level of consciousness he cannot escape the raging conflict of opposites in
his soul, as God wants to unite his opposites in man. As soon as

a more honest and complete consciousness beyond the collective has been established, man is no more an end in himself, but becomes an instrument of God, and this is really so and no joke about it.

C. G. JUNG (1875–1961)
Swiss psychiatrist and philosopher

The worst thing that can happen to a man who is already divided up into a dozen different compartments is to seal off yet another compartment and tell him that this one is more important than all the others. . . .

The first thing you have to do, before you even start thinking about such a thing as contemplation, is to try to recover your basic natural unity, to reintegrate your compartmentalized being into a coordinated and simple whole, and learn to live as a unified human person. This means that you have to bring back together the fragments of your distracted existence, so that when you say "I," there is really someone present to support the pronoun you have uttered.

It should be accepted as a most elementary human and moral truth that no man can live a fully sane and decent life unless he is able to say "no" on occasion to his natural bodily appetites. No man who simply eats and drinks whenever he feels like eating and drinking, who smokes whenever he feels the urge to light a cigarette, who gratifies his curiosity and sensuality whenever they are stimulated, can consider himself a free person. He has renounced his spiritual freedom and become the servant of bodily impulse. Therefore his mind and his will are not fully his own. They are under the power of his appetites. And through the medium of his appetites, they are under the control of those who gratify his appetites. Just because he can buy one brand of whisky rather than another, this man deludes himself that he is making a choice; but the fact is that he is a devout servant of a tyrannical ritual. He must reverently buy the bottle, take it home, unwrap it, pour it out for his friends, watch TV, "feel good," talk his silly uninhibited head off, get angry, shout, fight and go to bed in disgust with himself and the world. This becomes a kind of religious compulsion without which he cannot convince himself that he is really alive, really "fulfilling his personality." He is not "sinning" but simply makes an ass of himself.

THOMAS MERTON (1915–1968)
American Cistercian monk

First comes *impact* (contact, action when a thing thrown hits the thing at which it is thrown): then comes *coupling* (joining together: attention is fettered to the object so that there exists only the soul and the object which has impinged on it and occupied it); next comes *merging together* (the object which has impinged upon the soul and occupied the attention has provoked desire— and the soul has consented to it—has merged with it); then comes *captivity* (the object has captured the soul which desired it and is leading it to action like a fettered slave); finally comes *passion* (sickness of the soul) inculcated in the soul by frequent repetition (repeated gratification of the same desire) and by habit.

PHILOTHEUS OF SINAI (d. 297)

Something very fleeting arises abruptly and solicits our attention. From the subconscious the appeal rises to consciousness and makes an effort to be kept there. This is not yet sin, far from it, but it is the presence of a suggestion. It is in this first moment that the immediate reaction of one's attention is decisive. The temptation is going to leave or remain. The spiritual masters make use of an image that was familiar in the desert: "Strike the serpent on the head" before he enters the cell. If the serpent enters, the struggle will be much more laborious.

If our attention does not react, the following phase is indulgence. A willing attentiveness to the tempting solicitation causes a certain pleasure, becoming an equivocal attitude that is already cooperating. St. Ephrem speaks of the "pleasant conversation" of the soul with a persistent suggestion.

An enjoyment by anticipation, imaginary at the moment, marks the third stage. A tacit agreement, an unavowed consent, orients one toward an accomplishment deemed possible, for it is passionately desirable. Theoretically, the decision has indeed been made. In coveting the object, the sin has been mentally committed. This is the judgment of the Gospel on the impure gaze in which adultery has already been pre-consummated.

The fourth stage effectively consummates the act. It forms the beginning of a passion, of a thirst henceforth unquenchable. When it has become a habit, the passion neutralizes every resistance. The person disintegrates in powerlessness. Bewitched, he leans toward his implacable end: despair, fearful *accedia*, disgust or anxiety, madness or suicide, in all cases, spiritual death.

PAUL EVDOKIMOV (1901–1970)
Russian Orthodox theologian

There can be no non-attachment without inhibition. When the state of non-attachment has become "a second nature," inhibition will doubtless no longer be necessary; for impulses requiring inhibition will not arise. Those in whom non-attachment is a permanent state are few. For everyone else, such impulses requiring inhibition arise with a distressing frequency.

The technique of inhibition needs to be learnt on all the planes of our being. On the intellectual plane—for we cannot hope to think intelligently or to practice the simplest form of "recollection" unless we learn to inhibit irrelevant thoughts. On the emotional plane—for we shall never reach even the lowest degree of non-attachment unless we can check as they arise the constant movements of malice and vanity, of lust and sloth, of avarice, anger, and fear. On the physical plane—for if we are maladjusted (as most of us are in the circumstances of modern urban life), we cannot expect to achieve integration unless we inhibit our tendency to perform actions in the, to us, familiar, maladjusted way. . . . What is needed is a practical morality working at every level from the bodily to the intellectual.

ALDOUS HUXLEY (1894–1963)
English novelist, essayist, and poet

Renunciation does not take away. It gives. It gives the inexhaustible power of simple things.

MARTIN HEIDEGGER (1889–1976)
German existentialist philosopher

There are souls that form great projects of doing excellent services for our Lord by eminent deeds and extraordinary sufferings, but deeds and sufferings of which there is no present opportunity, and perhaps never will be, and upon this imagine that they have done a great matter in love, in which they are very often deceived—in this way, that embracing in desire what seems to them great future crosses, they studiously avoid the burden of such as are present, which are less. Is it not a great temptation to be so valiant in imagination and so cowardly in execution? Ah, God keep us from these imaginary fervours which very often breed in the bottom of our hearts a vain and secret self-esteem! Great works do not always lie in our way, but every moment we may do little ones excellently, that is, with great love. I beg you to remark the saint who gives a cup of water for God's sake to a poor thirsty traveller; he seems to do a small thing; but the intention, the sweetness, the love with which he animates his action, is so excellent that it turns this simple water into the water of life, and of eternal life. Bees gather honey from the lily, the iris, and the rose; but they get as much booty from the little minute rosemary flowers and thyme; they not only draw more honey from these, but even better honey, because in these little vessels the honey being more closely locked up is much better preserved. Truly in small and insignificant exercises of devotion charity is practised not only more frequently, but also as a rule more humbly too, and consequently more holily and usefully. Those condescensions to the humours of others, that bearing with the troublesome actions and ways of our neighbour, those victories over our own tempers and passions; . . . all this is more profitable to our souls than we can conceive, if heavenly love only have the management of them.

FRANCIS DE SALES (1567–1622)
Saint, bishop of Geneva, and doctor of the church

As for those who have naturally less exactness, they ought to observe a more inviolable law with regard to small matters. They are tempted to despise them; to count them as nothing. They do not enough consider the consequence of them; they do not recall to themselves the blind progress of the passions; they even forget their own remorseful experiences. They choose rather to attribute to themselves an imaginary steadiness, and to trust in their own strength, which has so often deceived them, than to be subject to a continual fidelity.

It is a trifle, they say. Yes, it is a trifle, but a trifle that is everything to you; a trifle to which you are so attached that it keeps you back from God, and that will prove your destruction. We often value a trifle more than a matter seemingly of great importance; we should, perhaps, find more difficult to renounce a favorite amusement than to bestow a large sum in alms.

It is not a greatness of soul which induces us to despise small things: on the contrary, it is by having a limited view that we regard anything as small which carries such important consequences. The more difficulty we find in attending to small things, the more we ought to fear our negligence, and mistrust ourselves. He that looks down on small things and ignores them, shall fall—little by little.

Fear not a continual attention to small things. At first some steadiness and courage will be necessary; but it is a self-denial that will constitute your peace and security; without it you cannot have either. God will by degrees render this state sweet and easy. Love is attentive without pain or contention.

FRANÇOIS FÉNELON (1651–1715)
French Roman Catholic archbishop of Cambrai

From a senior devil to his junior charge:

My dear Wormwood,

I am very pleased by what you tell me about this man's relations with his mother. But you must press your advantage. The Enemy will be working from the center outwards, gradually bringing more and more of the patient's conduct under the new standard, and may reach his behavior to the old lady at any moment. You want to get in first. Keep in close touch with our colleague Glubose who is in charge of the mother, and build up between you in that house a good settled habit of mutual annoyance; daily pinpricks. The following methods are useful.

I. Keep his mind on the inner life. He thinks his conversion is something *inside* him and his attention is therefore chiefly turned at present to the states of his own

mind—or rather to that very expurgated version of them which is all you should allow him to see. Encourage this. Keep his mind off the most elementary duties by directing it to the most advanced and spiritual ones. Aggravate that most useful human characteristic, the horror and neglect of the obvious. You must bring him to a condition in which he can practice self-examination for an hour without discovering any of those facts about himself which are perfectly clear to anyone who has ever lived in the same house with him or worked in the same office. . . .
Your affectionate uncle,
Screwtape

C. S. LEWIS (1898–1963)
English novelist and Christian apologist

It may sometimes happen that, having bowed and made peace, a monk continues to nurse a feeling of hurt against his brother and to cling to thoughts against him. This is resentment; and much care is needed not to become hardened in it and perish. A man who has at once made peace with another, after being irritated with him, has cured his anger, but has done nothing against resentment, and so he continues to be sore with his brother. For resentment is one thing, anger another, irritation another and being disturbed yet another. So that you may understand it more clearly, I will give you an example. To kindle a fire one takes first a small piece of charcoal: this is the word of the brother who offended you. If you can bear it, you extinguish the charcoal. But if you think, "Why did he say that? If that's the case, then I too shall say this and that to him. If he did not wish to offend me, he would not have said it. So I shall certainly offend him in return." There you are, putting on some kindling wood, or something else that one puts on to start a fire, and you've produced smoke, which is disturbance. Disturbance is the movement and stirring up of thoughts, which arouse and irritate the heart. And irritation is a vengeful uprising against the man who offended you, which gives rise to presumptuousness.

ABBA DOROTHEUS (sixth century)
Saint, ascetical writer, and founder of a Palestinian monastery

This dying has many degrees, and so has this life. A man might die a thousand deaths in one day, and find at once a joyful life corresponding to each of them. This is as it must be: God cannot deny or refuse this death. The stronger the death, the more powerful and thorough is the corresponding life, and the more intimate the death, the more inward is the life. Each life brings strength, and strengthens to a harder death. When a man dies to a scornful word, bearing it in God's name, or to some inclination inward or outward, acting or not acting against his own will, be it in love or grief, in word or act, in going or staying; or if he denies his desires of taste or sight, or makes no excuse when wrongfully accused; or anything else whatever it may be to which he has not yet died, it is harder at first to one who is unaccustomed to it and unmortified than to him who is mortified. . . . A great life makes reply to him who dies in earnest even in the least things, a life which strengthens him immediately to die a greater death; a death so long and strong, that it seems to him hereafter more joyful, good and pleasant to die than to live, for he finds life in death and light shining in darkness.

JOHANNES TAULER (1300–1361)
German Dominican contemplative

All endeavors merely to rectify the exterior impel the soul yet farther outward into that about which it is so warmly and zealously engaged; and thus its powers are diffused and scattered abroad; for its application being immediately directed to externals, it thus invigorates those very senses it is aiming to subdue.

This species of mortification can never subdue the passions, or lessen their activity. The only method to effect this is inward silence; by which the soul is turned wholly and altogether inward, to possess a present God. If it direct all its vigor and energy towards this center of its being, the simple act separates and withdraws it from the senses; the exercising of all its powers internally leaves the senses faint and impotent; and the nearer it draws to God, the farther is it separated from the senses, and the less are the passions influenced by them.

JOHANNES KELPIUS (1673–1708)
German recluse, mystic, and teacher

You could say that the body has been constructed like a musical instrument.

Musicians often cannot give adequate proof of their talent because the instrument they are playing is unfit for use: it is either spoilt with age, or damaged by being dropped, or completely ruined through damp or rust. If you put it in the hands of an artist of the first rank, such an instrument does not respond to his skill.

The same thing happens with the spirit. It functions through the body to display its skill in a spiritual way. But the spirit cannot exercise its normal activity except with an instrument which conforms to the order of nature.

Our spirit is fashioned in the image of the perfect Good. As long as it remains with the good, it keeps its likeness to the Model. When it strays from the good, it loses its original beauty.

Therefore, just as the spirit takes its proper perfection from its likeness to the beauty of the universal Model, so the body, ruled by the spirit, finds its proper embellishment in the beauty of the spirit.

GREGORY OF NYSSA (330–395)
Saint, bishop of Nyssa, and
Cappadocian father of the church

May the yoke of the Law of God be upon my shoulder,
the coming of the Holy Spirit on my head,
the sign of Christ on my forehead,
the hearing of the Holy Spirit in my ears,
the smelling of the Holy Spirit in my nose,
the vision of the people of heaven in my eyes,
the speech of the people of heaven in my mouth,
the work of the Church of God in my hands,
the good of God and of neighbor in my feet.
May God dwell in my heart and may I belong entirely to
    God the Father.
Amen.

BREASTPLATE PRAYER OF FURSA (eighth century)
Celtic saint

Prayer in which the body does not toil by means of the heart, and the heart by means of the mind, together with the intellect and the intelligence all gathered together in deep-felt groaning, but where instead prayer is just allowed to float across the heart, such prayer you should realize is just a miscarriage, for while you are praying, your mind is drawing you away to some other business that you are going to see to after praying. In such a case you have not yet managed to pray in a unified manner.

SIMEON THE GRACEFUL (sixth century)
Syrian Orthodox father

For if things are to go well with a man, one of two things must always happen to him. Either he must find and learn to possess God in works, or he must abandon all works. But since a man cannot in this life be without works, which are proper to humans and are of so many kinds, therefore he must learn to possess his God in all things and to remain unimpeded, whatever he may be doing, wherever he may be. And therefore if a man who is beginning must do something with other people, he ought first to make a powerful petition to God for his help, and put him immovably in his heart and unite all his intentions, thoughts, will and power to God, so that nothing else than God can take shape in that man.

MEISTER ECKHART (1260–1327)
German Dominican mystic and theologian

Is praying difficult?

A fourteenth-century Byzantine monk, who for a short time was Patriarch of Constantinople with the name of Callixtus II, answers this question with the illustration of the lute-player. "The lute-player bends over his instrument and listens attentively to the tune, while his fingers manipulate the plectrum and make the strings vibrate in full-toned harmony. The lute has turned into music; and the man who strums upon it is taken out of himself, for the music is soft and entrancing."

Anyone who prays must set about it in the same way. He has a lute and a plectrum at his disposal. The lute is his heart, the strings of which are the inward senses. To get the strings vibrating and the lute playing he needs a plectrum, in this case: the recollection of God, the Name of Jesus, the Word. . . . "The Word is, after all, very close to you, on your lips and in your heart" (Rom. 10:8).

You need only pick up the plectrum and pluck the strings. To persevere in the Word and in your heart, watching and praying. There is no other way of learning how to pray. You must return to yourself and to your true and deepest nature, to the human-being-in-Jesus that you already are, purely and simply by grace. "Nobody can learn how to see. For seeing is something we can do by nature. So too with prayer. *Authentic prayer* can never be learnt from someone else. It has its own instructor within it. Prayer is God's gift to him who prays."

ANDRÉ LOUF (1929–)
French Cistercian abbot

What the body of those who are still in the life of the spirit has to learn is always to do the opposite of what it wants to do, the opposite of what pleases it most. Otherwise the soul will slip back from the life of the spirit.

But once the soul has become completely free, the opposite is the case: then the soul has to do exactly what it pleases, or it will slip back from the life of peace. Once the soul has pro-gressed from virtue to love and from love to nothingness, it has to do exactly what pleases it, or it will lose its peace and freedom.

The soul is totally pure only when she has passed the thresh-old of doing the contrary of her desires and does what most pleases her. This is her crossing of the Red Sea, leaving her ene-mies drowned behind her. What pleases her then is my will for her, since she enjoys pure unity of will with God, in whom I have placed her. Having moved from grace to perfection, from the virtues to love, from love to nothingness, and from nothingness to the enlightenment of God, who at this stage gives her his light so completely that she can no longer see either herself or him, then her will has become mine.

MARGUERITE PORETE (? –1310)
French mystic

God of truth,
I ask that I may receive,
so that my joy may be full.
Meanwhile, let my mind meditate on it,
let my tongue speak of it,
let my heart love it,
let my mouth preach it,
my flesh thirst for it,
and my whole being desire it,
until I enter into the joy of my Lord,
who is God one and triune, blessed forever. Amen.

ANSELM OF CANTERBURY (c. 1033–1109)
Saint and founder of medieval Scholasticism

CYCLE TEN

FUEL FOR
THE FIRE

What is a person without a form? A form "into which and through which to pour out his life"? We consider here the need for method, for a rule of prayer, for training and discipline. Our type and temperament will determine the means, but for all, "the less one prays, the worse it goes."

I asked Metropolitan Anthony again about the work with the body, about the methods, the exercises that I knew were in the Christian tradition—somewhere, in some time. Where did they come from? Where have they gone? . . . Is there a text that has not yet been rediscovered which speaks about them in a way that could guide this new search for the practical mysticism of the Christian path?

I waited for him to continue. He said something about the Athonite Christians having this work with the body, and then paused once again. And once again, I waited for him.

Finally, he raised his eyes toward me. "You have been to our service. If you stand in the service with your hands down to the side, with your head slightly down—not too much—your weight evenly balanced . . . if one does this, one begins to see changes taking place in the body. The breathing changes, certain muscles relax, others become firm—not tense. All this comes from the religious impulse. . . ."

Again a pause.

He continued, speaking softly and deliberately. *"The exercises you ask about originated in this way, from the Fathers observing what happened to them when they were in a state of prayer."*

JACOB NEEDLEMAN (contemporary)
American philosopher of religion

The various methods described by the Fathers (sitting down, making prostrations, and the other techniques used when performing this prayer [Jesus Prayer]) are not suitable for everyone: indeed without a personal director they are actually dangerous. It is better not to try them. There is just one method which is obligatory for all: *to stand with the attention in the heart.* All other things are beside the point, and do not lead to the crux of the matter.

It is said of the fruit of this prayer, that there is nothing higher in the world. This is wrong. As if it were some talisman! Nothing in the words of the prayer and their uttering can alone bring forth its fruit. All fruit can be received without this prayer, and even without any oral prayer, but merely by directing the mind and heart towards God.

The essence of the whole thing is *to be established in the remembrance of God, and to walk in His presence.* You can say to anyone: "Follow whatever methods you like—recite the Jesus Prayer, perform bows and prostrations *(In Orthodox practice it is common to bow or prostrate oneself after making the sign of the Cross. This bowing or prostration takes two main forms: a profound bow from the waist, touching the ground with fingers of the right hand; a full prostration, touching the ground with the forehead.* [footnote in original]*),* go to Church: do what you wish, only strive to be always in constant remembrance of God." . . .

The Jesus Prayer is a good means to arrive at inner prayer, but in itself it is not inner but outer prayer. Those who attain the habit of the Jesus Prayer do very well. But if they stop only at this and go no further, they stop halfway. . . .

It is good that the Name of Jesus should cleave to your tongue. But with this it is still possible not to remember God at all and even to harbor thoughts which are opposed to Him. Consequently everything depends on conscious and free turning to God, and on a balanced effort to hold oneself in this.

The object of our search is the fire of grace which enters into the heart. When the spark of God Himself—grace—appears in the heart, it is the prayer of Jesus which quickens it and fans it into flame. But it does not itself create the spark—it gives only the possibility that it may be received, by recollecting the thoughts and making ready the soul before the face of the Lord. The essential thing is to hold oneself ready before God, calling out to Him from the depths of one's heart. This is what all those who seek the fire of grace must do; as to words or positions of the body during prayer, these have only secondary importance. God is concerned with the heart.

We can sometimes spend all the time set aside for prayer by the rule in reciting one psalm, composing our own prayer from each verse. Again, we can sometimes spend all the time allotted by the rule in reciting the Jesus Prayer with prostrations. We can also do a little of each of these things. What God asks for is the heart, and it is enough that it should stand before Him with reverence. Standing always before God with reverence is unceasing prayer: such is its exact description; and in this regard the rule of prayer is only fuel for the fire, or the throwing of wood into a stove.

THEOPHAN THE RECLUSE (1815–1894)
Russian Orthodox monk and saint

The recollection of Jesus and the unremitting invocation of His Name create as it were a divine atmosphere in our spirit, provided we do not stop calling inwardly upon Jesus, and that we continue in sobriety and watchfulness. Let us remain true at all times and in all places to this task of calling upon the Lord Jesus. Let us cry out to Him with heart aflame so that we may appropriate the holy Name of Jesus. . . . Blessed the heart in which the Name of Jesus ceaselessly resounds, as inseparably as the air cleaves to our body and the flame to the candle. The sun, moving across the firmament, engenders the day; the holy Name of Jesus, constantly appearing in our spirit, brings forth glorious notions without number.

HESYCHIUS OF SINAI (dates unknown)

A medieval priest and monk of the Order of St. Basil

This calling upon the Name of Jesus is actually a calling-in of Jesus Himself. The Blessed Ruisbroek uses this term to describe an analogous technique of prayer. He also calls it the *summoning-in*, the *importuning*, of Jesus. In this guise the Jesus prayer has been disseminated not only in the Christian East. It turns up just as frequently in the West, though less systematically than was the case in the East during the thirteenth and fourteenth centuries. One has only to think here of St. Bernard, for whom the Name of Jesus, in line with the passage in the Song of Songs, is an oil outpoured. Like oil, the Name gives light and warmth, it is nourishment and medicine. . . .

Invoking the Name of Jesus, therefore, very much resembles a spiritual communion. It strengthens and feeds you. It imparts to you Jesus Himself, who obtains an ever firmer footing in your heart. In the end the Name does more than express your own ardent longing for Jesus. It is the very Love of Jesus in you, an uncreated light, a consuming fire. This is the prayer that William of St. Thierry recommended to the first Carthusians: "During the prayer you must go and stand before God, face to face, and examine yourself in the light of His countenance. Then you will call on the Name of the Lord and with that Name strike upon the stone of your heart till fire leaps from it. You will keep fluttering about the recollection of the abundance of God's sweetness till He Himself causes that sweetness to well up within your heart."

ANDRÉ LOUF (1929–)
French Cistercian abbot

Father, Son and Holy Spirit can be reached only by Their
  names;
do not look further, to Their Persons,
just meditate on Their names.
If you investigate the person of God, you will perish,
but if you believe in the name, you will live.
Let the name of the Father be a boundary to you,
do not cross it and investigate His nature;
let the name of the Son be a wall to you,
do not cross it and investigate His birth from the Father;
let the name of the Spirit be a fence for you,
do not enter inside for the purpose of prying into Him.

EPHREM THE SYRIAN (303–373)
Spiritual and theological writer

The very idea of methodology in the spiritual life offends the "modern mind" which is in revolt against reason, discipline, and indeed, against all authority. The modern mind above all wants to "feel," for in feeling it makes itself—its own egoity—the criterion of its own state of soul, and feeling requires neither thinking nor discipline. The modernist forgets that John the Baptist cried (as in the wilderness of the modern world), *"Prepare ye the way of the Lord."* He forgets that Advent must precede Christmas and that Advent is a penitential season. He may admit to the need for methodology in science, in business, or even in madness, but denies its role in religion. Love and faith are reduced to "feeling" and feeling can never be methodological. What then is this preparation that must precede the coming of Christ? It is the training of the will which requires obedience, discipline, and virtue. It is the training of the intellect which requires the abandoning of Pride, Ignorance, and Intellectual Sloth. And if there is to be no method, there is to be no direction. Everyone becomes his own spiritual director, and it is a fact that a person who is his own lawyer, both in this world and the next, "has a fool for his advocate."

RAMA P. COOMARASWAMY (contemporary)
American physician, theologian, and author

The greater the authority of a father, the greater should be his self-effacement. A disciple can indeed formulate the true and only aim of his request: "Father, tell me what the Holy Spirit suggests to you in order to heal my soul." Abbot Poemen on his side specifies the art of a starets: "Never command, but be for all an example, never a lawgiver." A young man once went to an old ascetic to be instructed in the way of perfection, but the old man did not say a word. The other asked him the reason for his silence. "Am I then a superior to command you?" he answered. "I shall say nothing. Do, if you want, *what you see me do.*" From then on the young man imitated the old ascetic in everything and learned the meaning of silence and of free obedience.

A spiritual father is never "a director of conscience"; he is before all else a charismatic. He does not engender *his* spiritual son, he engenders a son of God. Both, *in common*, place themselves in the school of truth. The disciple receives the gift of spiritual attention, the father receives that of being the organ of the Holy Spirit. St. Basil advises to find "a friend of God," who gives the certitude that God speaks through him. "Call no one father" means that all fatherhood shares in the fatherhood of God, that all obedience is obedience to the Father's will in sharing in the acts of the obedient Christ. . . .

The advice explains the essential—no obedience to human elements, no idolatry of a spiritual father, even if he is a saint. Every counsel of a starets leads a man to a state of freedom before the face of God.

Obedience crucifies man's own will in order to arouse the final freedom—the spirit listening to the Holy Spirit.

PAUL EVDOKIMOV (1901–1970)
Russian Orthodox theologian

All the greatest masters of prayer bring home to us the simple, natural, unforced character of real intercourse with God. They say again and again that prayer is nothing else but a devout intent directed towards Him; and this intent expresses itself in various ways. The beginner must be shown these ways, and often be helped to use them; but in the mature man or woman of prayer their exercise is free and spontaneous. Perhaps there is no other department of the spiritual life in which St. Augustine's great saying, "Love, and do what you like," becomes more completely true. Julian of Norwich says at the end of her Revelations that what she has found and felt most fully is "the homeliness, courtesy and naturehood of God." . . .

A badly held, distracted attempt at the prayer of simplicity, involving tension and effort, and therefore self-consciousness, has far less spiritual content than an unforced, humble and natural vocal prayer. In prayer, will and grace cooperate. Neither a limp abandonment to the supposed direction of the Spirit, nor a vigorous determination to wrestle with God on our own account, will do for it. . . . Hence it is useless to endeavor by willed struggle, or by obeying the rules in ascetic manuals, to reach a level of prayer to which we are not yet impelled by grace. We cannot by stretching ourselves add an inch to our stature: the result will be strain, not growth. . . . Real inward silence is not achieved by any deliberate spiritual trick. It develops naturally; and most often from the full exercise of mental prayer, which is in its turn the child of properly practiced vocal prayer. Therefore I think that no one ought to set to work to practice such inward silence until they feel a strong impulse so to do. If we try such artificial methods, we probably drift into a mere quietistic reverie; and such reverie, though pleasant, has nothing in common with real contemplative prayer.

. . . We are never to struggle for a degree or condition of fervor in which we do not naturally find ourselves. People are often encouraged to do this by the indiscriminate reading of ascetic and mystical literature, a practice to which real dangers are attached. They browse among descriptions and counsels intended only for advanced souls, and struggle to produce states of consciousness far beyond their power. These states will arise within us naturally and simply, only when and if we are ready for them. In all normal cases, God feeds and leads the soul very gently. Growth is gradual. The many adjustments necessary to the full establishment of the prayerful consciousness take time; and often its advance is checked by periods of dullness, fatigue and incapacity which are explicable by psychology, and must be borne with patience as instruments of our purification. . . .

Self-will in prayer is a subtle temptation, known to most religious people. But there is always some way of turning to God which is within our reach, however distracted or weary we may be: and as a general rule, it is surely better to begin there, quite simply, though the crudity and childishness of our level of feeling and expression may deal a smart blow at our self-respect.

Constituted as we are, it is inevitable that our spiritual aptitude should fluctuate, as does the rest of our plastic and unstable psychic life. This limitation ought not to depress us, but it ought to keep us in humility; and humility is the one grace which gives wings to the simplest prayer.

EVELYN UNDERHILL (1875–1941)
English writer on mysticism

A person who resolves to begin regular morning exercises usually does so not because he already has physical fitness but in order to get something he does not have. Once one has something he can be anxious to keep it; previous to that, he is anxious to get it.

Therefore, begin your practice without expecting anything of yourself. If you are fortunate enough to sleep in a room by yourself, you can quite literally and without trouble follow the instructions of the prayer book:

When you awake, before you begin the day, stand with reverence before the All-Seeing God. Make the sign of the Cross and say:

In the Name of the Father, and of the Son, and of the Holy Ghost. Amen.

Having invoked the Holy Trinity, keep silence for a little, so that your thoughts and feelings may be freed from worldly cares. Then recite the following prayers without haste, and with your whole heart.

God, be merciful to me, a sinner.

Thereafter follow the other prayers [in *A Manual of Eastern Orthodox Prayers*] with the prayer to the Holy Spirit first, then to the Holy Trinity, and next the Our Father, which precedes the whole list of morning prayers. It is better to read a few of them quietly than all of them impatiently. They rest upon the gathered experience of the Church; through them you enter a great fellowship of praying folk. You are not alone; you are a cell in the body of the Church—that is, of Christ. Through them you learn the patience that is necessary not only for the body but also for the heart and mind, for the building up of your faith.

The complete and correct prayer is one in which the words of the prayer are accepted by both thought and emotion; attentiveness is therefore needful. Do not let your thoughts wander; imprison them again and again, and always begin anew from the point where you left off praying. You may read from the Psalter, in the same way, especially if you do not have a prayer book. Thus you learn patience and watchfulness.

A person standing at an open window hears the sounds from outside; it is impossible not to do so. But he can give the voices his attention or not, as he himself wishes. The praying person is continually beset by a stream of inappropriate thoughts, feelings and mental impressions. To stop this tiresome stream is as impracticable as to stop the air from circulating in an open room. But one can notice them or not. This, say the saints, one learns only through practice.

When you pray, you yourself must be silent. You do not pray to have your own earthbound desires fulfilled, but you pray: Thy will be done. It is not fitting to wish to use God as an errand boy. You yourself must be silent; let the prayer speak.

TITO COLLIANDER (1904–1989)
Finnish Orthodox writer

My mother would be asking us to sing our morning song to God down in the back-house, as Mary's lark was singing it up in the clouds, and as Christ's mavis was singing it yonder in the tree, giving glory to the God of the creatures for the repose of the night, for the light of the day, and for the joy of life. She would tell us that every creature on the earth below and in the ocean beneath and in the air above was giving glory to the great God of the creatures and the worlds, of the virtues and the blessings, and would *we* be dumb!

CATHERINE MACLENNAN (early 20th century)
Scottish crofter

Before the heart unlocks itself for the world, God wants to open it for himself; before the ear takes in the countless voices of the day, it should hear in the early hours the voice of the Creator and Redeemer. God prepared the stillness of the first morning for himself. It should remain his.

Before our daily bread should be the daily Word. Only thus will the bread be received with thanksgiving. Before our daily work should be the morning prayer. Only thus will the work be done as the fulfillment of God's command. The morning must yield an hour of quiet time for prayer and common devotion. That is certainly not wasted time. How else could we prepare ourselves to face the tasks, cares, and temptations of the day? And although we are often not "in the mood" for it, such devotion is an obligatory service to the One who desires our praises and prayers, and who will not otherwise bless our day but through his Word and our prayers.

It is wrong to say that we are being "legalistic" when we are concerned with the ordering of our Christian life and with our faithfulness in requirements of Scripture reading and prayer. Disorder undermines and destroys the faith: any theologian who confuses evangelical freedom with lack of discipline needs to learn that. Whoever wants to carry out properly any fully developed spiritual office, without bringing both self and work to ruin by mere activism, must learn early on the spiritual discipline of the servant of Jesus Christ. . . .

Proceeding from the Word of God, we pray everything that the Word teaches us; we bring the coming day before God and cleanse our thoughts and intentions before him; we pray above all to be in full communion with Jesus Christ. We do not want to forget to pray for ourselves; "ascribe to yourself honor according to your worth." Next, the broad field of intercession lies before us. Here our view expands to see persons and things near and far, in order to commend them to the grace of God. . . . each of us knows of persons who otherwise would scarcely have anyone to pray for them. Nor should we forget to thank God for those who help and strengthen us by their intercessions. We do not want to conclude the quiet time of prayer before we have repeated the Amen with great conviction. . . .

Now God has spoken his Word in the silence of the morning. . . . We can go to our day's work with confidence.

DIETRICH BONHOEFFER (1906–1945)
German Lutheran pastor and theologian

Let us go forward with the heart completely attentive and the soul fully conscious. For if attentiveness and prayer are daily joined together, they become like Elias' fire-bearing chariot, raising us to heaven. What do I mean? A spiritual heaven, with sun, moon and stars, is formed in the blessed heart of one who has reached a state of watchfulness, or who strives to attain it.

PHILOTHEUS OF SINAI (d. 297)

The soul of all exercises in the Lord is attention. Without attention all these exercises are sterile, dead. He who wants to be saved must so dispose himself that he preserve attention to himself, not only in seclusion but amid distraction itself, into which he is drawn sometimes by circumstances, against his will. Let the fear of God outweigh all other feelings on the scales of the heart—then it will be easy to preserve attention to oneself both in the silence of a cell and amid noise surrounding one on all sides.

On awakening . . . direct your thoughts to God, offer as a sacrifice to God the first fruits of the thoughts of your mind, which has not yet accepted upon itself any vain impressions. In silence, very carefully, having done all that is necessary for the body upon awakening from sleep, read the usual rule of prayer, concerning yourself not so much with the quantity of prayer as with the quality of it, i.e., that it be done with attention, and so that because of the attention, the heart might come to life with prayerful compunction and consolation. . . .

Whoever is attentive to himself must deny himself all daydreaming, in general, no matter how seductive and glittering; all daydreaming is wandering of the mind, outside truth, in a land of visions which do not exist and cannot come into existence, which lure the mind and deceive it. The results of daydreaming are loss of attention to oneself, mental distraction and hardness of heart during prayer; hence, spiritual sickness.

In the evening, on going to sleep, which is death for the life of that day, examine your actions during the day that has passed. For him who leads an attentive life, such an examination is not difficult, because that forgetfulness which is so characteristic of a distracted person is destroyed due to attention to himself. And thus, recalling all your sins in deed, word, thought, and feeling, offer repentance over them to God with the disposition and heartfelt promise of correction. Then, having read the rule of prayer, end with divine meditation a day begun with divine meditation. Great Agathon said, "It is impossible to progress in virtue without attention to oneself." Amen.

IGNATIUS BRYANCHANINOV (1807–1867)
Russian bishop

Anyone, however, who supposes that the institutionalized practices in Christian living are already outmoded simply on the grounds that they are uncomfortable and involve strict discipline is deceiving himself and will never attain to a genuine mode of Christian living unless the grace of God rescues him by means of some catastrophe, whether interior or exterior, from his impoverished and diminished form of existence, which has only a coloring of Christianity. Certainly there is no commandment of God or the Church directing us to say our prayers precisely when we get up or go to bed, or before meals. He who really is a man of prayer without these praiseworthy Christian customs may in all Christian freedom regard himself as dispensed from them. But will he be a man of prayer? Will he be able to lay the supremely decisive moments of his life before God in prayer if in his everyday life prayer is simply the outcome of a momentary prompting or merely the "liturgical" prayer of the Church's public services, or if he has not previously fixed his own times of prayer which he voluntarily engages himself to observe?

KARL RAHNER (1904–1984)
German Jesuit theologian

From the beginning two things have been the necessary form and mystery of Christian spirituality. Two things, even before the closing events of resurrection, ascension, and commission, wove disparate and often renegade believers into an inspirited body of the whole, connected to God and each other.

Like a double helix rendered elegant by complexity and splendid by authority, the amalgam of gospel and shared meal and the discipline of fixed-hour prayer were and have remained the chain of golden connection tying Christian to Christ and Christian to Christian across history, across geography, and across idiosyncrasies of faith. The former is known as the food and sustenance of the Church, the latter as its work. . . .

Fixed-hour prayer, while it is with the Eucharist the oldest surviving form of Christian spirituality, actually had its origins in the Judaism out of which Christianity came. Centuries before the birth of Jesus of Nazareth, the Hebrew psalmist wrote that "Seven times a day do I praise you" (Ps. 119:164). . . .

The first detailed miracle of the apostolic Church, the healing of the lame man on the Temple steps by Sts. Peter and John (Acts 3:1), occurred when and where it did because two devout Jews (who did not yet know they were Christians as such) were on their way to ninth-hour (three o'clock) prayers. Not many years later, one of the great defining events of Christianity—St. Peter's vision of the descending sheet filled with both clean and unclean animals—was to occur at noon on a rooftop because he had gone there to observe the sixth-hour prayers. . . .

Such readiness to accommodate circumstance was to become a characteristic of fixed-hour prayer. So too were some of the words Peter must have used. We know, for instance, that from its very earliest days, the Christian community incorporated the Psalms in their prayers (Acts 4:23–30); and the Psalter has remained as the living core of the daily offices ever since. Likewise, by c. A.D. 60, the author of the first known manual of Christian practice, the *Didache*, was teaching the inclusion of the Lord's Prayer at least three times each day, a usage that was to expand quickly to include all the offices. . . .

Within the third century, the Desert Fathers, the earliest monastics of the Church, began to pursue the universal Christian desideratum of living out St. Paul's admonition to "pray without ceasing" (I Thess. 5:17). To accomplish this, they devised the stratagem, within their communities, of having one group of monks pass the praying of an office on seamlessly to another group of monks waiting to commence the next office. The result was the introduction into Christian thinking of the concept of a continuous cascade of prayer before the throne of God. That concept was to remain into our own time as a realized grace for many, many Christians, both monastic and lay.

Christians today, wherever they practice the discipline of fixed-hour prayer, frequently find themselves filled with a conscious awareness that they are handing their worship, at its final "Amen," on to other Christians in the next time zone. Like relay runners passing a lighted torch, those who do the work of fixed-hour prayer do create thereby a continuous cascade of praise before the throne of God. To participate in such a regimen with such an awareness is to pray, as did the Desert Fathers, from within the spiritual community of shared texts as well as within the company of innumerable other Christians, unseen but present, who have preceded one across time or who, in time, will follow one.

FROM THE PREFACE TO *THE DIVINE HOURS*
PHYLLIS TICKLE (contemporary)
American Episcopalian writer

It is supremely to be hoped that the Liturgy of the Hours may pervade and penetrate the whole of Christian prayer, giving it life, direction and expression, and effectively nourishing the spiritual life of the people of God.

We have, therefore, every confidence that an appreciation of that "unceasing" prayer which our Lord Jesus Christ entrusted to his Church will take on new life, since the Liturgy of the Hours, distributed as it is over suitable intervals of time, continually strengthens and supports that prayer. The very celebration of the Liturgy of the Hours, especially when a community is assembled for this purpose, expresses the genuine nature of the praying Church and is seen as a wonderful sign of that Church.

Christian prayer is above all the prayer of the whole human community, which Christ joins to himself. . . . This prayer takes its unity from the heart of Christ, for our Redeemer desired "that the life he had entered upon in his mortal body with supplications and with his sacrifice should continue without interruption through the ages in his mystical body, which is the Church." Because of this, the prayer of the Church is at the same time "the prayer of Christ and his body to the Father." We must recognize, therefore, as we celebrate the Office, our own voices echoing in Christ, his voice echoing in ours.

To manifest this quality of our prayer more clearly, "the warm and living love for holy Scripture" which is the atmosphere of the Liturgy of the Hours must come to life in all of us, so that Scripture may indeed become the chief source of all Christian prayer. In particular, the praying of the psalms, which continually ponders and proclaims the action of God in the history of salvation, must be embraced with new warmth by the people of God. . . .

Because the life of Christ in his mystical body also perfects and elevates for each member of the faithful his own personal life, any conflict between the prayer of the Church and personal prayer must be entirely rejected, and the relationship between them strengthened and enlarged. . . . If the prayer of the Divine Office becomes genuine personal prayer, the relation between the liturgy and the whole Christian life also becomes clearer. The whole life of the faithful, hour by hour during day and night, is a kind of *leitourgia* or public service, in which the faithful give themselves over to the ministry of love toward God and men, identifying themselves with the action of Christ, who by his life and self-offering sanctified the life of all mankind.

The Liturgy of the Hours clearly expresses and effectively strengthens this most profound truth, embodied in the Christian life. . . .

In a celebration in common or in individual recitation the essential structure of this liturgy remains the same, that is, it is a conversation between God and man. . . . In this way the apostle's exhortation is obeyed: "Let the word of Christ dwell in you in all its richness, as you teach and advise each other in all wisdom by psalms, hymns and spiritual canticles, singing thankfully in your hearts to God" (Col. 3:16).

From the GENERAL INSTRUCTION OF THE
ROMAN CATHOLIC *LITURGY OF THE HOURS*

Now the duty of having stated times of private prayer . . . seems to us to be a form, or at least a light matter, to observe or omit; whereas in truth, such creatures are we, there is the most close and remarkable connection between small observances and the permanence of our chief habits and practices. It is easy to see why it is irksome; because it presses upon us and is inconvenient. It is a duty which claims our attention continually, and its irksomeness leads our hearts to rebel; and then we proceed to search for reasons to justify our dislike of it. Nothing is more difficult than to be disciplined and regular in our religion. It is very easy to be religious by fits and starts, and to keep up our feelings by artificial stimulants; but regularity seems to trammel us and we become impatient. This is especially the case with whom the world is yet new, and who can do as they please. Religion is the chief subject which meets them, which enjoins regularity; and they bear it only so far as they can make it like things of this world, something curious, changeable, or exciting.

When you have given over the practice of stated prayer, you gradually become weaker without knowing it. . . . you lose the direction of your conscience, which being ill-used, at length refuses to direct you.

JOHN HENRY NEWMAN (1801–1890)
English Roman Catholic cardinal

When prayer seems impossible that is no reason for panic or despair, for making a great effort, for attempting devices or techniques, for awaiting some mysterious and sovereign urge. It is enough to fall back on the most simple and childlike obedience asked of us, that of hearing the word.

But then we must be careful. Our intellect, always defective in the things of the Spirit, will trick us into thinking that if there is obedience then there must be an obligation, a compulsion, a *duty* to pray. Then we fall back into the confusion between law and commandment. Obedience in Christ is the opposite to a duty or an obligation. There is no compulsion. There is the hearing of a word which I receive and which commands me, before which it is mine to obey without pressure or penalty. There is not a duty of prayer. There is an understanding of a responsibility, an entering into communion and dialogue. . . .

It cannot be doubted that to declare it a duty to pray kills the possibility of prayer, that duty is impersonal and sterilizing (and not in this domain alone!). It diverts the word and command of God into a moral perspective in which God has not placed them. We well know what happened to the family prayers in the old Protestant families, at which the children were obliged to be present. From the very outset that compulsion frustrated participation in the prayer. The latter can only be free and voluntary. . . .

Hence this commandment, since it is of God, calls us to a free obedience, to a voluntary consent, to a response that one cannot hesitate to call spontaneous, even though incited. There is no question of a duty or of threats. . . .

This obedience, in fact, transforms my condition, in the sense that everything in my life which was an obstacle to prayer—impossibilities, lukewarmness, all the causes, justifications, conditions, dispositions and situations, inward as well as outward, which keep me from praying—is called into question.

Listening to the commandment, and the decision to obey it, by no means imply passivity, but direct combat against the whole context in which my inability to pray was located. Obedience is in no sense a submissive, passive, insipid, feeble attitude. Obedience is an active struggle with all that impedes the reality of life in Christ: hence, in this connection, with every obstacle to prayer.

JACQUES ELLUL (1912–1994)
French philosopher and theologian

The only way to pray is to pray; and the way to pray well is to pray much. If one has no time for this, then one must at least pray regularly. But the less one prays, the worse it goes.

JOHN CHAPMAN (1865–1933)
English Benedictine spiritual adviser and biblical scholar

What is a person without the form that shapes him, the form that surrounds him inexorably like a coat of armor and which nonetheless is the very thing that bestows suppleness on him and which makes him free of all uncertainty and all paralyzing fears, free for himself and his highest possibilities? What is a person without this? What is a person without a life-form, that is to say, without a form which he has chosen for his life, a form into which and through which to pour out his life, so that his life becomes the soul of the form and the form becomes the expression of his soul?

HANS URS VON BALTHASAR (1905–1988)
Swiss Roman Catholic theologian

True prayer changes into a constant attitude, into a state of mind that structures and molds our whole being liturgically. Here is seen the great truth that to *have* is still a symbol, the reality is to *be*. According to spiritual teachers, it is not enough to *have* prayers, rules, habits; one must *be* prayer incarnate. It is in his very structure that man sees himself as a liturgical being, as the man of the *Sanctus,* the one who by his whole life and his whole being prostrates and adores, one who can say: "I sing praise to my God while I live." To make of one's life a liturgy, a prayer, a doxology, is to make of it a sacrament of perpetual communion. "God descends to the soul in prayer and the spirit rises to God."

PAUL EVDOKIMOV (1901–1970)
Russian Orthodox theologian

The word of God should lead us first of all to contemplation and meditation. Instead of taking the words apart, we should bring them together in our innermost being; instead of wondering if we agree or disagree, we should wonder which words are directly spoken to us and connect directly with our most personal story. Instead of thinking about the words as potential subjects for an interesting dialogue or paper, we should be willing to let them penetrate into the most hidden corners of our heart, even to those places where no other word has yet found entrance. Then and only then can the word bear fruit as seed sown in rich soil. Only then can we really "hear and understand" (Matt. 13:23). . . .

Secondly, we simply need quiet time in the presence of God. . . . This asks for much discipline and risk-taking because we always seem to have something more urgent to do and "just sitting there" and "doing nothing" often disturbs us more than it helps. But there is no way around this. Being useless and silent in the presence of our God belongs to the core of all prayer. In the beginning we often hear our own unruly inner noises more loudly than God's voice. This is at times very hard to tolerate.

But slowly, very slowly, we discover that the silent time makes us quiet and deepens our awareness of ourselves and God. Then, very soon, we start missing these moments when we are deprived of them, and before we are fully aware of it an inner momentum has developed that draws us more and more into silence and closer to that still point where God speaks to us.

Contemplative reading of the holy scriptures and silent time in the presence of God belong closely together. The word of God draws us into silence; silence makes us attentive to God's word.

HENRI NOUWEN (1932–1996)
Dutch Roman Catholic priest, professor, and counselor

I have come to see that I do not limit my mind enough simply to prayer, that I always want to do something myself in it, wherein I do very wrong. . . . I wish most definitely to cut off and separate my mind from all that, and to hold it with all my strength, as much as I can, to the sole regard and simple unity. By allowing the fear of being ineffectual to enter into the state of prayer, and by wishing to accomplish something myself, I spoilt it all.

JANE DE CHANTAL (1572–1641)
French saint and founder of the Order of the Visitation

If you are praised, be silent. If you are scolded, be silent. If you incur losses, be silent. If you receive profit, be silent. If you are satiated, be silent. If you are hungry, also be silent. And do not be afraid that there will be no fruit when all dies down; there will be! Not everything will die down. Energy will appear; and what energy!

FEOFIL, THE FOOL FOR CHRIST (1788–1853)
Russian priest, saint, ascetic, and visionary

The immediate person thinks and imagines that when he prays, the important thing, the thing he must concentrate upon, is that *God should hear* what HE *is praying for*. And yet in the true, eternal sense it is just the reverse: the true relation in prayer is not when God hears what is prayed for, but when *the person praying* continues to pray until he is *the one who hears*, who hears what God wills. The immediate person, therefore, uses many words and, therefore, makes demands in his prayer; the true man of prayer only *attends*.

SØREN KIERKEGAARD (1813–1855)
Danish theologian

We ought to pray until the Holy Spirit descends upon us . . . when he has come to visit us, we cease praying.

SERAPHIM OF SAROV (1759–1833)
Russian Orthodox priest and saint

CYCLE ELEVEN

PURE FIRE WITH NEITHER FLAME NOR SMOKE

"True silence is found only in a pure heart," a contemporary Carthusian tells us, and the great Spanish mystics, John of the Cross and Teresa of Ávila, repeat again and again that the concentration necessary for spiritual prayer is "the fruit of moral purification of the will." There is a wealth of teachings about the difference between self-willed passivity and true contemplation, a difference that brings us to the heart of Christian prayer: "a work of the whole being."

And so, for the first time in my life perhaps (although I am supposed to meditate every day!), I took the lamp and, leaving the zone of everyday occupations and relationships where everything seems clear, I went down into my inmost self, to the deep abyss whence I feel dimly that my power of action emanates. But as I moved further and further away from the conventional certainties by which social life is superficially illuminated, I became aware that I was losing contact with myself. At each step of the descent a new person was disclosed within me of whose name I was no longer sure, and who no longer obeyed me. And when I had to stop my exploration because the path faded from beneath my steps, I found a bottomless abyss at my feet, and out of it came—arising I know not from where—the current which I dare to call my life. . . .

At that moment, as anyone else will find who cares to make this same interior experiment, I felt the distress intrinsic to an atom lost in the universe, the distress which makes human wills founder daily under the crushing number of living things and of stars. And if something saved me, it was hearing the voice of the Gospel, guaranteed by divine successes, speaking to me from the depth of the night: *ego sum, noli timore* (It is I, be not afraid). . . . In the life which wells up in me and in the matter which sustains me, I find much more than your gifts. It is you yourself whom I find, who makes me participate in being, you who molds me. . . .

O God, whose call precedes the very first of our movements, grant me the desire to desire being—that, by means of that divine thirst which is your gift, the access to the great waters may open wide within me.

PIERRE TEILHARD DE CHARDIN (1881–1955)
French paleontologist and Jesuit priest

The more reason sinks into humility before God, and the more unworthy reason holds itself to be before God, so much more does reason die to its own desire; and so much more is reason pierced through by God's Spirit, who brings it to the highest knowledge, so that it may see the great wonders of God. God's Spirit acts only in resigned humility, which neither seeks nor desires itself, which in itself desires to be simple before God. Thus it is that God's Spirit grasps and leads into His wonders. . . .

God has not created us for self-dominion but as instruments of His wonder by which He Himself wishes to reveal His wonders.

JACOB BOEHME (1575–1624)
German Lutheran theosophist

To be silent before God means to humbled before God, to feel the pain of contrition; but, beyond all measure, there is the joy of love and grace. . . .

With that we are led to ask: What do we need to do in order to reach this state of silent waiting for God? In answer, I can only say a little out of my quite modest experience. None of us is so rushed that it would be impossible to allow for even ten minutes in the day, in the morning or the evening, in which arrangements could be made for silence, in order to place oneself in the presence of Eternity, allow it to speak, question it, and thereby look deep within and far beyond oneself. . . . Whoever earnestly works at this day by day will be overwhelmed by the golden harvest of the fruit of those times. . . .

If it is possible for there to be rest and silence anywhere, then it is only possible where there is wholeness, and that is only in God. All human strivings and drives are finally directed toward God and can only find their complete satisfaction in him. Augustine, the great father of the church, expressed this most beautifully when he said: "Lord God, you have made all things for yourself, and our hearts are restless until they find their rest in you." May God grant us all to know this rest, may he draw us into his solitude and silence.

DIETRICH BONHOEFFER (1906–1945)
German Lutheran pastor and theologian

To promote that inwardness not only exterior silence but also interior silence is needed. The latter is much more important, and unfortunately also less familiar than the former. For our interior world is not of itself attuned to God, except for the deep core where we may accept our existence from the hands of God. That core, however, is surrounded by a screen of desires and thoughts that do not directly set our feet on the path to God.

Like our body, so our inwardness still bears the marks of sin. Therefore, an interior vigilance is needed, so that we do not yield to whatever thought or desire announces itself. A certain poverty or sobriety of thought and desires will free or scoop out within us a deep inner emptiness into which the life of the Spirit within us will bubble up, like an unstoppable spring of water, from the bottom of our heart. Perhaps the idea of the spring is a good image for the silence, one which always has to do with the Spirit. . . .

To persevere in the impasse also means not scrambling back to the little byways and paths where we used to attempt prayer with some degree of success. More specifically it means not falling back on our intellect, our imagination, our feelings. . . . The ancient biblical and patristic idiom here employs the verb *hypomenein* and the noun *hypomone* (literally "to stay under something"). One could almost translate this as, to dive under in the impasse and remain there, waiting until something else comes to surprise us. . . .

In order to pray more and better we must often do less, let go of more things, give up numerous good intentions, and be content to yield to the inner pressure of the Spirit the moment he bubbles up in us and tries to win us over and take us in tow. Ultimately all our attempts at prayer and all our methods must come to a dead end and wither away in order that the Spirit of Jesus may facilitate and validate his own prayer in our heart.

ANDRÉ LOUF (1929–)
French Cistercian abbot

There was Presented to me a Person, angling upon the Brink of a River, to catch fish; but his Labor was fruitless and he gave up hope. Then came another Person and said, "Be not discouraged, but follow me: Behold, and see, I have got an Angle that has such a Bait that all the Fish in the River will fall upon it." And accordingly I beheld multitudes in a cluster brought up by it. Then cried out that first Person, "Surely the Lord, who is the great Fish-taker, in truth is come here, and has wrought this Miracle indeed." Whereupon the Person went into the Deep, and having vanished down into it, drew up the Fish and cried, "If you will here follow me, you shall the Principal Fish take; but under Water you must learn to Dive, and again know how to Rise." Consider, and find out this Parable: for here is Meat for the Strong.

JANE LEAD (1624–1704)
English mystic

I can only say that the soul conceives itself to be near God, and that it is left with such a conviction that it cannot possibly help believing. All the faculties (thought, imagination, memory) are in abeyance, and so suspended, as I have said, that their operations cannot be followed. If the soul has previously been meditating on any subject, it vanishes from the memory at once, as completely as if it had never been thought of. If it has been reading, it is unable to remember it or dwell on the words; and it is the same with vocal prayer. So the restless little moth of memory has its wings burned, and it can flutter no more. The will must be fully occupied in loving, but does not understand how it loves. If it understands, it does not understand how it understands, or at least, cannot comprehend anything of what it understands. . . .

Let it be observed too that however long the soul may enjoy this suspension of the faculties, the actual time is, in my opinion, very short. Half an hour would be a very long period of rapture, longer, I think, than any I ever experienced. Actually, it is very difficult to judge the time, since the senses are in abeyance. But I do not think that it can ever be long before one of them recovers. It is the will that maintains the contact. But the other two faculties soon begin to trouble it once more. But, as the will is calm, they become suspended again, and they are quiet for a little longer. But eventually they spring into life again. In this way some hours may be—and are—spent in prayer. For once the two faculties have begun to grow drunk on the taste of this wine, they are very ready to give themselves up again in order to enjoy some more. Then they keep company with the will, and the three rejoice together.

TERESA OF ÁVILA (1515–1582)
Spanish Carmelite saint and mystic

"He is all and does all if you could but see Him," said one of the mystics. . . . Deep down in men's souls is a persistent sense that this is true: and when this sense rises up into consciousness, we are moved by love and worship for the Home and Father of our souls. So the first essential of true worship is that which is given us so wonderfully in the vision of Isaiah—the Glory of the Lord must fill the temple.

This is equally true whether God be sought alone on the mountain, or in the corporate silence of a Quaker meeting, or under the veils of sacramental devotion. Every time, the only thing that matters is the unchanging Glory of God. Man has to tune in to that universal voice of adoration which says all the time—whether we notice it or not—Holy, holy, holy, Lord God of hosts! Heaven and earth are full of Thy Glory; Glory be to Thee, oh Lord most High! The Sanctus is the classic norm of all human worship.

EVELYN UNDERHILL (1875–1941)
English writer on mysticism

For God is silence, and in silence is he sung and glorified by means of that psalmody and praise of which he is worthy. I am not speaking of the silence of the tongue, for if someone merely keeps his tongue silent, without knowing how to sing and give praise in mind and spirit, then he is simply idle in his silence. . . . He is just keeping an exterior silence and he does not know how to sing or give praise in an interior way, seeing that the tongue of his "hidden person" has not yet learned to stretch itself out even to babble. . . . just as the tongue placed in an infant's mouth is still because it does not yet know speech . . . so it is with that interior tongue of the mind; it will . . . simply be placed there, ready to learn the first babbling of spiritual utterance.

Thus there is a silence of the tongue, there is a silence of the whole body, there is the silence of the soul, there is the silence of the mind, and there is the silence of the spirit. . . .

The silence of the spirit is . . . when all its movements are stirred solely by Being; in this state it is truly silent, aware that the silence which is upon it is itself silent.

ABRAHAM OF NATHPAR (c. sixth century)
Syriac father of the church

It is normal that intellectual activity be gradually stilled during prayer. . . . Sometimes this experience is especially strong and inevitably one finds oneself exposed to what I might call the temptation of silence itself. . . .

The first temptation is to make of silence an activity, even if we are entirely convinced we are doing the opposite. Basing ourselves on the fact that intellectual activity has ceased and that our heart is at rest, we imagine that we have achieved a genuine silence of all our being. In fact, even if it has a real value, this silence is the result of a tension on the part of the will which is the most subtle, but equally the most pernicious, of activities. Instead of keeping our heart attentive and alert, we maintain ourselves in an artificial state in which we are not receptive to the

Lord but are relying on our own resources. In the case of people with strong and active wills, this can prove a major obstacle to attaining a state of readiness and openness to receive the Lord. Materially speaking, this silence is impressive, but it is a silence turned in on itself and dependent upon itself.

Another temptation is to make silence an end in itself. . . . My inner state is what matters and not the relationship of loving receptivity which I have with God. I am no longer even praying; I am merely contemplating myself!

A similar temptation consists in making silence a reality in itself. Silence is everything! Once all the "noise" of the senses, the mind and the imagination has been stilled, a genuine feeling of joy arises, and that is enough for us. . . . There is no more prayer. There is nothing left but the casting of an idol called Silence. . . .

God alone suffices; everything else is nothing. Genuine silence is the manifestation of this basic reality of all prayer. Silence truly exists in the heart once all the impurities which were opposed to the reign of the Father have disappeared.

True silence is only found in a pure heart, a heart that resembles the heart of God.

This is why a really pure heart is able to maintain complete silence, even when it is immersed in all sorts of activity, because there is no longer any discord between it and God. Even if its intelligence and feeling remain active, in conformity with the will of God, true silence continues to reign in such a heart. "Blessed are the pure in heart, for they shall see God."

A CARTHUSIAN (contemporary)

The true contemplative is not the one who prepares his mind for a particular message that he wants or expects to hear, but who remains empty because he knows that he can never expect or anticipate the word that will transform his darkness into light.

He does not even anticipate a special kind of transformation. He does not demand light instead of darkness. He waits on the Word of God in silence, and when he is "answered," it is not so much by a word that bursts into his silence. It is by his silence itself suddenly, inexplicably revealing itself to him as a word of great power, full of the voice of God.

But we must not take a purely quietistic view of contemplative prayer. It is not mere negation. Nor can a person become a contemplative merely by "blacking out" sensible realities and remaining alone with himself in darkness. First of all, one who does this of set purpose, as a conclusion to practical reasoning on the subject and without an interior vocation, simply enters into an artificial darkness of his own making. He is not alone with God, but alone with himself. He is not in the presence of the Transcendent One, but of an idol: his own complacent identity. He becomes immersed and lost in himself, in a state of inert, primitive, and infantile narcissism. His life is "nothing," not in the dynamic, mysterious sense in which the "nothing," *nada*, of the mystic is paradoxically also the all, *todo*, of God. It is purely the nothingness of a finite being left to himself and absorbed in his own triviality.

THOMAS MERTON (1915–1968)
American Cistercian monk

All creatures are naturally inclined toward rest and therefore both the good and the bad seek rest in many different ways. Now notice that whenever a person is bare and imageless in his senses and devoid of activity in his higher powers, he enters a purely natural state of rest. . . .

Consider now the way in which a person practices this natural rest. It consists in sitting quietly in a state of idleness, without any interior or exterior exercises, in order to find rest and have it remain undisturbed. But it is not lawful to practice this kind of rest, for it produces blind ignorance in a person and makes him sink down into himself in inactivity. Such rest is nothing other than a state of empty idleness into which a person falls and in which he becomes forgetful of himself, of God, and of all things as regards any activity. This kind of rest is contrary to that supernatural rest in which a person possesses God, for the latter is a loving immersion of oneself characterized by a simple act of gazing in incomprehensible resplendence. This rest in God—which is always sought actively with fervent desire, found in blissful inclination, eternally possessed in a loving immersion of oneself, and still sought even when already possessed—this rest is raised as high above merely natural rest as God is raised above all creatures.

For this reason all those persons are deceived who have the intention of immersing themselves in a state of natural rest, neither seeking God through desire nor finding him in blissful love. The rest which they possess consists in an emptying of their inmost being, something to which they are inclined by both nature and custom. One cannot find God in this state of natural rest, but it does bring a person into that state of emptiness which can be attained by all persons . . . no matter how evil, provided only that they can live in their sins without suffering the reproaches of conscience and can empty themselves of images and all activity.

The rest which one attains in this state of emptiness is both satisfying and deep. . . . But if a person seeks to practice and possess it without performing works of virtue, then he falls into spiritual pride and a state of self-complacency from which hardly anyone ever recovers. . . .

Those guilty of this deviation are, in their own estimation, contemplatives. They think they are the holiest persons alive, but in fact they live in a way that is contrary to and unlike God, all the saints, and all who are good. . . . Because of the natural rest which they feel and possess within themselves in a state of emptiness, they conclude that they are free and are united with God without intermediary. They also believe that they are above all the practices of the holy Church, above God's commandments, above the law, and above all virtuous works which might be practiced in any manner, for they consider this state of emptiness to be so great a thing that it must not be disturbed by any works, however good they might be, since the emptiness is nobler than all virtue. They therefore live in a state of pure passivity without performing any activity directed either to God or neighbor, just as if they were a tool which is itself idle and awaits the time when its master wishes to work, for if they did anything themselves, then God would be hindered in his own work. For this reason they are empty of every virtue, so empty that they have no wish either to praise or thank God. They do not know, love, will, pray, or desire, for in their opinion they already possess everything that they could pray for or desire.

Charity is a bond of love which raises us up above ourselves; through it we renounce ourselves and become united with God and God with us, whereas natural love turns back upon itself and upon its own pleasure and so remains ever alone. It is true that in exterior activity natural love resembles charity as closely as two hairs on the same head, but the intentions in the two cases are different: With his heart uplifted, a good person constantly seeks, intends, and desires the glory of God, whereas in the case of natural love a person is always intent on himself and his own profit.

JOHN RUUSBROEC (1293–1381)
Flemish mystic and theologian

A hound that runs after the hare only because he sees other hounds run, when he becomes weary, stays and rests, or turns home again; but if he runs because he sees or is in view of the hare, he will not spare himself till he has caught her. So it is in the spiritual course. Whoever has grace, be it ever so little, and knowingly leaves it, and begins another exercise or takes up a practice of another kind for which he has not as yet received a gift or grace, but only because he sees, reads, or hears that others do so, may perhaps run awhile till he be weary, but then he will turn home again, and if he is not careful, may hurt his feet with such fancies before he gets home. But he that continues working upon such grace as he has, and humbly begs by prayer persever-antly for more, and after feeling his heart stirred to follow after the grace which he desired, he may securely run, if he keep him-self humble.

Therefore, desire of God as much as you will or can, with-out measure or moderation at all concerning any thing that belongs to His love or Heaven's bliss, for he that can desire most of God shall feel and receive most; but work as you may and cry God mercy for that which you cannot do. Thus St. Paul seems to mean, when he said: Every one hath a proper gift of God, one so, and another so. Therefore it is needful that we know the gifts that are given us by God, that we may work in them, for by those we shall be saved—some by bodily works, and by deeds of mercy, some by great bodily penance, some by sorrow and weep-ing for their sins all their lifetime, some by preaching and teach-ing, some by divers graces and gifts of devotion shall be saved and come to bliss.

WALTER HILTON (1343–1396)
English contemplative writer

He who would pass from this state and seek to advance further in order to satisfy spiritual ambitions that are denied him will, in my opinion, lose both the one and the next. Since these spiritual blessings are supernatural, man is not capable of achieving them himself. He will thus be left desolate and in great aridity. It seems to be a kind of spiritual pride when we seek to ascend higher. Remember God descends so low He allows us, being what we are, to draw near unto Him. . . .

Let us not rise if God does not raise us. This is the language of true spirituality. He will understand me who has had any experience. And if I do not know how to explain it or if what I have said does not make sense, this one with experience understands. . . .

In mystical theology, the understanding ceases from its acts because God suspends it. But we must not imagine that we can bring about this suspension. That must not be done. Nor must we allow the understanding to cease from its acts. In that case, we shall be stupid and cold and the result will be neither the one nor the other. But when our Lord suspends the understanding and makes it to cease from its acts, He puts before it that which astonishes and occupies it. Without making any reflections, then, the mind can comprehend in a moment more than we would comprehend in all our years with all the efforts of the world.

TERESA OF ÁVILA (1515–1582)
Spanish Carmelite saint and mystic

"If any man will follow My road, let him deny himself and take up his cross and follow Me. For he that will save his soul shall lose it; but he that loses it for My sake, shall gain it." Oh, that one could show us how to understand, practice and experience what this counsel is which our Savior here gives us concerning self-denial, so that spiritual persons might see in how different a way they should conduct themselves upon this road from that which many of them think proper! For they believe that any kind of retirement and reformation of life suffices; and others are content with practicing the virtues and continuing in prayer and pursuing mortification; but they attain not to detachment and poverty or selflessness or spiritual purity (which are all one), which the Lord here commends to us; for they prefer feeding and clothing their natural selves with spiritual feelings and consolations, to stripping themselves of all things, and denying themselves all things, for God's sake. For they think that it suffices to deny themselves worldly things without annihilating and purifying themselves of spiritual attachment.

Wherefore it comes to pass that, when there presents itself to them any of this solid and perfect spirituality, consisting in the annihilation of all sweetness in God, in aridity, distaste, and trial, which is the true spiritual cross, and the detachment of the spiritual poverty of Christ, they flee from it as from death, and seek only sweetness and delectable communion with God. This is not self-denial and detachment of spirit, but spiritual gluttony. . . . For to seek oneself in God is to seek the favors and refreshments of God; but to seek God in oneself is not only to desire to be without both of these for God's sake, but to be disposed to choose, for Christ's sake, all that is most distasteful, whether in relation to God or to the world; and this is love of God.

JOHN OF THE CROSS (1542–1591)
Spanish saint and mystic

Later I discovered and am still discovering up to this very minute that it is only by living completely in this world that one learns to believe. One must abandon every attempt to make something of oneself, whether it be a saint, a converted sinner, a churchman (the priestly type, so-called!), a righteous man or an unrighteous one, a sick man or a healthy one. This is what I mean by worldliness—taking life in one's stride, with all its duties and problems, its successes and failures, its experiences and helplessness.

It is in such a life that we throw ourselves utterly in the arms of God and participate in his sufferings in the world and watch with Christ in Gethsemane. That is faith, that is *metanoia,* and that is what makes a man and a Christian.

DIETRICH BONHOEFFER (1906–1945)
German Lutheran pastor and theologian

The devout Christian of the future will either be a "mystic," one who has "experienced" something, or he will cease to be anything at all. For devout Christian living as practiced in the future will no longer be sustained and helped by the unanimous, manifest, and public convictions and religious customs of all, summoning each one from the outset to a personal experience and a personal decision. . . .

The mystical approach of which we are speaking must impart the correct "image of God," based upon the accepted experience of man's basic orientation to God, the experience that the basis of man's existence is the abyss: that God is essentially the inconceivable; that his inconceivability grows, and yet does not derogate from the fact that the more rightly God is understood the more nearly does his self-bestowing love touch us; the experience that in mapping the course of one's life one can never confine God to specific points in it without being brought up against the fact that when one does so the sum fails to come out right; the experience that he only becomes our "happiness" when we pray to him and love him unconditionally; but also the fact that he . . . is not simply the one who is remote as opposed to one who is near. . . .

The mystical approach of which we have been speaking must teach us in the concrete to maintain a constant closeness to *this* God; to say "thou" to him, to commit ourselves to his silence and darkness, not to be anxious lest we may lose him by the very fact of calling him by a name, as though he cannot, if he wills (as in fact he has willed), also enter into our eternal duality precisely because he does not constitute one element among others in our scheme of things.

KARL RAHNER (1904–1984)
German Jesuit theologian

My yoke is easy, and my burden is light (Matt. 11:30). . . .

Both St. John of the Cross and St. Teresa of Ávila do not tire of repeating that the concentration necessary for spiritual prayer is the fruit of moral purification of the will. It is therefore useless to strive to concentrate oneself if the will is infatuated with something else. . . . It is the silenced will which effects the silence of thought and imagination in concentration. This is why the great ascetics are also the great masters of concentration. All this is obvious and stands to reason. However, what occupies us here is not just concentration in general but particularly and especially *concentration without effort.* What is this?

Look at a tightrope walker. He is evidently completely concentrated, because if he were not, he would fall to the ground. His life is at stake, and it is only perfect concentration which can save him. Yet do you believe that his thought and his imagination are occupied with what he is doing? Do you think that he reflects and that he imagines, that he calculates and that he makes plans with regard to each step that he makes on the rope?

If he were to do that, he would fall immediately. He has to eliminate all activity of the intellect and of the imagination in order to avoid a fall. . . . It is the intelligence of his rhythmic system—the respiratory and circulatory system—which replaces that of his brain during his acrobatic exercises. In the last analysis, it is a matter of a miracle—from the point of view of the intellect and the imagination—analogous to that of St. Dionysius, apostle of the Gauls and first bishop of Paris, whom tradition identifies with St. Dionysius the Areopagite, disciple of St. Paul. In particular, he was

> beheaded with the sword before the statue of Mercury, confessing his faith in the Holy Trinity. And at once the body of Dionysius stood erect, and took his head in its hands; and with an Angel guiding it and a great light going before, it walked for two miles, from the place called Montmartre to the place where, by its own choice and by the providence of God, it now reposes.

Now, the tightrope walker, he too has the head—that is to say, the intellect and imagination—severed for the time of the exercise of his skill, and he also walks from one point to another, carrying his head in his hands, under the guidance of another intelligence than that of his head, which acts through the body's rhythmic system. For the tightrope walker, the juggler, and the magician, their skill and ability are, fundamentally, analogous to the miracle of St. Dionysius; because with them as with St. Dionysius, it is a matter of transposing the center of directing consciousness from the head to the chest—from the cerebral system to the rhythmic system. . . .

Concentration *without effort*—that is to say where there is nothing to suppress and where contemplation becomes as natural as breathing and the beating of the heart—is the state of consciousness (i.e., thought, imagination, feeling, and will) of perfect calm, accompanied by the complete relaxation of the nerves and the muscles of the body. It is the profound silence of desires, of preoccupations, of the imagination, of the memory, and of discursive thought. One may say that the entire being becomes like the surface of calm water, reflecting the immense presence of the starry sky and its indescribable harmony. And the waters are deep, they are so deep! And the silence grows, ever increasing . . . what silence! Its growth takes place through regular waves which pass, one after the other, through your being: one wave of silence followed by another wave of more profound silence, then again a wave of still more profound silence. Have you ever *drunk silence?* If in the affirmative, you know what concentration without effort is.

To begin with there are moments, subsequently minutes, then "quarters of an hour" for which complete silence or "concentration without effort" lasts. With time, the silence or concentration without effort becomes a fundamental element always present in the life of the soul. It is like the perpetual service at the church of Sacre-Coeur de Montmartre which takes place, whilst in Paris one works, one trades, one amuses oneself, one sleeps, one dies. . . . It is in like manner that a "perpetual service" of silence is established in the soul, which continues all the same when one is active, when one works, or when one converses. This "zone of silence" being once established, you can draw from it both for rest and for work. Then you will have not only concentration without effort, but also activity without effort.

ANONYMOUS (20th century)
Christian hermeticist

According to St. Maximus, contemplation without action, theory which is not applied in practice, differs in no way from imagination, from fantasy without any real substance; similarly, action, if it is not inspired by contemplation, is as sterile and rigid as a statue. "The very life of the spirit being the work of the heart," says St. Isaac the Syrian, "it is purity of heart which gives integrity to the contemplation of the spirit." Thus the active life consists in the purifying of the heart, and this activity is conscious, being directed by the spirit, the contemplative faculty which enters into and unites itself with the heart, coordinating and uniting the human being in grace.

By means of action, according to Evagrius Ponticus, man may attain finally to a state of impassability to the freedom of his nature no longer subject to passions, nor affected by anything. But this impassability is not a passive condition. On the level of the spiritual life, where it is operative, the opposition between active and passive no longer has any meaning: these two contrary dispositions belong to the domain of fallen nature, which is subject to sin. The spirit, which thus regains its integrity, is no longer affected by anything whatever, it no longer "suffers"; but, on the other hand, it is not "active" in the usual sense of the word. . . . The human spirit, in its normal condition, is neither active nor passive: it is vigilant. This is the "sobriety," "the attention of the heart," the faculty of discernment and of the judgment in spiritual matters, which are characteristic of human nature in its state of wholeness.

VLADIMIR LOSSKY (1903–1958)
Russian Orthodox theologian

A heart that would contemplate must be bright as a mirror, shimmer like some still stretch of water crystal clear, so that in it and through it the mind may see itself, as in and through a mirror, an image in the image of God. The heart that covets the sight of God as in a mirror must keep itself free from cares, from harmful, unnecessary and even necessary ones. It must keep itself ever alert through reading, meditation and prayer. Blessed are the pure of heart; they shall see God. May he grant that we do so. Amen.

ISAAC OF STELLA (d. 1169)
*English Cistercian father and
leading thinker in Christian humanism*

In meditation there is a wrestling of ignorance with knowledge; and the light of truth gleams as in a fog of error. So fire is kindled with difficulty on a heap of green wood; but then, fanned with stronger breath, the flame burns higher, and we see volumes of smoke rolling up, with flame flashing through. Little by little the damp is exhausted, and the leaping fire dispels the smoke. Then *victrix flamma*, darting through the heap of crackling wood, springs from branch to branch, and with lambent grasp catches upon every twig; nor does it rest until it penetrates everywhere and draws into itself all that it finds that is not flame. At length the whole combustible material is purged of its own nature and passes into the similitude and property of fire; then the din is hushed, and the voracious fire, having subdued all and brought all into its own likeness, composes itself to a high peace and silence, finding nothing more that is alien or opposed to itself. First there was fire with flame and smoke; then fire with flame, without smoke; and at last pure fire with neither flame nor smoke.

HUGH OF BALMA (13th century)
Carthusian abbot

The painful sense and feeling of what you are, kindled into a working state of sensibility by the Light of God within you, is the Fire and Light from whence your Spirit of Prayer proceeds. In its first kindling nothing is found or felt but pain, wrath, and darkness, as it is to be seen in the first kindling of every heat or fire. And therefore its first prayer is nothing else but a sense of penitence, self-condemnation, confession, and humility. This prayer of humility is met by the Divine Love, the mercifulness of God embraces it; and then its prayer is changed into hymns and songs and thanksgivings. When this state of fervor has done its work, has melted away all earthly passions and affections, and left no inclination in the soul but to delight in God alone, then its prayer changes again. It has now come so near to God, has found such a union with Him, that it does not so much pray as live in God. Its prayer is not any particular action, is not the work of any particular faculty, not confined to times, or words, or place, but is the work of its whole being, which continually stands in fullness of faith, in purity of love, in absolute resignation, to do, and be, what and how its beloved pleases. This is the last state of the Spirit of Prayer, and is its highest union with God in this life.

WILLIAM LAW (1686–1761)
English contemplative and cleric

Lord, you are my Lord and my God,
    and I have never seen you.
You have created and re-created me,
    all the good I have comes from you,
    and still I do not know you.
I was created to see you,
    and I have not yet accomplished that for which I was
    made. . . .
Let me discern your light,
    whether from afar or from the depths.
Teach me to seek you,
    and as I seek you, show yourself to me,
    for I cannot seek you unless you show me how,
    and I will never find you
    unless you show yourself to me.
Let me seek you by desiring you,
    and desire you by seeking you;
    let me find you by loving you,
    and love you in finding you.

ANSELM OF CANTERBURY (c. 1033–1109)
Saint and founder of medieval Scholasticism

ALL THE WAY TO HEAVEN IS HEAVEN

Father Alexander Men, a Russian priest killed in 1990, often said that Christianity is "in its infancy," like an arrow well launched, but only beginning its course. It has a great, and incomparable, aspiration to break down the barriers of egoism, to end "our trance of selfishness," to teach us all that "our lives are meant to be poured out," to be spent for others—to make one Body of many members.

> *There came a woman having an alabaster box of ointment of spikenard very precious; and she brake the box, and poured it on His head* (Mark 14:3).

Sometimes an act, which may not seem very important to someone who does not know the meaning of it, may mean a tremendous amount to the person who does it. To this poor woman the breaking of the alabaster cruse and the pouring of the rich ointment on our Saviour's head symbolized the giving of the whole treasure of her womanhood, the wonder of her life.

Our life is meant to be poured out, to be spent. All the great lives we have ever known have been poured out for others. When our Lord said those strange words about the harlots and publicans going into the kingdom of heaven before the Pharisees, His meaning appears to be that it is better to spend badly than not to spend at all. He seems to say: "You Pharisees have hoarded your lives, so that no one has been the richer for them. These people have squandered their lives, their sins are many, but nevertheless they have spent them." It may even be that it is better to spend money badly than to be a miser, to spend talent unwisely rather than not spend it at all. We can, and it is a very sad thing, spend our treasure badly, but we can learn by that spending.

Here is this woman, who has spent the treasure of her womanhood badly. Now she comes to Jesus, and in the light of His purity she sees the darkness and squalor of her life. But she pours out her treasure on His head, and in that act finds peace, and not only did she get a blessing for herself but the whole house was filled with the odor of her spending. So the whole Church is enriched by every sacrificed and consecrated life.

FATHER ANDREW (1869–1946)
English Anglican priest

Our trance of selfishness must end, for we are all being organized, by the one true life, in the one true body. In the body of Christ, self-seeking is a monstrosity! The whole body must be "fitly joined together and compacted by that which every joint supplies . . . unto the edifying of itself in love." Our Lord has need of each one in his great, mystical body; and they must all be one in him, the Anointed.

There is a life, and this world comprehends it not. It has a body without defect, want, misery, anger, or death. The Holy Spirit is its air and spirit; it is filled with love and joy.

This life has been from eternity, uprising and blossoming! It is not of this earth, but substantial—the eternal life! And all who have received this life, at the end of the age, will be presented pure and without blemish, one body in Christ!

To all you who are in the process of birth are these lines written; that each one may be strengthened, and bud in the life of God, and grow, and bear fruit in the Tree of paradise so that each branch and twig in this fair Tree may contribute, help and shelter all the other branches and twigs, that this Tree may become a great Tree! Then shall we all rejoice, one with another, with "joy unspeakable and full of glory"! AMEN!

JACOB BOEHME (1575–1624)
German Lutheran theosophist

The human body by contact with this body of Christ, which is no longer limited by space and time, has within it the seed of the divine life. As St Paul says: "We ourselves, who have the first fruits of the Spirit, groan inwardly as we wait for ... the redemption of our bodies." And this "groaning" is part of the travail of all nature, which waits to be delivered "from its bondage to decay and obtain the glorious liberty of the children of God." This is the cosmic drama, this transformation of nature, of matter and the body, so as to become the outward form of the divine Spirit, the body of the Lord. And this transformation is taking place in our own bodies. In every human being matter is being transformed daily into Spirit. We take in matter through our bodies as food, and that matter goes to feed the brain, and the brain produces thought. Thought itself is matter become Spirit. But for most of us this process remains incomplete. Matter is never fully assimilated by Spirit, and at death the matter unassimilated by the Spirit returns to the earth. But in the body of Christ we can see that transformation of matter by Spirit taking place, which is the destiny of us all at the end of time.

BEDE GRIFFITHS (1906–1993)
English Benedictine monk

There is yet to come, in fuller measure, the down-shining inspiration of God's Spirit, giving sensibility and power to all it touches. . . . This view of Christ as saving his people—as working in them, working for them, working by the great round of providence, working by his special manifestations, and working in them *to will and to do*—the aspect of Christ as one having a saving nature, and that spirit in which he says, "I came not to condemn the world," in which he calls men to him, and which he manifested in laying down his life that he might save the world—this aspect of Christ is the most precious to me, for my own sake, and for the sake of my fellow men.

HENRY WARD BEECHER (1813–1887)
American Congregational minister

All this is what lay behind my question to Metropolitan Anthony, but before I could begin to speak about it in detail he was already replying:

"You ask what in yourself can respond to the sacrifice of God? But this sacrifice, as you call it, is *love*. What is the proper response to love?"

At first, I thought Metropolitan Anthony was expecting me to answer. I had no answer.

"The proper response to love," he continued, "is to accept it. There is nothing to *do*. The response to a gift is . . . to accept it. Why would you wish to do anything?"

JACOB NEEDLEMAN (contemporary)
American philosopher of religion

The first thing I wish to discuss, as far as my limited understanding will allow, is the nature of the essence of perfect prayer. For we come across some people who believe that the whole thing consists in thought; and thus, if they are able to think a great deal about God, however much the effort may cost them, they immediately imagine they are spiritually minded; while, if they become distracted, and their efforts to think of good things fail, they at once become greatly discouraged and suppose themselves to be lost. . . . I have written elsewhere of what I believe to be the reasons for this wandering of the imagination and so I am not discussing that now; I am only anxious to explain that the soul is not thought, nor is the will controlled by thought, it would be a great misfortune if it were. The soul's profit, then, consists not in thinking much, but in loving much.

TERESA OF ÁVILA (1515–1582)
Spanish Carmelite saint and mystic

You do not ask for the psychologically impossible—since what I am asked to cherish in the vast and unknown crowd is never anything save one and the same personal being which is yours.

Nor do you call for any hypocritical protestations of love for my neighbor, because—since my heart cannot reach your person except at the depths of all that is most individually and concretely personal in every "other"—it is to the "other" *himself*, and not to some vague entity around him, that my charity is addressed.

No, you do not ask anything false or unattainable of me. You merely, through your revelation and your grace, force what is most human in me to become conscious of itself at last. Humanity was sleeping—it is still sleeping—imprisoned in the narrow joys of its little closed loves. A tremendous spiritual power is slumbering in the depths of our multitude, which will manifest itself only when we have learnt to *break down the barriers* of our egoisms and, by a fundamental recasting of our outlook, raise ourselves up to the habitual and practical vision of universal realities.

Jesus, Savior of human activity to which you have given meaning, Savior of human suffering to which you have given living value, be also the Savior of human unity; compel us to discard our pettinesses, and to venture forth resting upon you, into the uncharted ocean of charity.

PIERRE TEILHARD DE CHARDIN (1881–1955)
French paleontologist and Jesuit priest

Often I have said to people, "I will pray for you," but how often did I really enter into the full reality of what that means? When I really bring my friends and the many I pray for into my innermost being and feel their pains, their struggles, their cries in my own soul, then I leave myself, so to speak, and become them, then I have compassion.

Compassion lies at the heart of our prayer for our fellow human beings. When I pray for the world, I become the world; when I pray for the endless needs of the millions, my soul expands and wants to embrace them all and bring them into the presence of God. But in the midst of that experience I realize that compassion is not mine but God's gift to me. I cannot embrace the world, but God can. I cannot pray, but God can pray in me. When God became as we are, that is, when God allowed all of us to enter into the intimacy of the divine life, it became possible for us to share in God's infinite compassion.

In praying for others, I lose myself and become the other, only to be found by the divine love which holds the whole of humanity in a compassionate embrace.

HENRI NOUWEN (1932–1996)
Dutch Roman Catholic priest, professor, and counselor

What better discipline in goodness can we conceive for a human spirit . . . than to live and labor for a brother's welfare? To find our deepest joy, not in the delights of sense, nor in the gratification of personal ambition, nor even in the serene pursuits of culture and science—nay, not even in seeking the safety of our own souls, but in striving for the highest good of those who are dear to our Father in heaven, and the moral and spiritual redemption of that world for which the Son of God lived and died—say, can a nobler school of goodness be discovered than this? . . . Live in this, find your dearest work here, let love to God and man be the animating principle of your being; and then, let death come when it may, and carry you where it will, you will not be unprepared for it. The summons that calls you into regions unknown, need awaken in your breast no perturbation or dismay; for you cannot in God's universe go where love and truth and self-devotion are things of naught, or where a soul, filled with undying faith in the progress and identifying its own happiness with the final triumph of goodness, shall find itself forsaken.

JOHN CAIRD (1820–1898)
Scottish Presbyterian minister

My soul, as soon as it is out of my body, is in Heaven, and does not wait for the possession of Heaven, nor for the fruition of the sight of God, till it ascends through air, and fire, and Moon, and Sun, and Planets, and Firmament, to that place which we conceive to be Heaven, but without the thousandth part of a minutes stop, as soon as it issues, is in a glorious light, which is Heaven (for all the way to Heaven is Heaven . . .).

As my soul shall not go *towards* Heaven, but go by Heaven to Heaven, to the Heaven of Heavens, so the true joy of a good soul in this world is the very joy of Heaven; and we go thither, not that being without joy, we might have joy infused into us, but that, as Christ says, Our joy might be full, perfected, sealed with an everlastingness; for, as he promises, That no man shall take our joy from us, so neither shall Death itself take it away, nor so

much as interrupt it, or discontinue it, but as in the face of
Death, when he lays hold upon me, and in the face of the Devil,
when he attempts me, I shall see the face of God (for, every
thing shall be a glass, to reflect God upon me), so in the agonies
of Death, in the anguish of that dissolution, in the sorrows of
that valediction, in the irreversibleness of that transmigration, I
shall have a joy, which shall no more evaporate, than my soul
shall evaporate, A joy, that shall pass up, and put on a more glorious garment above, and be joy super-invested in glory. Amen.

JOHN DONNE (1572–1631)
English poet and dean of St. Paul's Cathedral, London

All is magnetism, all is sentiment, instinct and attraction, and the
freedom of the will has the government of it. There is nothing
in the universe but magnetism and the impediments of it. For as
all things come from God, and all things have something of God
and goodness in them, so all things have magnetical effects and
instincts both towards God and one another. This is the life, the
force, the power, the nature of everything. . . . We discover this
magnetism in some things, where it breaks out sensibly; but it is
everywhere for the same reason that it is anywhere, though we are
too busy with the fictions of our own minds to see it, or too
much employed in such things as resist and suppress its force.

But because this magnetism is a secret life that wants to
increase its strength before it can sensibly show its power; and
because we have an activity of reason within us that is soon in
action, and concerns itself with everything, and takes all upon it
as if it did all; because it can look at all and dispute about all;
therefore it is that this magnetism, or instinct towards God and
goodness, has much difficulty to show itself sufficiently, and
only stirs now and then within us, or when sickness, distress, or
some great outward shock has so dashed in pieces all images of

reason, and stopped the activity of our minds, that the secret power of the soul has liberty to awake in it.

This is that trumpet of God which will raise and separate the dead; and then, all impediments being removed, everything will take its place.

WILLIAM LAW (1686–1761)
English contemplative and cleric

"A full measure, pressed down, shaken together and running over, will be poured into your lap" (Luke 6:38). And that measure, as I have heard, will be without measure.

But what I should like to know, however, is the nature of that which is to be measured out, what that immense reward is which has been promised. "The eye has not seen, O God, besides you, what things you have prepared for them that love you." Tell us then, since you do the preparing, tell us what it is you prepare. We believe, we are confident, that in accordance with your promise, "we shall be filled with the good things of your house." But—I persist in asking—what are these good things, what are they like? Would it be with corn and wine and oil, with gold and silver or precious stones? But these are things that we have known and seen, that we have grown weary of seeing. We seek for the things that no eye has seen and no ear has heard, things beyond the mind of man. To search after these things, whatever they may be, is a source of pleasure and relish and delight. "They will all be taught by God," says Scripture, "and he will be all in all. . . ."

Who indeed can comprehend what an abundance of goodness is contained in that brief expression: "God will be all in all"?

BERNARD OF CLAIRVAUX (1091–1153)
Cistercian abbot, saint, and theologian

The appearances of Jesus after the Resurrection are often understood, by Christians, as being for the purpose of proof of the Resurrection (or by unbelievers thought to be the product of wishful dreaming by the disciples) but as we read the Gospel we find something much deeper.

They are not just "proofs," still less the result of the disciples' desire to see Jesus, but they are because Jesus so desired to come to his brothers and sisters, to his friends (as he called them at the Last Supper) and to be with them, and to resume the fellowship of their holy community.

So he again eats with them, sharing bread and fish by the sea, not to prove something but because he desires to begin again the sharing of life: "with desire I have desired to eat with you" (Luke 22:15), and this time without end.

So when he speaks to Thomas about the blessedness of those who will come after, the scene opens and includes us, and we find that it is to be with us also and to share our life, that he desires, and for this that he is Risen.

Therefore I say to you, as a word given me and you from the Lord, "The Lord says, with desire have I desired to be with you this day and, see!, I am here!"

Let each of us today know that it is to appear to us, to be with us, that Christ is Risen. This is his deep desire and love, to be with you and with me. Let us also know that his desire in Resurrection is to be with us as a spiritual family, as a community, to share our life and to meet us each through each other!

Let our community today know itself as meeting the Lord because of His desire to be here with us, and as one with the disciples by the sea, and one with the whole family of Christ in all times . . . a family of love without limit . . . a story which begins at the Resurrection but has no end . . . and indeed, in us, let it begin again this day (because only of His love and desire)! Amen.

SERAPHIM SIGRIST (contemporary)
American Eastern Orthodox bishop

Easter Sermon of John Chrysostom

Let all the pious faithful everywhere, and everyone who loves God, rejoice in the splendor of this feast; let the wise servants blissfully enter into the joy of their Lord; let those who have borne the burden of Lent now receive their pay, and those who have toiled since the first hour, let them now receive their due reward; let any who came after the third hour be grateful to join in the feast, and those who have come after the sixth, let them not be afraid of being too late, for the Lord is gracious and He receives the last just as the first.

He gives rest to those who come in the eleventh hour as well as to those who have toiled since the first: yes, He takes pity on the last and He serves the first; He rewards the one and is generous to the other; He repays the deed and praises the effort.

Come, all of you: enter into the joy of the Lord. You the first and you the last, receive alike your reward; you rich and you poor, dance together; you who are sober and you who are weak, celebrate the day; you who have kept the fast and you who have not, rejoice today.

The table is richly loaded: enjoy its royal banquet. The calf is well-fattened, so let no one go away hungry. May all of you enjoy the banquet of faith; may all of you receive the riches of His goodness.

Let no one grieve over their poverty, for the universal kingdom has been revealed; let no one weep over their sins, for pardon has shone from the grave; let no one fear death, for the death of our Savior has set us free. The Lord has destroyed it by enduring it, He has despoiled Hades by going down into its realm, He has angered it by allowing it a taste of His powerful presence.

When Isaiah foresaw all this, he proclaimed: "O Hades, you were furious at encountering Him in the nether world." Hades is indignant because it has been frustrated, it is angry because it has been mocked, it is wrathful because it has been destroyed, it is enraged because it has been reduced to nothing, it is filled with ire because it is now captive.

It seized a body, and lo! It discovered God; it seized earth, and, behold! It met up with heaven; it seized the visible, and was overcome by the invisible.

O death, where is your sting? O Hades, where is your victory? Christ is risen and you are abolished, Christ is risen and life is freed, Christ is risen and the tomb is emptied of the dead: for Christ, being raised from the dead, has become the leader and reviver of those who had fallen asleep.

To him be glory and power for ages of ages.

AMEN

ACKNOWLEDGMENTS
AND SOURCES

To Sr. Catherine Patten, R.S.H.M., Phyllis Tickle, Bishop Seraphim Sigrist, and Mother Mary Clare, persons of prayer who helped orient, steady, and refine my search in these pages, I express my gratitude. They are living exemplars of the fruit of prayer, and their generosity, openness of heart, and humility were, and remain, a support and an inspiration.

Also, my thanks to the patient and helpful staff of St. Mark's Library at the General Theological Seminary in New York City, to my clear-sighted editor, Toinette Lippe, and to the publishers whose works appear excerpted here, especially to the Cistercian Publications, faithful guardians of a precious legacy. L.K.

ABRAHAM OF NATHPAR (c. sixth century)
Syriac father of the church.

p. 204: From *The Syriac Fathers on Prayer and the Spiritual Life,* introduced and translated by Sebastian Brock, Kalamazoo, Mich.: Cistercian Publications, 1987. Reprinted by permission of the publisher.

AGAPII (19th century)
Monk of Valamo monastery, Russia.

p. 148: From *The Art of Prayer: An Orthodox Anthology*, compiled by Igumen Chariton of Valamo, translated by E. Kadloubovsky and E. M. Palmer, edited and with an introduction by Timothy Ware, London: Faber and Faber Ltd., 1966.

ALBERT THE GREAT (c. 1200–1280)
Theologian, bishop, saint, and one of the teachers of Meister Eckhart at the University of Paris.

p. 86: From *On Cleaving to God*, attributed to Albert the Great, translated by John Richards, cited on ccel.org.

ANDREW, FATHER (1869–1946)
English Anglican priest.

p. 221: From *A Gift of Light: A Collection of Thoughts from Father Andrew*, selected and edited by Harry C. Griffith, New York: Morehouse-Barlow, 1968. Reprinted by permission of Harry C. Griffith.

ANDREWES, LANCELOT (1555–1626)
Anglican bishop of Winchester and Ely.

p. 39: From Sermon Four on Repentance: Ash Wednesday, 1619.

ANGELA OF FOLIGNO (1248–1309)
Umbrian mystic.

p. 148: From *The Book of Divine Consolation of the Blessed Angela of Foligno*, translated by Mary G. Steegmann, New York: Duffield & Co., 1909. Edited and adapted by L.K.

ANONYMOUS (20th century)
Christian hermeticist, who wished this book to be published posthumously.

pp. 3, 118, 119, 153, and 214: From *Meditations on the Tarot: A Journey into Christian Hermeticism*, translated by Robert Powell. New York: Jeremy P. Tarcher, a division of Penguin Putnam, 2002. Reprinted by permission of Robert Powell.

ANSELM OF CANTERBURY (c. 1033–1109)
Saint and founder of medieval Scholasticism.

pp. 8, 176, and 219: From *The Prayers and Meditations of St. Anselm with the Proslogion,* translated by Benedicta Ward (Penguin Classics, 1973). Copyright © 1973 by Benedicta Ward. Reprinted by permission of Penguin Books, Ltd.

AUGUSTINE OF HIPPO (354–430)
Carthaginian saint, philosopher, and doctor of the church.

p. 19: From *Confessions* by Augustine, translated by F. J. Sheed, Indianapolis; Cambridge: Hackett Publishing Company, Inc., 1993.

p. 108: From "A Discourse on the Psalms," cited in *A Path to Contemplation* by John T. Catoir, New York: Alba House, 1988.

p. 145: From *Prayer: Personal and Liturgical* by Agnes Cunningham, Wilmington, Del.: M. Glazier, 1985.

p. 158: From "Commentary on the First Epistle of John," in *Spiritual Classics from the Early Church,* introduced and compiled by Robert Atwell, O.S.B., London: Church House Publishing, 1995.

BALTHASAR, HANS URS VON (1905–1988)
Swiss Roman Catholic theologian.

p. 6: From *Christian Meditation* by Hans Urs von Balthasar, translated by Mary Theresilde Skerry, San Francisco: Ignatius Press, 1989. Reprinted by permission of the publisher.

pp. 56 and 104: From *Prayer* by Hans Urs von Balthasar, translated by Graham Harrison, San Francisco: Ignatius Press, 1986. Reprinted by permission of the publisher.

p. 196: Cited in *The Undivided Heart: The Western Monastic Approach to Contemplation* by Michael Casey, Petersham, Mass.: St. Bede's Publications, 1994. Reprinted by permission of the author.

BASIL THE GREAT (330–379)
Doctor of the church, saint, and bishop of Caesarea.

p. 51: From *Drinking from the Hidden Fountain: A Patristic Breviary* by Thomas Spidlik, translated by Paul Drake, Kalamazoo, Mich.: Cistercian Publications, 1994. Reprinted by permission of New City, 57 Twyford Avenue, London W3 9PZ, England.

p. 103: From "On the Holy Spirit, 9, 22–23," in *Spiritual Classics from the Early Church,* introduced and compiled by Robert Atwell, O.S.B., London: Church House Publishing, 1995.

p. 134: From *Prayer of the Heart* by George A. Maloney, Notre Dame, Ind.: Ave Maria Press, 1981. Reprinted by permission of the author.

BEECHER, HENRY WARD (1813–1887)
American Congregational minister.

p. 224: From *Morning and Evening Exercises, Selected from the Published and Unpublished Writings of the Rev. Henry Ward Beecher,* edited by Lyman Abbott, New York: Harper & Brothers, Publishers, 1891.

BERNANOS, GEORGES (1888–1948)
French novelist and polemicist.

p. 71: From *Diary of a Country Priest* by Georges Bernanos, New York: Macmillan & Co., 1937.

BERNARD OF CLAIRVAUX (1091–1153)
Cistercian abbot, saint, and theologian.

p. 14: Sermon Eighty-Four from *On the Song of Songs,* vol. 4, by Bernard of Clairvaux, translated by Irene Edmonds, Kalamazoo, Mich.: Cistercian Publications, 1971–1980. Reprinted by permission of the publisher.

p. 20: From *Bernard of Clairvaux: Selected Works,* translation and foreword by G. R. Evans, introduction by Jean LeClercq, preface by Ewart H. Cousins, New York: Paulist Press, 1987. Reprinted by permission of Paulist Press, www.paulistpress.com

p. 99: Sermon Seventy-Four, *On the Song of Songs,* vol. 4.

p. 150: From *The Very Thought of Thee: From Three Great Mystics, Bernard of Clairvaux, Jeremy Taylor, Evelyn Underhill*, arranged and edited by Douglas V. Steere and J. Minton Batten, Nashville, Tenn.: The Upper Room, 1953.

p. 229: Sermon Two, *On the Song of Songs*, vol. 1, translated by Kilian Walsh.

BIANCHI, ENZO (contemporary)
Italian Benedictine prior at Bose.

pp. 50 and 55: From *Praying the Word: An Introduction to Lectio Divina* by Enzo Bianchi, translated by James W. Zona, Kalamazoo, Mich.; Spencer, Mass.: Cistercian Publications, 1998. Reprinted by permission of the publisher.

BLOOM, ANTHONY (1914–)
Russian Orthodox monk and metropolitan of Sourozh.

p. 36: From *The Courage to Pray* by Metropolitan Anthony and Georges Lefebvre, translated by Dinah Livingstone, London: Darton, Longman & Todd, 1984; Crestwood, N.Y.: St. Vladimir's Seminary Press, 1984. Reprinted by permission of the publishers.

pp. 61 and 73: From *School for Prayer* by Metropolitan Anthony Sourozh, published and copyright 1970 and 1999 by Darton, Longman & Todd, Ltd., London, and Paulist Press. Reprinted by permission of Darton, Longman & Todd, Ltd., London and Paulist Press, www.paulistpress.com.

pp. 70 and 84: From *God and Man* by Metropolitan Anthony of Sourozh, London: Darton, Longman & Todd, 1983; Crestwood, N.Y.: St. Vladimir's Seminary Press, 1983.

BOEHME, JACOB (1575–1624)
German Lutheran theosophist.

p. 38: From *The Way to Christ* by Jacob Boehme, translated and with an introduction by Peter Erb, New York: Paulist Press, 1978. Reprinted by permission of Paulist Press, www.paulistpress.com.

pp. 200 and 202: From *On the Suprasensual Life* by Jacob Boehme, translated by William Law, London: Printed for M. Richardson, 1764–1781. Edited and adapted by L.K.

Acknowledgments and Sources

BOLSHAKOFF, SERGIUS (20th century)
Russian Orthodox monk and writer.

p. 143: From *Russian Mystics* by Sergius Bolshakoff, introduction by Thomas Merton, Kalamazoo, Mich.: Cistercian Publications, 1977. Reprinted by permission of the publisher.

BONAVENTURE (1221–1274)
Italian scholastic theologian, saint, cardinal, and doctor of the church.

p. 109: From "The Soul's Journey to God" in *Bonaventure*, translated and with an introduction by Ewart Cousins, preface by Ignatius Brady, New York: Paulist Press, 1978, www.paulistpress.com.

BONHOEFFER, DIETRICH (1906–1945)
German Lutheran pastor and theologian.

pp. 47, 187, and 201: From *Meditating on the Word* by Dietrich Bonhoeffer, edited and translated by David McI. Gracie, Cambridge, Mass.: Cowley Publications, 1986.

p. 72: From *Life Together* by Dietrich Bonhoeffer, translated and with an introduction by John W. Doberstein, New York; London: Harper & Row, 1954.

p. 212: Cited in *The New Theologian* by Ved Mehta, New York: Harper & Row, 1965.

BRYANCHANINOV, IGNATIUS (1807–1867)
Russian bishop.

p. 188: From "A Rule of Attention to Oneself" by Bishop Ignaty Bryanchaninov, *Parish Life*, August 1989.

BULTMANN, RUDOLPH KARL (1884–1976)
German Protestant theologian and New Testament scholar.

p. 126: From *Jesus and the Word* by Rudolf Bultmann, translated by Louise Pettibone Smith and Erminie Huntress Lantero, New York: Charles Scribner's Sons, © 1958.

Acknowledgments and Sources

A CARTHUSIAN (contemporary)

　p. 44: From *Interior Prayer: Carthusian Novice Conferences*, translated by Sister Maureen Scrine, Kalamazoo, Mich.: Cistercian Publications, 1996.

　pp. 145 and 205: From *The Wound of Love: A Carthusian Miscellany*, Kalamazoo, Mich.: Cistercian Publications; London: Darton, Longman & Todd, 1994.

CAIRD, JOHN (1820–1898)
Scottish Presbyterian minister.

　p. 226: From *A Diary of Readings* by John Baillie, New York: Charles Scribner's Sons, 1955.

CASEY, MICHAEL (contemporary)
Australian Benedictine monk of Tarrawarra Abbey.

　p. 52: From *The Undivided Heart: The Western Monastic Approach to Contemplation* by Michael Casey, Petersham, Mass.: St. Bede's Publications, 1994. Reprinted by permission of the author.

CASSIAN, JOHN (360–435)
Monk and founder of monasteries near Marseilles.

　pp. 116, 120, and 148: From *John Cassian: The Conferences*, translated and annotated by Boniface Ramsey, New York: Paulist Press, © 1997. Reprinted by permission of Paulist Press, www.paulistpress.com

CAUSSADE, JEAN-PIERRE DE (1675–1751)
French Jesuit.

　p. 86: From *Spiritual Letters of Jean-Pierre de Caussade*, translated by Kitty Muggeridge, Wilton, Conn.: Morehouse-Barlow, 1986.

CHAPMAN, JOHN (1865–1933)
English Benedictine spiritual adviser and biblical scholar.

　pp. 90 and 196: From *The Spiritual Letters of Dom Chapman*, New York and London: Sheed and Ward, Ltd., 1935.

CHRYSOSTOM, JOHN (345–407)

Father of the Eastern church, saint, and bishop of Constantinople.

p. 231: From the Easter sermon of John Chrysostom, version courtesy of the Monks of New Skete.

CLIMACUS, JOHN (520–603)

Father of the Eastern church.

pp. 27 and 161: From *The Ladder of Divine Ascent* by John Climacus, translation by Colm Luibheid and Norman Russell, notes on translation by Norman Russell, introduction by Kallistos Ware; preface by Colm Luibheid, New York: Paulist Press, 1982. Reprinted by permission of Paulist Press, www.paulistpress.com.

CLUTTON-BROCK, ARTHUR (1868–1924)

English essayist, critic, and journalist.

p. 13: From *A Diary of Readings* by John Baillie, New York: Charles Scribner's Sons, 1955.

COLLIANDER, TITO (1904–1989)

Finnish Orthodox writer.

p. 185: From *Way of the Ascetics* by Tito Colliander, translated by Katherine Ferré, introduction by Kenneth Leech, San Francisco: Harper & Row, 1960. Copyright © 1960 by Tito Colliander. Introduction copyright © 1982 by Kenneth Leech. Reprinted by permission of HarperCollins Publishers, Inc., and St. Vladimir's Seminary Press, 575 Scarsdale Road, Crestwood, N.Y. 10707, 1-800-204-2665.

COMENIUS, JOHN AMOS (1592–1670)

Czech educator and bishop of Bohemian Unity of Brethren.

p. 27: From *The Labyrinth of the World and the Paradise of the Heart* by John Comenius, translated and with an introduction by Howard Louthan and Andrea Sterk, preface by Jan Milic Lochman, New York: Paulist Press, © 1998. Reprinted by permission of Paulist Press, www.paulistpress.com.

CONGAR, YVES (1904–1997)
French Dominican theologian and cardinal.

pp. 60 and 99: From *I Believe in the Holy Spirit* by Yves Congar, translated by David Smith, New York: Seabury Press; London: G. Chapman, 1983. English translation copyright by Geoffrey Chapman, a division of Cassell, 1983. Reprinted by permission of HarperCollins Publishers, Inc.

COOMARASWAMY, RAMA P. (contemporary)
American physician, theologian, and author.

p. 181: From *The Invocation of the Name of Jesus: As Practiced in the Western Church* by Rama P. Coomaraswamy, Louisville, Ky.: Fons Vitae, 2000.

CYPRIAN (c. 200–258)
Father of the church and bishop of Carthage.

pp. 119 and 121: From *Spiritual Classics from the Early Church*, introduced and compiled by Robert Atwell, O.S.B., London: Church House Publishing, 1995.

CYRIL OF JERUSALEM (c. 315–387)
Bishop of Jerusalem, saint, and catechetical writer.

p. 101: From *Fathers Talking: An Anthology* by Aelred Squire, Kalamazoo, Mich.: Cistercian Publications, 1986.

p. 122: Cited in *A Method of Prayer* by Eugraph Kovalevsky, based on the third French edition by Esther Williams, edited to conform to the fifth French edition by Robin Amis and Raymond Hèbert, Newburyport, Mass.: The Praxis Press, 1993. Reprinted by permission of L. G. Amis.

DAUJAT, JEAN (20th century)
French Dominican monk.

p. 9: From *Prayer* by Jean Daujat, translated by Martin Murphy, New York: Hawthorn Books, 1964.

DE CHANTAL, JANE (1572–1641)
French saint and founder of the Order of the Visitation.

    p. 144: From *Entretien*, xxxiv. Cited in *The Art of Mental Prayer* by Bede Frost, London: Alban Press, 1988.

    p. 198: From *Selected Letters*, cited in *The Art of Mental Prayer*.

DEFOE, DANIEL (1660–1731)
English novelist, pamphleteer, and journalist.

    p. 21: From *Robinson Crusoe* by Daniel Defoe, London: Penguin Books, 1994.

DELP, ALFRED (1907–1945)
German Jesuit theologian and writer.

    p. 88: From *Invitation to Christian Spirituality*, edited by John R. Tyson, New York; Oxford: Oxford University Press, 1999.

DENIS (fifth century)
Syrian monk, mystic, and teacher.

    p. 98: From *Prayer: Personal and Liturgical* by Agnes Cunningham, Wilmington, Del.: M. Glazier, 1985.

DÉSURMONT, T. R. P. (20th century)
French priest and modern exponent of the Redemptionist tradition.

    p. 26: From *Retour Continuel à Dieu.* Cited in *The Art of Mental Prayer* by Bede Frost, London: Alban Press, 1988.

DONNE, JOHN (1572–1631)
English poet and dean of St. Paul's Cathedral, London.

    p. 227: From The Second Prebend Sermon preached at St. Paul's, January 29, 1625.

DOROTHEUS, ABBA (sixth century)
Saint, ascetical writer, and founder of a Palestinian monastery.

p. 108: From *Early Fathers from the Philokalia*, selected and translated from the Russian text by E. Kadloubovsky and G. E. H. Palmer, London: Faber and Faber Ltd., 1954.

p. 125: From *Drinking from the Hidden Fountain: A Patristic Breviary* by Thomas Spidlik, translated by Paul Drake, Kalamazoo, Mich.: Cistercian Publications, 1994. Reprinted by permission of New City, 57 Twyford Avenue, London W3 9PZ, England.

p. 170: From *Early Fathers from the Philokalia*.

DOSTOEVSKY, FYODOR (1821–1881)
Russian novelist.

p. 76: From *The Brothers Karamazov* by Fyodor Dostoevsky, translated by Constance Garnett, New York: Macmillan, 1923.

ECKHART, MEISTER (1260–1327)
German Dominican mystic and theologian.

pp. 41, 97, 157, and 174: From *Meister Eckhart: Teacher and Preacher*, edited by Bernard McGinn with the collaboration of Frank Tobin and Elvira Borgstadt, preface by Kenneth Northcott, New York: Paulist Press, 1986. Reprinted by permission of Paulist Press, www.paulistpress.com.

ELLUL, JACQUES (1912–1994)
French philosopher and theologian.

pp. 68, 155, and 194: From *Prayer and Modern Man* by Jacques Ellul, translated by C. Edward Hopkin, New York: Seabury Press, 1970. Copyright © 1970 by Jacques Ellul. Reprinted by permission of HarperCollins Publishers, Inc.

EMERSON, RALPH WALDO (1803–1882)
American poet and essayist.

p. 93: From *The Esoteric Emerson*, edited by Richard G. Geldard, Hudson, N.Y.: Lindisfarne Press, 2000.

Acknowledgments and Sources

EPHREM THE SYRIAN (303–373)
Spiritual and theological writer.

pp. 44 and 181: From *The Luminous Eye: The Spiritual World Vision of Saint Ephrem* by Sebastian Brock, Kalamazoo, Mich.: Cistercian Publications, © 1992. Reprinted by permission of the publisher.

ERIUGENA, JOHN THE SCOT (810–877)
Irish theologian, original thinker, and scholar.

p. 5: From *Johannis Scotti Erivgenae Periphyseon*, edited by I. P. Sheldon-Williams, The Dublin Institute for Advanced Studies, Dublin, 1981. Cited in *The Enlightened Mind: An Anthology of Sacred Prose*, edited by Stephen Mitchell, New York: HarperCollins, 1991.

EVDOKIMOV, PAUL (1901–1970)
One of the most representative figures of the Russian Orthodox church in the West.

pp. 29, 165, 182, and 196: From *Ages of the Spiritual Life* by Paul Evdokimov; original translation by Sister Gertrude, revised translation by Michael Plekon and Alexis Vinogradov, Crestwood, N.Y.: St. Vladimir's Seminary Press, 1998. Reprinted by permission of St. Vladimir's Seminary Press, 575 Scarsdale Road, Crestwood, N.Y. 10751.

p. 109: From *The Sacrament of Love*, translated by Anthony P. Gythiel and Victoria Steadman, Crestwood, N.Y.: St. Vladimir's Seminary Press, 1985.

FÉNELON, FRANÇOIS (1651–1715)
French Roman Catholic archbishop of Cambrai.

pp. 13, 85, 90, 108, and 168: From *Extracts from the Writings of Francis Fénelon, Archbishop of Cambrai*, edited by John Kendall, Philadelphia: Kimber, Conrad & Co., 1804.

FEOFIL, THE FOOL FOR CHRIST (1788–1853)
Russian priest, saint, ascetic, and visionary.

p. 198: Cited on cybercom.net/~htm/pearls/pearls_9.htm.

FLAVEL, JOHN (1630–1691)
English writer and preacher.

p. 132: From *On Keeping the Heart*, circulated in the United States by the American Tract Society, cited on ccel.org. Edited by L.K.

FOX, GEORGE (1624–1691)
English religious leader and founder of the Society of Friends.

p. 105: From *A Journal or Historical Account of the Life, Travels, Sufferings, Christian Experiences, and Labour of Love, etc., of George Fox*, Philadelphia: Friends' Book Store, 189?.

FRANCIS OF ASSISI (1182–1226)
Italian monk, saint, and founder of the Franciscan order.

p. 112: From *St. Francis of Assisi: The Legends and Lauds*, edited, selected, and annotated by Otto Karrer, translated by N. Wydenbruck, New York: Sheed & Ward, 1952.

FRANCIS DE SALES (1567–1622)
Saint, bishop of Geneva, and doctor of the church.

p. 10: From *Introduction to the Devout Life* by Francis de Sales, Library of Spiritual Works for English Catholics, London: Rivingtons, 1876.

p. 89: From *Treatise on the Love of God* by St. Francis de Sales, translated by Reverend Henry Benedict Mackey, O.S.B., Rockford, Ill.: Tan Books and Publishers, Inc., 1997.

p. 117: From *Introduction to the Devout Life*.

p. 167: Ibid.

FROST, BEDE (1877–?)
English Benedictine.

p. 155: From *The Art of Mental Prayer* by Bede Frost, London: Alban Press, 1988.

Acknowledgments and Sources

FURSA (eighth century)
Celtic saint.

p. 173: From *Prayers from the Heart* by Richard J. Foster, San Francisco: HarperSanFrancisco, 1994.

GILBERT OF HOYLAND (d. 1172)
Cistercian abbot.

p. 15: From *In the School of Love: An Anthology of Early Cistercian Texts,* selected and annotated by Edith Scholl, introduction by M. Basil Pennington, Kalamazoo, Mich.; Spencer, Mass.: Cistercian Publications, 2000.

GILBERT, HUGH, O.S.B. (contemporary)
Benedictine abbot of Pluscarden Abbey, Scotland.

p. 52: From "The Life of Spiritual Combat," an interview by Philip Zaleski in *Parabola, Myth, Tradition, and the Search for Meaning,* vol. 24, no. 2, May 1999.

GREGORY OF NYSSA (330–395)
Saint, bishop of Nyssa, and Cappadocian father of the church.

p. 172: From *Drinking from the Hidden Fountain: A Patristic Breviary* by Thomas Spidlik, translated by Paul Drake, Kalamazoo, Mich.: Cistercian Publications, 1994. Reprinted by permission of New City, 57 Twyford Avenue, London W3 9PZ, England.

GRIFFITHS, BEDE (1906–1993)
English Benedictine monk.

pp. 9, 137, 160, and 223: From *Return to the Center* by Bede Griffiths, London: Collins, 1976; Springfield, Ill.: Templegate, 1977. Reprinted by permission of the Bede Griffiths Trust.

GUARDINI, ROMANO (1885–1968)

Italian-born German Roman Catholic monsignor and professor of Christian philosophy at the universities of Breslau, Berlin, Tübingen, and Munich.

pp. 63 and 140: From *Prayer in Practice* by Romano Guardini, translated by Prince Leopold of Lowenstein-Wertheim, New York: Pantheon Books, © 1957 by Pantheon Books and renewed 1985 by Random House, Inc. Used by permission of Pantheon Books, a division of Random House, Inc. Now available from Sophia Institute Press as *The Art of Praying*.

GUIGO DE PONTE (d. 1297)

Carthusian monk and spiritual writer.

p. 45: From *The Ladder of Monks and Twelve Meditations by Guigo II*, translated and with an introduction by Edmund Colledge, O.S.A., and James Walsh, S.J., Garden City, N.Y.: Image Books, 1978.

GURNALL, WILLIAM (1617–1679)

English pastor.

p. 142: From *The Christian in Complete Armour* by William Gurnall, M.A. Cited on ccel.org.

HADEWIJCH (13th century)

Flemish Beguine and contemplative writer.

p. 65: From *The Complete Works: Hadewijch*, translated and with an introduction by Columba Hart, preface by Paul Mommaers, New York: Paulist Press, © 1980. Reprinted by permission of Paulist Press, www.paulistpress.com.

HALLESBY, OLE (1879–1961)

Norwegian seminary professor and writer imprisoned for his resistance to the Nazi regime.

p. 31: From *Prayer* by Ole Hallesby, translated by Clarence J. Carlsen, Minneapolis, Minn.: Augsberg Fortress, © 1994. Reprinted by permission.

HEIDEGGER, MARTIN (1889–1976)

German existentialist philosopher.

    p. 167: From an article in *World Review*, 1950.

HESYCHIUS OF SINAI (dates unknown)

A medieval priest and monk of the Order of St. Basil.

    p. 180: Cited in *Teach Us to Pray* by André Louf, Cambridge, Mass.: Cowley Publications, 1992. Reprinted by permission of the publisher.

HILTON, WALTER (1343–1396)

English contemplative writer.

    p. 209: From *The Scale of Perfection* by Walter Hilton, edited by Evelyn Underhill, London: John M. Watkins, 1923.

HOPKINS, GERARD MANLEY (1844–1889)

English Jesuit priest and poet.

    pp. 2 and 156: From "The Principle or Foundation," an address based on the Spiritual Exercises of St. Ignatius Loyola.

HÜGEL, BARON FRIEDRICH VON (1852–1925)

English Roman Catholic religious writer.

    p. 89: From *Letters from Baron Friedrich von Hügel to a Niece*, edited and with an introduction by Gwendolen Green, London and Toronto: J. M. Dent & Sons, Ltd., 1929.

HUGH OF BALMA (13th century)

Carthusian abbot.

    p. 217: From the first of Hugh's *Nineteen Sermons on Ecclesiastes*, translated by H. O. Taylor in *The Medieval Mind*, Cambridge, Mass.: Harvard University Press, 1949.

Acknowledgments and Sources

HUXLEY, ALDOUS (1894–1963)
English novelist, essayist, and critic.

    p. 129: From *The Perennial Philosophy* by Aldous Huxley, New York and London: Harper & Brothers, 1945.

    p. 166: From *Ends and Means* by Aldous Huxley, London: Chatto & Windus, 1937.

ISAAC OF NINEVEH (d.c. 700)
Monastic writer.

    p. 24: From *The Syriac Fathers on Prayer and the Spiritual Life,* introduced and translated by Sebastian Brock, Kalamazoo, Mich.: Cistercian Publications, 1987. Reprinted by permission of the publisher.

ISAAC OF STELLA (d. 1169)
English Cistercian father and leading thinker in Christian humanism.

    p. 217: From *In the School of Love: An Anthology of Early Cistercian Texts,* selected and annotated by Edith Scholl, introduction by M. Basil Pennington, Kalamazoo, Mich.; Spencer, Mass.: Cistercian Publications, © 2000.

JOHN, ACTS OF
A collection of traditional wisdom sayings, parables, and proverbs attributed to Jesus.

    p. 16: From *The Other Gospels: Non-Canonical Gospel Texts,* edited by Ron Cameron, Philadelphia: The Westminster Press, 1982.

JOHN OF THE CROSS (1542–1591)
Spanish saint and mystic.

    p. 68: From *The Spiritual Canticle & Poems* by Saint John of the Cross, translated by E. Allison Peers, London: Burns and Oates, 1978.

    p. 156: Cited in *The Perennial Philosophy* by Aldous Huxley, New York and London: Harper & Brothers, 1945.

p. 211: From *The Ascent of Mount Carmel* by St. John of the Cross, translated and edited by E. Allison Peers, New York: Triumph Books, 1991.

JOHN PAUL II (1920–)
Polish pope, theologian, and philosopher.

p. 126: From the encyclical letter "Veritatis Splendor," addressed by the Supreme Pontiff Pope John Paul II to all the bishops of the Catholic Church regarding certain fundamental questions of the church's moral teaching. Vatican City: Libreria Editrice Vaticana, 1993.

JONES, RUFUS (1863–1948)
American Quaker.

p. 72: From *Rufus Jones Speaks to Our Time: An Anthology*, edited by Harry Emerson Fosdick, New York: Macmillan, 1952.

JUNG, C. G. (1875–1961)
Swiss psychiatrist and philosopher.

p. 65: Excerpt from a letter to Dorothee Hoch, from Jung, C. G., *Selected Letters of C. G. Jung*, copyright © 1975 by Princeton University Press. Reprinted by permission of Princeton University Press.

p. 163: Excerpt from a letter to Fr. Victor White, ibid. Reprinted by permission of Princeton University Press.

KELPIUS, JOHANNES (1673–1708)
German recluse, mystic, and teacher.

p. 171: From *A Method of Prayer*, edited and with an introduction by E. Gordon Alderfer, New York: Harper Brothers, 1950. In association with Pendle Hill.

KIERKEGAARD, SØREN (1813–1855)
Danish theologian.

p. 94: From *From the Fathers to the Churches*, edited by Brother Kenneth, CGA, London: Collins, 1983.

p. 105: From *The Prayers of Kierkegaard*, edited and with a new interpretation of his life and thought by Perry D. LeFevre, Chicago: University of Chicago Press, 1976.

p. 198: From *Prayer and Meditation* by F. C. Happold, Harmondsworth: Penguin, 1971.

KOVALEVSKY, EUGRAPH (1912–1970)
Russian founder of the French Catholic Orthodox Church.

pp. 121, 136, and 151: From *A Method of Prayer* by Eugraph Kovalevsky, based on the third French edition by Esther Williams, edited to conform to the fifth French edition by Robin Amis and Raymond Hèbert, Newburyport, Mass.: The Praxis Press, 1993.

LAUD, WILLIAM (1573–1645)
English archbishop of Canterbury.

p. 26: From *The Works of the Most Reverend Father in God, William Laud, D.D., sometime lord archbishop of Canterbury*, vol. 3, cited in *The Secret Place of the Most High* by Arthur John Gossip, New York: Charles Scribner's Sons, 1947.

LAW, WILLIAM (1686–1761)
English contemplative and cleric.

p. 8: From *The Spirit of Prayer, or The Soul Rising out of the Vanity of Time, into the Riches of Eternity*, by William Law, M.A., London, 1749. Adapted by L.K.

p. 19: From *The Spirit of Prayer.*

pp. 50, 87, and 103: From *Liberal and Mystical Writings of William Law*, with an introduction by William Scott Palmer, London: Longmans, Green, & Company, 1908.

p. 161: From *Liberal and Mystical Writings.* Adapted by L.K.

p. 218: From *Liberal and Mystical Writings.*

p. 228: Ibid.

LEAD, JANE (1624–1704)
English mystic.

  p. 202: Cited on passtheword.org.

LEBER, ERIC (contemporary)
American layperson.

  p. 116: From a letter to the editor in *Tricycle: The Buddhist Review,* Summer 2000.

LEWIS, C. S. (1898–1963)
English novelist and Christian apologist.

  p. 169: From *The Screwtape Letters* by C. S. Lewis, New York: Macmillan, 1961.

LITURGY OF THE HOURS (Roman Catholic)

  pp. 66 and 192: From the English translation of "The General Instruction of The Liturgy of the Hours" from *The Liturgy of the Hours,* © 1974, International Committee on English in the Liturgy. Used by permission. All rights reserved.

LOUF, ANDRÉ (1929–)
French Cistercian abbot.

  pp. 1, 54, 81, 174, and 180: From *Teach Us to Pray* by André Louf, Cambridge, Mass.: Cowley Publications, 1992. Reprinted by permission of the publisher.

  pp. 34 and 201: From *Tuning In to Grace: The Quest for God* by André Louf, translated by John Vriend, Kalamazoo, Mich.: Cistercian Publications, 1992. Reprinted by permission of the publisher.

LOSSKY, VLADIMIR (1903–1958)
Russian Orthodox theologian.

  pp. 32, 135, and 216: From *The Mystical Theology of the Eastern Church* by Vladimir Lossky, Cambridge: James Clarke, © 1957, and subsequently by St. Vladimir's Seminary Press in 1998. Reprinted by permission of St. Vladimir's Seminary Press, 575 Scarsdale Road, Crestwood, N.Y. 10707, 1-800-204-2665.

LUTHER, MARTIN (1483–1546)
German leader of the Protestant Reformation.

    p. 123: From *The Large Catechism by Dr. Martin Luther,* translated by F. Bente and W. H. T. Dau, published in *Triglot Concordia: The Symbolical Books of the Evangelical Lutheran Church,* St. Louis: Concordia Publishing House, 1921.

MACDONALD, GEORGE (1824–1905)
Scottish novelist and poet.

    p. 59: From *George MacDonald, an Anthology* by C. S. Lewis, New York: Macmillan, 1947.

MACLENNAN, CATHERINE (early 20th century)
Scottish crofter.

    p. 186: Cited in *The Celtic Way of Prayer* by Esther de Waal, New York: Doubleday, 1997.

MALONEY, GEORGE A. (1924–)
American Jesuit.

    p. 135: From *Prayer of the Heart* by George A. Maloney, Notre Dame, Ind.: Ave Maria Press, 1981. Reprinted by permission of the author.

MARY CLARE, MOTHER (1907–1988)
English Anglican nun.

    p. 141: From *Encountering the Depths* by Mother Mary Clare, Harrisburg, Penn.: Morehouse Publishing Co., 1993.

MERTON, THOMAS (1915–1968)
American Cistercian monk.

    pp. 46 and 49: From *Spiritual Direction and Meditation* by Thomas Merton, Collegeville, Minn.: Liturgical Press, © 1960, 1987. Reprinted by permission of the publisher.

    pp. 92 and 142: From *The Monastic Journey* by Thomas Merton, edited by Patrick Hart, Kalamazoo, Mich.: Cistercian Publications, © 1977 by

The Trustees of the Merton Legacy Trust. Reprinted by permission of The Merton Legacy Trust.

p. 164: First passage: From *Thomas Merton's Dark Path* by William H. Shannon, New York: Farrar, Straus, Giroux, © 1987. Second passage: From *New Seeds of Contemplation* by Thomas Merton, copyright © 1961 by the Abbey of Gethsemani, Inc. Reprinted by permission of New Directions Publishing Corp.

p. 206: From *Contemplative Prayer* by Thomas Merton, Garden City, N.Y.: Image Books, 1971.

MICHAEL, ELDER OF VALAAM (1877–1962)
Russian Orthodox monk.

p. 141: From *Interior Silence: Elder Michael, The Last Great Mystic of Valaam* by Maria Stakhovich and Sergius Bolshakoff, Ouzinkie, Alaska: New Valaam Monastery; Platina, Calif.: St. Herman of Alaska Brotherhood, 1992.

NEEDLEMAN, JACOB (contemporary)
American philosopher of religion.

pp. 177 and 224: From *Lost Christianity* by Jacob Needleman, Garden City, N.Y.: Doubleday, 1980. Reprinted by permission of the author.

NEWMAN, JOHN HENRY (1801–1890)
English Roman Catholic cardinal.

p. 130: From *Prayers, Poems, Meditations* by John Henry Newman, selected and introduced by A. N. Wilson, New York: Crossroad, 1990.

p. 194: From a sermon cited in *Sacred Reading: The Ancient Art of Lectio Divina* by Michael Casey, Liguori, Mo.: Triumph Books, 1996.

NICHOLAS OF CUSA (1401–1464)
German cardinal, theologian, and mathematician.

p. 6: From *The Vision of God* by Nicholas of Cusa, translated by Emma Gurney Slater, New York: E. P. Dutton, 1928.

Acknowledgments and Sources

NIEBUHR, REINHOLD (1892–1971)
American Christian ethicist and theologian.

p. 93: From *An Interpretation of Christian Ethics* by Reinhold Niebuhr, New York: Harper & Bros., 1935.

NOUWEN, HENRI (1932–1996)
Dutch Roman Catholic priest, professor, and counselor.

p. 197: From *Reaching Out* by Henri J. M. Nouwen, copyright © 1975 by Henri J. M. Nouwen. Used by permission of Doubleday, a division of Random House, Inc.

p. 226: From *Genesee Diary: Report from a Trappist Monastery* by Henri J. M. Nouwen, Garden City, N.Y.: Doubleday, 1976.

O'CONNOR, FLANNERY (1925–1964)
American novelist and short-story writer.

p. 92: From *A Good Man Is Hard to Find and Other Stories* by Flannery O'Connor, New York: Harcourt, Brace, 1955.

PATRICK (d. 457)
Saint of Ireland.

p. 79: Cited in *I Believe in the Holy Spirit* by Yves Congar, translated by David Smith, New York: Seabury Press; London: G. Chapman, 1983.

PHILOTHEUS OF SINAI (d. 297)

pp. 165 and 188: Cited in *The Mystical Theology of the Eastern Church* by Vladimir Lossky, Cambridge: James Clarke, 1957, and subsequently by St. Vladimir's Seminary Press in 1998. Reprinted by permission of St. Vladimir's Seminary Press, 575 Scarsdale Road, Crestwood, N.Y. 10707, 1-800-204-2665.

PHILOXENUS OF MABBUG (c. 440–c. 523)
Syrian bishop, saint, and theologian.

p. 51: From *Drinking from the Hidden Fountain: A Patristic Breviary* by Thomas Spidlik, translated by Paul Drake, Kalamazoo, Mich.: Cistercian Publications, 1994. Reprinted by permission of New City, 57 Twyford Avenue, London N3 9PZ, England.

POIRET, PIERRE (1646–1719)
French philosopher, preacher, and mystic.

p. 114: From *The Protestant Mystics,* selected and edited by Anne Jackson Fremantle, with an introduction by W. H. Auden, Boston: Little, Brown, 1964.

PORETE, MARGUERITE (?–1310)
French mystic.

p. 175: From *A Mirror for Simple Souls: The Mystical Work of Marguerite Porete,* edited and translated by Charles Crawford, introduction by Anne L. Barstow, New York: Crossroad, 1990.

RAHNER, KARL (1904–1984)
German Jesuit theologian.

p. 23: From *Everyday Faith* by Karl Rahner, New York: Herder and Herder, 1968.

p. 36: From "Thoughts on the Theology of Christmas," in *Theological Investigations,* vol. 3, by Karl Rahner, translated, and with an introduction by Cornelius Ernst, Baltimore: Helicon Press, 1961.

pp. 64, 189, 213: From "Christian Living Formerly and Today," *Theological Investigations,* vol. 3.

p. 77: From "The Apostolate of Prayer," *Theological Investigations,* vol. 3.

p. 106: From "Reflections on the Experience of Grace," *Theological Investigations,* vol. 3.

p. 131: From *On Prayer* by Karl Rahner, Collegeville, Minn.: Liturgical Press, 1993.

RUSSIAN PILGRIM (ANONYMOUS) (c. 1850)

p. 39: From *The Way of a Pilgrim,* translated from the Russian by R. M. French, with a foreword by George Craig Stewart, Milwaukee, Wis.: Morehouse Publishing, 1931.

RUUSBROEC, JOHN (1293–1381)
Flemish mystic and theologian.

p. 5: From *The Adornment of the Spiritual Marriage* by Jan van Ruysbroek, translated by C. A. Wynschank, edited by Evelyn Underhill, London: John M. Watkins, 1951.

p. 207: From *John Ruusbroec: The Spiritual Espousals and Other Works,* translated and with an introduction by James A. Wiseman, preface by Louis Dupré, New York: Paulist Press, © 1985. Reprinted by permission of Paulist Press, www.paulistpress.com.

SAGNE, JEAN-CLAUDE (contemporary)
French Roman Catholic theologian.

p. 61: Cited in *I Believe in the Holy Spirit* by Yves Congar, translated by David Smith, New York: Seabury Press; London: G. Chapman, 1983.

SCUPOLI, LAWRENCE [LORENZO] (1530–1610)
Italian Roman Catholic priest.

p. 107: From *The Spiritual Combat, and a Treatise on Peace of the Soul* by Lawrence Scupoli, a translation, revised by William Lester and Robert Mohan, New York: Paulist Press, 1978, www.paulistpress.com.

SERAPHIM OF SAROV (1759–1833)
Russian Orthodox priest and saint.

p. 198: From *The Mystical Theology of the Eastern Church* by Vladimir Lossky, Cambridge: James Clarke, 1957, and subsequently by St. Vladimir's Seminary Press in 1998. Reprinted by permission of St. Vladimir's Seminary Press, 575 Scarsdale Road, Crestwood, N.Y. 10707, 1-800-204-2665.

SERGIEFF, JOHN (ST. JOHN OF KRONSTADT) (1829–1909)
Priest of the Russian Orthodox Church.

p. 104: From *A Treasure of Russian Spirituality,* compiled and edited by G. P. Fedotov, London: Sheed & Ward, 1950.

SIGRIST, SERAPHIM (contemporary)
American Eastern Orthodox bishop, author of Theology of Wonder, *deeply involved in Christian renewal in Russia.*

    p. 230: From his Easter letter to the Hosanna Orthodox Community, Moscow, 2001.

SIMEON THE GRACEFUL (sixth century)
Syrian Orthodox father.

    p. 173: From *The Syriac Fathers on Prayer and the Spiritual Life,* translated and with an introduction by Sebastian Brock, Kalamazoo, Mich.: Cistercian Publications, 1987. Reprinted by permission of the publisher.

SIMEON THE NEW THEOLOGIAN (949–1022)
Byzantine saint, mystic, and spiritual writer

    p. 102: From Cat. XXXVI, Thanksgiving 2 (113, 335–349), cited in *I Believe in the Holy Spirit* by Yves Congar, translated by David Smith, New York: Seabury Press; London: G. Chapman, 1983.

    p. 139: From *Writings from the Philokalia on Prayer of the Heart,* translated by E. Kadloubovsky and G. E. H. Palmer, London: Faber and Faber Ltd., 1951. Cited in *Lost Christianity* by Jacob Needleman, Garden City, N.Y.: Doubleday, 1980.

SPEYR, ADRIENNE VON (1902–1967)
Swiss mystic, physician, and writer.

    p. 11, 59, and 114: From *The World of Prayer* by Adrienne von Speyr, translated by Graham Harrison, San Francisco: Ignatius Press, 1985.

SUSO, HENRY (1300–1366)
One of the foremost German contemplatives, follower of Eckhart.

    p. 11: From *Henry Suso: The Exemplar, with Two German Sermons,* edited and translated by Frank Tobin, New York: Paulist Press, 1989. Reprinted by permission of Paulist Press, www.paulistpress.com.

SWEDENBORG, EMANUEL (1688–1772)
Swedish scientist and mystical thinker.

  p. 84: From *A Thoughtful Soul: Reflections from Swedenborg*, edited by George F. Dole, introduction by Huston Smith, West Chester, Penn.: Chrysalis Books, 1996.

TAULER, JOHANNES (1300–1361)
German Dominican contemplative.

  p. 171: From "I Die Daily," a sermon in *A Lectionary of Christian Prose*, compiled by A. C. Bouquet, Derby, England: Peter Smith, 1965.

TEILHARD DE CHARDIN, PIERRE (1881–1955)
French paleontologist and Jesuit priest.

  pp. 159, 199, and 225: From *The Divine Milieu: An Essay on the Interior Life* by Pierre Teilhard de Chardin. Copyright © 1957 by Edition du Seuil, Paris. English translation copyright © 1960 by Wm. Collins Sons & Co., London, and Harper & Row Publishers, Inc., New York. Renewed © 1988 by Harper & Row Publishers, Inc. Reprinted by permission of HarperCollins Publishers, Inc.

TEMPLE, WILLIAM (1881–1944)
English archbishop of Canterbury.

  p. 129: From *Christ the Truth* by William Temple, New York: Macmillan, 1924.

TERESA OF ÁVILA (1515–1582)
Spanish Carmelite saint and mystic.

  p. 117: From *The Way of Perfection* in *The Complete Works of Saint Teresa of Jesus*, translated and edited by E. Allison Peers from the critical edition of P. Silverio de Santa Teresa, London: Sheed & Ward, 1946.

  pp. 203 and 210: From *The Life of St. Teresa* in *The Complete Works of Saint Teresa of Jesus.*

  p. 224: From *Book of the Foundations* in *The Complete Works of Saint Teresa of Jesus.*

Acknowledgments and Sources

THEOPHAN THE RECLUSE (1815–1894)
Russian Orthodox monk and saint.

    p. 178: First passage: From *The Art of Prayer: An Orthodox Anthology*, compiled by Igumen Chariton of Valamo, translated by E. Kadloubovsky and E. M. Palmer, edited and with an introduction by Timothy Ware, London: Faber and Faber Ltd., 1966. Second passage: From *The Mystical Theology of the Eastern Church* by Vladimir Lossky, Cambridge: James Clarke, © 1957, and subsequently by St. Vladimir's Seminary Press in 1998. Reprinted by permission of St. Vladimir's Seminary Press, 575 Scarsdale Road, Crestwood, N.Y. 10707, 1-800-204-2665. Third passage: From *The Art of Prayer*.

TICKLE, PHYLLIS (contemporary)
American Episcopalian writer.

    pp. 39 and 190: From *The Divine Hours: Prayers for Autumn and Wintertime*, compiled and with a preface by Phyllis Tickle, New York: Doubleday, © 2000 by Tickle Incorporated. Used by permission of Doubleday, a division of Random House, Inc.

TILLICH, PAUL (1886–1965)
German-American Protestant theologian.

    p. 33: From *Best Sermons*, edited by G. Paul Butler, New York: McGraw-Hill, 1955.

    p. 91: From *The New Being* by Paul Tillich, New York: Charles Scribner's Sons, 1955.

    p. 98: From *The Eternal Now* by Paul Tillich, New York: Charles Scribner's Sons, 1963.

ULANOV, ANN BELFORD, AND BARRY ULANOV (contemporary)
American Jungian and Christian writers.

    pp. 76 and 82: From *Primary Speech: A Psychology of Prayer* by Ann Belford Ulanov and Barry Ulanov, Atlanta, Ga.: J. Knox, © 1982 by John Knox Press. Used by permission of Westminster John Knox Press.

UNDERHILL, EVELYN (1875–1941)

English writer on mysticism.

pp. 183 and 204: From *The Letters of Evelyn Underhill*, edited and with an introduction by Charles Williams, Westminister, Md.: Christian Classics, 1989.

UNKNOWN ENGLISH MYSTIC (14th century)

pp. 43 and 147: *The Cloud of Unknowing*, from *The Cloud of Unknowing*, edited and with an introduction by James Walsh, preface by Simon Tugwell, New York: Paulist Press, © 1981. Reprinted by permission of Paulist Press, www.paulistpress.com.

p. 62: *Letter of Private Direction* from *The Pursuit of Wisdom and other works* by the author of *The Cloud of Unknowing*, translated, edited, and annotated by James A. Walsh, S.J.; preface by George A. Maloney, S.J., New York: Paulist Press, 1998, www.paulistpress.com.

p. 138: *Assessment of Inner Stirrings* from *The Pursuit of Wisdom and Other Works*, by the author of *The Cloud of Unknowing;* translated, edited, and annotated by James A. Walsh, preface by Simon Tugwell, New York: Paulist Press, 1998. Reprinted by permission of Paulist Press, www.paulistpress.com.

UNSEEN WARFARE

In its original form *Unseen Warfare* was Lorenzo Scupoli's 16th-century work, *Combattimento spirituale*. In the 18th century, Nicodemus, a monk of Mount Athos, translated, edited, and adapted it to the needs of Orthodox readers. Later, in the 19th century, Theophan the Recluse translated *Unseen Warfare* into Russian, and also substantially adapted and added to it. The English version is translated from Theophan's Russian version.

p. 162: From *Unseen Warfare*, translated by E. Kadloubovsky and G. E. H. Palmer, introduction by H. A. Hodges, London: Faber and Faber Ltd., 1952. Reprinted by permission of Faber and Faber Ltd.

VARLAAM, IGUMEN (19th century)
Monk of Valamo monastery, Russia.

    p. 149: From *The Art of Prayer: An Orthodox Anthology*, compiled by Igumen Chariton of Valamo, translated by E. Kadloubovsky and E. M. Palmer, edited and with an introduction by Timothy Ware, London: Faber and Faber Ltd., 1966.

"VENI CREATOR" HYMN (UNKNOWN) (ninth century)

    p. 80: Cited in *I Believe in the Holy Spirit* by Yves Congar, translated by David Smith, New York: Seabury Press; London: G. Chapman, 1983.

WARE, KALLISTOS (1934–)
Greek Orthodox archbishop.

    p. 24: From *The Orthodox Way* by Kallistos Ware, London; Oxford: Mowbrays, 1979.

WATSON, THOMAS (d. 1686)
English Puritan divine.

    p. 111: From *A Body of Practical Divinity* by Thomas Watson, London, 1692. Cited on the Electronic Public Library of the Institute of Practical Bible Education, www.iclnet.org.

WESLEY, JOHN (1703–1791)
English founder of the Methodist Movement.

    p. 130: From sermon 105 "On Conscience."

WHYTE, ALEXANDER (1836–1921)
Scottish Evangelical minister.

    pp. 75 and 150: From *Lord, Teach Us to Pray: Sermons on Prayer* by Alexander Whyte, D.D., L.L.D., London: Hodder and Stoughton, Ltd., 1922.

YATES, MILES LOWELL (1890–1956)
American Episcopalian minister.

    p. 67: From *God in Us: The Theory and Practice of Christian Devotion* by Miles L. Yates, Greenwich, Conn.: Seabury Press, 1959.

YEATS, W. B. (1865–1939)
Irish poet.

    p. 5: From *Autobiographies* by W. B. Yeats, London: Macmillan, 1955.

YELCHANINOV, ALEXANDER (1881–1934)
Russian priest and spiritual guide in exile in France.

    p. 26: From *A Treasure of Russian Spirituality,* compiled and edited by G. P. Fedotov, London: Sheed & Ward, 1950.

ABOUT THE EDITOR

For more than twenty years, LORRAINE KISLY has studied and worked with the texts of the great religious traditions. She was the editor of *Parabola: Myth, Tradition, and the Search for Meaning;* the founding publisher of *Tricycle: The Buddhist Review* and editor of Tricycle Books; and publisher of Pilgrim Press. Her earlier collection, *Ordinary Graces: Christian Teachings on the Interior Life,* was published in 2000. She lives in rural Pennsylvania.